Moral
Injuries

Moral Injuries

WHEN GOOD CONSCIENCE SUFFERS IN A WORLD OF HURT

Michael Valdovinos

HARPER
An Imprint of HarperCollins*Publishers*

Without limiting the exclusive rights of any author, contributor or the publisher of this publication, any unauthorized use of this publication to train generative artificial intelligence (AI) technologies is expressly prohibited. HarperCollins also exercise their rights under Article 4(3) of the Digital Single Market Directive 2019/790 and expressly reserve this publication from the text and data mining exception.

Names and identifying characteristics of some individuals have been changed to protect their privacy.

MORAL INJURIES. Copyright © 2026 by The Nothing, LLC. All rights reserved. No part of this book may be used or reproduced in any manner whatsoever without written permission except in the case of brief quotations embodied in critical articles and reviews. For information, address HarperCollins Publishers, 195 Broadway, New York, NY 10007. In Europe, HarperCollins Publishers, Macken House, 39/40 Mayor Street Upper, Dublin 1, D01 C9W8, Ireland.

HarperCollins books may be purchased for educational, business, or sales promotional use. For information, please email the Special Markets Department at SPsales@harpercollins.com.

hc.com

FIRST EDITION

Designed by Elina Cohen

Library of Congress Cataloging-in-Publication Data has been applied for.

ISBN 978-0-06-341987-2

Printed in the United States of America

26 27 28 29 30 LBC 5 4 3 2 1

FOR A.L.L.—MY CONSTANT REASONS

PAST, PRESENT, AND WHATEVER COMES NEXT

Pain and suffering are always inevitable for a large intelligence and a deep heart. The really great men must, I think, have great sadness on earth.

—Fyodor Dostoyevsky, *Crime and Punishment*

CONTENTS

INTRODUCTION	XI
CHAPTER 1 AWAKENING: *Conscience in Crisis*	1
CHAPTER 2 EVOLVING: *The Biology of Morality*	35
CHAPTER 3 CIVILIZING: *The Power of Moral Communities*	59
CHAPTER 4 SOCIALIZING: *The Nature and Nurture of Moral Identity*	81
CHAPTER 5 HURTING: *Moral Injury's Crescendo Effect*	121
CHAPTER 6 HEALING: *From Moral Distress to Moral Resilience*	149
CHAPTER 7 RECKONING: *The Future of Moral Injury*	179
ACKNOWLEDGMENTS	201
NOTES	205
REFERENCES	217
INDEX	233

INTRODUCTION

> Now conscience wakes despair
> That slumbered; wakes the bitter memory
> Of what he was, what is, and what must be
> Worse; of worse deeds worse sufferings must ensue!
>
> —JOHN MILTON

I first became aware of the term "moral injury" during my seven years of active duty in the U.S. Air Force, when I deployed to Afghanistan. There, in my capacity as a special operations psychologist, I was assigned to a team of mental health experts tasked with upholding the Geneva Conventions in detention and interrogation operations. This mission was supposed to be the culmination of my military career. Sort of *Top Gun*, minus the planes.

Prior to my deployment I had fully bought into the idealistic notion of the United States as a positive force for Afghanistan, helping the people there to dethrone the Taliban, eradicate the specter of al-Qaeda, and prevent their country from further morphing into a sanctuary for nefarious forces. I arrived in March 2014 believing that our intervention was a moral counterbalance to the Taliban's imposition of ideology through coercive means. Not only was I going to combat terrorism, but I'd also help to cultivate enduring stability and democratic ideals across a conflict-ridden landscape. For me, the lodestar of this mission was the prospect of uplifting Afghan lives through robust infrastructure development, education, and the advancement of human rights—an aspiration I regarded with a sense of privilege as an officer entrusted, in small part, with its realization.

I naively assumed that the Afghan people welcomed our assistance. I wanted to give my all to our humanitarian mission, and I considered it an added honor to represent my community as one of the few Mexican American U.S. Air Force officers on base deep in Afghanistan's Parwan Province.

That pride lasted just three days. I lost it the first time I took a good look through binoculars over the blast walls of Bagram Air Base. The scene that stretched outside our base reminded me of my grandparents' Mexican neighborhood: a dusty village with dirt roads, a cluster of mud-brick houses set against the backdrop of snowcapped mountains. I was too far away to hear, but I could see motorcycles, goats, and men clad in traditional garb moving through the streets. None looked toward the base. In fact, they seemed intent on ignoring the very existence of this gigantic foreign military operation in their midst. Neither threat nor foe, these ordinary human beings were just trying to live in peace. And while we were ostensibly there to help them, our presence was having the opposite effect. Just the year before, in 2013, 118 Afghan civilians, including 37 children, had been killed in U.S. air strikes.

The awful paradox of our presence suddenly struck me: However well-intentioned we might be, these people didn't need or want us there. Our idealistic goals were more than overshadowed by the palpable dangers and disruptions we brought into their daily lives. And not only by the physical threats our operations posed but also by the deeper, more profound disturbance to their societal norms. Our modern American military culture was completely alien to theirs. They belonged there; we did not.

Then, too, that simple village, its mud-brick homes unchanged over centuries, was a stark reminder that geopolitical ambitions rarely yielded positive consequences for the people of Afghanistan. A long line of foreign invaders, from the colonial British of Kipling's era to the Soviets who'd triggered the rise of the Taliban we were now fighting, had taught Afghans to approach outside offers of "assistance" with healthy skepticism.

The gap between my idealistic sense of mission and the reality of our reception filled me with a jarring sense of dissonance. A sudden rush of guilt and shame swept through me as my conscience engaged. What the hell were we doing in this country? We weren't going to change anybody's mind. That was, at best, a wishful excuse. This realization forced me to question the whole moral foundation of our mission and the authenticity of the narratives that had led us there.

And that's when it hit: I was part of an invading force perpetuating harm on a whole society for reasons that might not be legitimate—at a cost of billions to U.S. taxpayers. As such, I was among those *responsible for the harm* befalling these people.

But that wasn't all. As I stood frozen under the blazing Afghan sun, a lifetime of more personal mortification seized me in an emotional whirlwind. I thought of my dad, who told me the one time I tried to stop him from beating me, "I'll always be able to kick your ass more times than you can call the cops." I thought of my mom, who'd been brutalized by her own father growing up and who carried PTSD and depression long before they were made worse by witnessing a rape by the coyotes who led her to the United States. Day after day as a kid I sat with her, trying to pull her from the depths of her despair, but I hadn't been strong enough. The wrongs stacked against us were just too many and too big.

I'd seen how systemic wrongs, too, hurt undocumented migrants like my parents. How they paid into Social Security systems they'd never benefit from, supporting a government that then turned around and attacked them. How they couldn't call the police or go to the ER when injured, for fear of being deported. How they picked America's crops, prepared America's food, cleaned America's homes and businesses, cared for America's elders and children, their labor exploited even as cynical politicians trashed their mere existence. America asked these people—my people—to be invisible, indispensable, and disposable all at once. And then blamed them for not belonging.

I carry this wound as a Mexican American, as a child of immigrants. I feel it in my bones. I know firsthand that Latino immigrants don't want to come to the United States illegally; it's just that the legal pathways are so limited, outdated, and backlogged that they're left with no viable option but to risk a route that's more dangerous and more expensive and carries lifelong consequences.

Whenever I saw my people living in fear, sleeping three families to a room, working jobs that broke their bodies, I felt ashamed of America's failure to fix this broken system. I also felt shame around my own safety. All my life I'd tried to help in the ways I could—offering translation and sharing what little institutional fluency I'd gained. But it never felt like enough. It never healed enough. It never restored the dignity or justice that was systematically being denied.

If you've ever witnessed massive harm and realized your tools were too small, too late, too few to stop the damage, then you've felt the same sense of helplessness and despair I felt that day at Bagram. But my experience as a U.S. service member deepened my distress.

I joined the Air Force not out of blind patriotism but as an acknowledgment that this country with no face, no handshake, no welcome, had nevertheless given my family a fighting chance. In the military, I was relieved to discover that if I fell, someone—regardless of color, class, ideology, or gender—would pick me up, no questions asked. So service, for me, became a ritual of belonging and gratitude. But it was also, inevitably, laced with ambivalence as I wore the uniform of a nation that routinely detains and deports other men who look like me. That funds ICE raids in neighborhoods like my family's. That calls the labor of my parents illegal. You'd think after a lifetime of exposure, I'd be numb to this contradiction, but the pain of it only kept drilling deeper.

I thought then of a trauma nurse I'd treated after completing my doctoral work in psychology. This nurse had served on the front lines in Afghanistan at the height of Operation Enduring Freedom. Years later she was still plagued by emotional and spiritual sorrow, remorse, and shame over the patients she'd lost, even though she was not directly responsible for any of the human carnage she had witnessed. Although I could treat her PTSD, I'd had no tools to alleviate her unbearable moral burden.

All at once I felt slammed by the full weight of a life spent confronting pain I couldn't prevent. The guilt was immense, not because I'd done harm, per se, but because the scope of suffering seemed as insurmountable as a tsunami. However sincere or determined, my efforts to help had collided again and again with realities I could not change. And now in this moment, I was reckoning with the unbearable distance between intention and outcome. I yearned for atonement, but what could possibly atone for the quantity of sorrow and harm that surrounded me?

Reeling, I was overwhelmed by a sense of profound sadness at life itself—at the never-ending cycles of violence, hatred, and anguish. I had spent years trying to ease others' pain, but in that moment I felt I'd barely made a dent. My whole body seemed to be sinking.

Then, suddenly, the experienced therapist in me snapped to attention. I took a step back, catching hold of myself and eyeing the weeping me in bewilderment. While it was true that I'd survived a painful childhood, I'd worked through this pain in therapy and was largely managing flare-ups of my own PTSD and anxiety. Therapy, coupled with psychological training, had taught me how to better recognize and challenge the negative thought patterns and behaviors that once held me back and caused me to crash. I understood the powerful connection between my thoughts, feelings, and behaviors, and I knew how to break cycles of anxiety, stress, or unhelpful habits. Cognitive behavior therapy had given me strategies to manage emotional pain, and I believed I approached psychological challenges with a balanced, proactive mindset. Earlier in my military career, I'd proven my resilience by enduring a grueling survival training program that broke many of my fellow airmen. And I'd treated hundreds of emotionally wounded patients with measurable success.

So, why was I falling apart now?

I collected myself and headed back to the bay inside the Bagram detention center. Then I did what anyone does when faced with a conundrum. I asked Google.

"Military," I typed in the search box. "Guilt." "Shame." "Remorse." "Loss of trust."

And that's when the answer popped onto the screen: "Moral Injury."

I was experiencing the crescendo effect of a lifetime of moral distress. *El acierto.* Bull's-eye.

The term "moral injury" was coined in the 1990s by the Veterans Affairs psychiatrist Jonathan Shay and his colleagues. They used it to describe a syndrome that they'd detected among Vietnam War veterans, though the patterns of moral betrayal and violation felt by these soldiers stretch back to the dawn of human warfare. Too often—even routinely—on the battlefield, soldiers are forced to choose between obeying a superior's command and honoring their own moral and spiritual convictions. Many of these orders relate to the taking of human life. Civilized societies the world over treat murder as a serious moral breach, yet even soldiers who aren't trained for combat contribute to their military's collective mission, which often involves lethal force. The moral crisis is heightened, of course, for service members who are explicitly directed to kill.

It may be possible to reconcile the conflict between protecting and ending human life, if you believe that the war you're waging is just and that human casualties are unavoidable in the pursuit of a greater good. Or if you're convinced that everyone you've ever targeted was an enemy combatant who directly threatened your own life. But warfare is rarely that clear-cut, and human emotion less so. When the events you experience contradict the principles you thought you were living by and fighting for—that you yourself *stood for*—the resulting crisis of conscience can produce mental health repercussions that persist for decades.

Moral injury occurs when we make choices that so violate our conscience and produce such unbearable consequences that we come to see ourselves as *irredeemably bad* people. What's more, victims, witnesses, and perpetrators are all equally susceptible. To understand how this can be, consider that a victim of rape or child abuse may feel as responsible as a perpetrator for not avoiding or stopping the abuse. A soldier may feel like a victim if ordered to commit a war crime, but becomes perpetrator if, in violation of their conscience, they execute the command. A colleague who witnesses a team member being sexually harassed at work may feel complicit in the abuse if they dare not act to protect their friend.

Our moral choices may be so involuntary that we feel as if we had no choice at all, but our conscience holds us accountable regardless. All it knows or cares about is that something has happened to crack or smash our moral compass, making it impossible to feel like a *good person*. Ultimately, it's this fracturing of our core moral identity that causes the emotional pain of moral injury.

Like PTSD, moral injury can cause depression, avoidance, anxiety, isolation, insomnia, and can lead to self-medication with sex, drugs, or alcohol, but it also tends to generate more distinctive burdens of guilt, shame, anger, and alienation. Significantly, moral injury destroys our social equilibrium by causing us to distrust not only others but, even more disturbingly, ourselves. This instability rocks our sense of *both* the common good and our own goodness, and that has the potential to damage relationships at home, at work, and throughout our communities.

The issue is complicated by the fact that we're not all equally susceptible to moral injury. Nor does this pain universally arise from a single set of circumstances. Just as moral values vary widely around the world, so do the transgressions that trigger moral injury. But each of us does have a *personal conscience*. And that's the critical factor in moral injury.

When we find ourselves caught up in high-stakes, consequential events that make us feel we've irredeemably betrayed our *own* moral values, that's when we suffer profound psychological and emotional harm.

Of course, what constitutes a "high-stakes, consequential event" can also vary. For some, the breach of a principle like honesty between friends might feel like a high-stakes violation, even if no one is physically harmed by it. Others require a catastrophic consequence, like loss of life, before their conscience cracks.

Back at Bagram, even as I began the painful process of tracing my own moral distress, I realized that my history gave me a counterintuitive advantage in unraveling this complexity. All the pressures that had shaped me and my family—from navigating immigration and racial prejudice to physical abuse, childhood poverty, and bearing witness to my mom's lifelong, intractable depression, to a career in the military—also gifted me with valuable insights into this trauma of conscience. I understood, for instance, that moral injury transcends geographic and occupational boundaries. Whether we dwell in the hustle bustle of urban life or in the tranquility of rural landscapes, whether our personal duties lead us to Zoom meetings or construction sites, the shadow of moral struggle reaches us all. Like soldiers fielding contradictory orders, each of us must deftly maneuver between the sometimes-harsh demands of daily survival and the quiet, persistent murmur of our inner conscience.

Life also had taught me that personal agency accounts for only part of our moral landscape. Whether in the rigid discipline of the military or in the nuanced complexity of civilian duties, a vast matrix of external forces shapes almost all our "individual" decisions. These influences echo with historical oppressions like colonialism, racism, sexism, and economic injustice. They include institutional cultures, corporate hierarchies, military protocols, religious dogmas, and countless other systems and structures that can both shape and overpower one's personal moral compass. And when trusted authorities within these systems betray our faith by compelling conduct that we deem immoral, the cognitive dissonance can feel unbearable.

It can be tempting to lash out against such injustice, but blind rage has a habit of turning inward and producing toxic consequences. The opposite response is to take the path of least resistance—just go along for the sake of security or comfort by surrendering or contorting your beliefs. But in my work as a psychotherapist I've found that moral healing lies neither in muting one's inner voice nor in acts of vengeance against systemic betrayals. Relief comes instead through reflection and the channeling of conscience into *constructive* change that embodies deeper understanding, forgiveness, and repair.

———

After I returned to civilian life, I continued to study and treat moral injury at the Palo Alto Veterans Affairs Medical Center and later at Weill Cornell Medical College, where I served as a clinician in the

Program for Anxiety and Traumatic Stress Studies and associate director of the New York-Presbyterian Military Family Wellness Center, before moving back to California to co-direct behavioral medicine training at UCSF Sutter Health's Family Medicine Residency. Then, after the coronavirus pandemic wound down, I moved from health care into technology, where my global role in health and well-being policy gave me a front-row seat to the new complexities shaping digital life.

All these experiences have convinced me that the political, economic, and social fault lines running through society today pose moral threats we could not have imagined even as recently as the year 2000. From school shootings to vigilante mobs and escalating hate crimes, deepfakes to identity theft, climate denial to environmental demolition, catalysts for moral injury surround us.

Even more troubling, the fractures in society are causing us to demean and attack each other's most deeply held beliefs, causing untold moral conflict within families, neighborhoods, and nations. These disputes are now so pervasive that the word "immoral" has become a meaningless epithet hurled across party lines. Like the proverbial frog in the pot, many of us don't even realize the danger we're in as the moral waters rise to a boil. But the danger is real and steadily escalating. Our society is long overdue for a moral reckoning.

As an Air Force veteran and board-certified, licensed clinical psychologist, I have now been studying, treating, and personally confronting moral injury for more than a decade. In the chapters that follow, I'll share with you what I've learned at the intersection of trauma, technology, and treatment. But to be clear, this is a book about the *psychology* of moral injury. I will not be giving out philosophical, political, or theological advice. I'm not going to define which values constitute "morality" for you, nor will I tell you what behaviors or beliefs are "right" or "wrong." The specific settings of your moral compass are a matter for you and your faith leader, for you and your family, for you and your own conscience to determine. My concerns in this book are, instead, the psychological value of the compass itself and the emotional repair that needs to occur when your compass, for whatever reason, is smashed.

Along the way, you'll find stories of healing and resilience, as well as shared expertise from pioneers in the nascent field of moral injury research, prevention, and treatment. At a time when our collective conscience is under relentless attack, my goal in writing this book is to provide you with a beacon of hope and a path through moral suffering that is literally battle tested.

Moral Injuries

CHAPTER 1

AWAKENING

Conscience in Crisis

> The real problem of humanity is the following: we have paleolithic emotions; medieval institutions; and god-like technology. And it is terrifically dangerous, and it is now approaching a point of crisis overall.
>
> —EDWARD O. WILSON

It was 7:00 a.m., the start of another horrific pandemic day in mid-2020, when I arrived at Sonoma County Regional Hospital to meet with the family medicine residents who were on their inpatient rotations. At the time, there were few known treatments for COVID-19. The residents' own personal protective equipment was in short supply, and patients were dying for lack of ventilators. The hospital administrators were concerned that "morale was tanking" on the front lines of the war against the coronavirus, so I'd been asked to lead a process session aimed at dispelling the overwhelming specters of doom and sorrow that haunted the medical staff as they battled the seemingly unstoppable tide of death.

The residents' lounge, typically a zone of much-needed decompression, now felt frigid and lifeless. Most of the dedicated young men and women who filled the room stared without expression. Overwhelmed by the sense of defeat, remorse, and moral betrayal that consumed their pandemic lives, these doctors were as traumatized as if they'd been wounded in combat.

I sat down, took some deep breaths, and initiated a round of check-ins. Some of the residents wrestled up words to express their grief and anger, while others could only sob as their emotions now overflowed. Some felt enraged by what they considered massive transgressions by authorities who ought to be doing more to safeguard both patients and health-care workers. Others blamed themselves for failing to live up to the oath they'd sworn, to do everything in their power to heal the sick. A few spoke of feeling robbed, their family practice residencies derailed by the relentless grip of COVID.

After everyone had spoken, I let a few moments of silence pass. Then I said quietly, "Listen, gang. I commend you for what you've done and forgive you for what you can't do."

With that, all of us wept.

Though not physically sick, those young doctors were clearly suffering—emotionally, mentally, and spiritually. Their feelings were chaotic, confusing storms of both anger over the moral betrayals of others *and* shame and guilt over their own culpability, as well as helpless despair over losses they could not prevent. Unable to quell their consciences, they felt condemned, as if they were personally responsible for the cosmic *wrong* of the situation. If they were truly good people, the moral judge of conscience declared, they'd have found a way to stem the tide of death and failure, but since they hadn't, they must be *morally bad*.

There was nothing rational about this thinking, of course, but there was nothing rational about the moral dilemma that engulfed them, either. The very irrationality of their thoughts was itself a symptom of conscience in crisis. What those anguished doctors were experiencing was the deeply disorienting syndrome of *moral injury*.

Morals, the personal values and beliefs that guide our sense of right and wrong, serve as pillars of our identity. We rely on them to direct our choices and actions, and in return they shape our character, by which I mean the unique set of qualities that distinguish our sense of self. The more consistently we abide by a secure moral code, the stronger our sense of integrity and the better our moral health.

But moral codes are not uniform. They vary widely both in content and in structure. We don't all have the same codes, nor do we guard every value within our own codes equally.

Your most deeply rooted moral values are the product of your own innate temperament, your family's faith and cultural history, and your personal experience, all genetically threaded together. Your values may resemble those of your neighbors, or they may be fundamentally different; either way, if they run deep enough—and I mean beyond your head and even your heart to the very intuitions you feel in your gut—then they become intrinsic to your moral identity as a *good* human. If you fail to honor these core values, then you'll feel like a *bad person*.

That feeling of personal *badness* is the essence of moral injury.

We'll discuss the evolution and diversity of moral values in later chapters, but the point I need to impress on you here is that moral injury serves as a warning that the deepest roots of your moral identity have been badly damaged. The doctors who reeled under the moral assault of COVID were a self-selecting group who shared a profoundly idealistic code, which they believed defined them as *good people*. This code stressed compassion, service, dignity, and fairness, as distilled in their Hippocratic oath to "first do no harm." Yet every day during the early weeks of the pandemic the residents found themselves violating their oath by allowing patients to suffer and die on their watch. And this sense of violation wounded them.

Not their fault! you might well argue, but their consciences didn't care. Those whose code of service ran deepest felt as if they'd lost their bearings. They were emotionally fallen, and some could not get up.

The mechanics of moral injury work something like this: If you have a deeply rooted moral value that you see being violated, even if you're not at fault, your conscience will react with a flash of emotional pain to shock you to attention. When you do something that contradicts your own moral code, the flash warns that you're betraying yourself. When others violate your code, your conscience announces that you've been betrayed. Either way, you'll physically and psychically *hurt* as your conscience struggles to protect the integrity of your moral identity. If you're unable to stop, prevent, or reverse the violation, the protest of conscience will escalate, like a siren that won't quit, and your pain will build. This unique form of stress can have psychological repercussions. When moral health breaks, mental health suffers.

Moral breakdown is precisely what those young residents in 2020 were experiencing, and they were hardly alone. Whether we realized it or not, the pandemic gave us all a crash course in moral distress. As formerly routine events, like getting vaccinated or going to work, morphed into life-or-death decisions that endangered some groups while protecting others, nearly every move we made during COVID represented a potential moral dilemma. Those who staked their virtue on helping to minimize the pandemic's death toll found themselves locked in battle with those who would protect their family's economic security at all costs. Those who saw themselves first as defenders of their community's liberty felt menaced by those who would subject them to blanket mandates for the sake of strangers. Then, as the pervasive atmosphere of uncertainty and alarm threatened everyone's moral equilibrium, even mundane interactions between family members, neighbors, and co-workers became fraught.

The moral friction between us was aggravated by our collective ignorance. Because so little was known about the coronavirus, no one could evaluate public or private health decisions with much medical certainty. The resulting panic and anger at government leaders and authority figures led to a widespread sense of betrayal and splintering of trust in our institutions. This deepened preexisting economic and social fissures. Choices as personal as wearing a protective mask then became moral litmus tests that tore friends, families, and communities apart.

Among those who went into lockdown, isolation magnified feelings of alienation and distrust, and among those whose livelihoods forced them to risk daily exposure to the virus, mortal risk heightened feelings of moral resentment and fear. All these extreme emotions deepened the collective trauma of witnessing widespread death and being helpless to stop it. Millions felt profound remorse over the loss of loved ones who might have been saved if only we'd all been able to make better decisions.

Even now, as the cumulative pandemic death toll continues to climb—over 7 million lost to COVID worldwide and more than 1.2 million in the United States alone—many are still struggling to recover their moral balance after those cataclysmic years. Yet few have any idea they're wrestling with a syndrome called "moral injury."

WHAT IS MORAL INJURY?

When it was first named in the 1990s, moral injury was defined broadly as "the strong cognitive and emotional response that can occur following events that violate a person's moral or ethical code." It was treated in tandem with post-traumatic stress disorder (PTSD) as a condition that primarily afflicted combat veterans.

By then, PTSD was understood to be the body's long-term physical and psychological reaction to mortal threats such as explosions, gunfire, and other violent assaults. The annals of military history dating back to *The Iliad* describe soldiers being haunted by shattering traumas experienced on the battlefield. Before the term "post-traumatic stress disorder" was coined, doctors called this syndrome shell shock.

But as the psychiatrist Jonathan Shay worked with Vietnam vets, he noticed that certain severe symptoms, like rage, depression, shame, and alienation, were showing up even among vets who'd never been under fire. These former soldiers typically were less jumpy—"hyperaroused," in therapy-speak—than those with PTSD, but they were often racked by remorse and guilt, as well as crippling self-doubt, which could lead to even greater risk for substance abuse and suicide.

Shay looked deeper into this subset of service members and found that many struggled with a relentless sense of moral failure or betrayal over events that they considered unforgivable. Some, following orders, had committed "crimes of obedience," such as killing civilians or abandoning teammates, in violation of their personal convictions. Others had witnessed serious ethical transgressions, which they hadn't been able or willing to stop. Still others had themselves been victimized or betrayed by fellow soldiers or commanders they'd trusted to do the right thing. Some had experienced all these crushing moral blows, sometimes within or around a single incident.

As these soldiers described the situations that haunted them, Shay began to understand the psychic toll of moral betrayal. Years later, in a radio interview, he instructed listeners to imagine that someone they trusted and had sworn to obey was ordering them to do something unconscionable.

"You will discover your body reacts," Shay said. "Your guts churn, your heart begins to pound, you may get sweaty." What he was describing was a powerful stress reaction.

When faced with danger, our bodies release stress hormones to prepare us for action. The primary fight-flight-or-freeze response is a well-known survival mechanism triggered largely by adrenaline and cortisol. It helped energize and focus our ancestors, especially lone hunters who met menacing predators and had little choice but to engage in battle, run away, or blend into the undergrowth. The trouble was, while fighting, fleeing, and freezing were often necessary reactions for individual survival, these impulses were less useful for those who tended the tribe's children and elders. Compared with male hunters, the mostly female caregivers typically lacked the freedom, speed, and strength to physically bolt or battle their attackers, even if they had been willing to abandon their dependents. What they needed instead was an instinctive boost to help keep everyone safe and working together to find a way out or around the threat—to engage social behavior as a protective strategy.

That boost took the form of a secondary wave of gentler stress hormones, which University of California researcher Shelley Taylor in 2000 dubbed the "tend-and-befriend" response. The so-called love hormone, oxytocin, plays a central role here. Oxytocin promotes bonding, empathy, compassion, reciprocity, and collaboration. Other researchers have suggested that its release under stress helps to explain why some women try to placate their attackers when being sexually assaulted and why children may bond with abusive family members instead of attempting to fight or flee them.

But while tend and befriend may soften the initial panic enough for us to plot alternative avenues of escape from danger, it does not replace or cancel the primary fight-flight-freeze response. The reactive turbulence that Jonathan Shay described is a mix of *all* these stress hormones surging through the body, searching for ways to help us survive under potentially intolerable pressure.

As Shay indicated, that pressure doesn't have to be physical. It can be emotional or psychological. The threat can also be moral.

Subtle neurological differences do distinguish the syndrome of moral injury—the body's response to *moral* threat—from PTSD, which is a reaction to *mortal* danger. While moral injury tends to activate regions of the brain that are involved in social processing—especially the anterior cingulate cortex, which helps monitor social attention, and the ventromedial prefrontal cortex, which is active in emotional responses—PTSD is primarily tied to regions of the brain like the amygdala that register and react to fear and physical trauma. But the kinship between these two syndromes does tell us that we need both a healthy, intact conscience *and* a healthy, intact physical body to survive. If our moral equilibrium suffers, so will our sanity and general well-being. That's why our brains are wired to warn us when we're in moral peril, almost as if we were under physical assault. It's also why we breathe easier when we find morally acceptable solutions to disturbing ethical dilemmas, much as our bodies flood with relief when we escape mortal danger.

Unfortunately, we can rarely fight, flee, or freeze our way to moral reconciliation. And in urgent life-threatening situations, the primary stress responses designed for physical survival can overrule conscience. The soldier who comes face-to-face with his enemy will likely shoot without thinking about the age, identity, or family of his target. But stress hormones will not stop the protest of moral pain if, after the fact, the soldier discovers that his "enemy" was an innocent child.

The kind of pressure that Shay highlights is particularly insidious when it involves an internal conflict between our moral *identity* and the actions we feel *compelled* to take. Medics under fire, for example, might be ordered to kill any civilians who block their company's escape, but as physicians they've sworn an oath to "first, do no harm" and their moral instincts as caregivers also favor nonviolence. The moral injury that arises then from an order to kill is not only a reaction to the resulting casualties but also, for medics, a response to the assault on their core identity. *Is it right for me to defy the authority of an officer who may be wrong? Is it right for me to protect a civilian life at the expense of my unit? Is it right for me to kill civilians just because I'm obeying orders?* Caught between the need to obey and defend their fellow soldiers and their moral commitment to protect innocent life, field doctors could wind up receiving medals for "valor under fire" yet still feel they've betrayed their own conscience. Over time, such gnawing, unresolved dilemmas might erode their sense of dignity, self-worth, and integrity. Many soldiers who feel they've violated their primary values on the battlefield will experience persistent psychological trauma, including guilt, anger, and profound disillusionment, long after they leave the service. Such moral dissonance can rupture their sense of self, leading to deep struggles with existential questions about the meaning, purpose, and even value of life.

To complicate the picture, violent, high-stakes situations like combat can cause PTSD and moral injury to overlap. On the battlefield, for example, a soldier might experience both the mortal threat of coming under fire and the moral threat of killing innocent bystanders. That combination can produce a mixed bag of symptoms—the jumpiness, flashbacks, and avoidance symptomatic of PTSD on top of the guilt, shame, and sense of personal betrayal that hallmark moral injury. Sometimes, too, the moral piece will emerge only later, when triggered by a reminder or revelation about the original incident; this delay can make the pain confusing and challenging to identify.

Resolution of moral conflict generally requires thoughtful engagement, creativity, and empathy, all of which are boosted by the tend-and-befriend response. Unfortunately, the more aggressive primary stress hormones remain in the mix, and they can impede conciliatory thinking. So, between the stress reactions themselves, a contest begins. Even as oxytocin promotes rational decision-making or problem-solving, elevated levels of adrenaline and corticosteroids may impair the ability to think clearly. This chemical tension can lead to frustration and impulsive or defensive behavior that we later regret.

If we witness but fail to halt a violent assault, for example, we might lash out, impulsively accusing or denigrating *others* for refusing to intervene. Alternatively, we might retreat into isolation, heaping guilt and shame onto ourselves. Then, especially if we lack social support, loneliness could short-circuit the more helpful tend-and-befriend mechanisms, allowing the harsher stress responses to spiral.

This "stress mess" can intensify the social strain of moral conflict and block constructive solutions. People often lean toward more aggressive or defensive behavior when they feel their dignity is under assault, when they've lost control, or when they experience overwhelming anger, guilt, or shame. This pattern applies to groups, too, making violence, including mass eruptions like riots, one possible outcome.

But it's essential to remember that we're also wired to reflect on our actions, learn from mistakes, and find better ways to handle tough situations. There are always nonviolent paths available. And responses that channel empathy, understanding, and reparation tend to lead to better moral outcomes.

Constructive paths can be hard to find, though, if life keeps piling on new layers of moral distress. Soldiers in the fog of war, like pandemic doctors and nurses, may be under so much pressure to follow orders and react quickly that they have no capacity to consider the moral ramifications of each action. Rapid-fire incidents can lead to one dubious moral choice after another, and with each round, the levels of stress hormones in the body rise, eventually leading to burnout, depression, and despair.

Noting that these symptoms in Marine vets can look a lot like acute grief or PTSD, the psychologist Brett Litz decided to tease the strands apart in his research at the Veterans Affairs Boston Healthcare System. By working backward to identify the traumatic events that first triggered their symptoms, Litz found that about a third of the Marines under his care had personally experienced physical danger. Another third were traumatized by the loss of a close friend or relative. But fully one-third were suffering primarily from stress reactions linked to events they could not reconcile with their conscience. One-third of the Marines, in other words, suffered from moral injury.

Why is this distinction important? The most important reason is that effective diagnosis and treatment of moral injury can save lives.

According to the Department of Veterans Affairs, people with moral injury are significantly more likely than those with PTSD alone to contemplate or attempt self-harm or suicide.

One dramatic example was the suicide of Matthew Livelsberger, a thirty-seven-year-old Green Beret who shot himself in a Tesla Cybertruck, which he'd wired to blow up outside the Trump hotel in Las Vegas on New Year's Day 2025. Livelsberger had been deployed twice to Afghanistan since 2006. He left notes on his cell phone stating that he needed to "cleanse" his mind "of the brothers I've lost and relieve myself of the burden of the lives I took." Such thoughts and desperate acts are strong indications of moral injury.

"Self-harm might arise," according to Litz, "because you feel unforgivable and damned, and you may feel at a very deep level that you deserve to suffer." The behavior that follows the indictment of oneself as a *bad person*, then, can be a form of self-punishment. "They may abuse drugs, they may drive dangerously, some may not even care whether they live or die."

In 2020, about seventeen U.S. veterans died by suicide every day—a rate 150 percent higher than the general population's. Health-care workers, including nurses and health technicians, also have an elevated risk for suicide. So do veterinarians, who routinely face the moral hurdle of euthanizing rather than treating sick or injured animals. And so do first responders, including police, firefighters, and emergency medical technicians, whose duties frequently present them with moral dilemmas, including the choice between following orders and saving lives. Researchers studying traumatic experiences such as child abuse and sexual assault have confirmed that these moral injuries, too, raise the risk for suicidal behavior for predators and victims alike.

Another important reason to improve our understanding of moral injury is to lower stress and prevent burnout, especially in high-pressure occupations. Researchers point to widespread moral injury in the ranks of chronically overworked and understaffed air traffic controllers on duty when plane accidents happen; among social workers and teachers who lack the resources or legal authority to protect all the children in their charge; among journalists and photographers assigned to impartially cover humanitarian crises that leave them feeling helpless and guilty for not intervening; and among border patrol agents who've committed "crimes of obedience," such as separating migrant children from their parents. Moral injury is an occupational hazard, too, for lawyers and employees of individuals who've committed heinous crimes. Legal defenders are often caught between loyalty to the principle of due process and certainty of their client's guilt. Staff aides of war criminals may be torn between fear for their own and relatives' lives and opposition to their bosses' moral transgressions. In such situations, personal clarity starts to dissolve under the weight of professional duty and obedience. It's likely that moral injury haunts countless bodyguards of tyrants, mobsters' lawyers, and even lower-level staff members of powerful organizations and individuals who prey on the weak, ignorant, and vulnerable. Such jobs carry a high burnout rate, and moral injury is one big reason why.

THE INVISIBLE EPIDEMIC

Many clinicians—and I'm one of them—believe that society is suffering from an invisible epidemic of moral distress. That's especially true as I write this in America, where we seem to be caught in a collective feedback loop of grievance, outrage, and despair. Too many of us focus on the eruption of these moral emotions instead of on the forces that are stoking them. We ask, What is happening? when the more urgent question is, What have we allowed to happen to us?

Many Americans today feel betrayed. And betrayal is the hallmark of moral violation—not just personal but institutional and systemic moral violation, too. Ordinary citizens feel used and ignored by a host of titanic forces, from corporate giants to political opportunists who have steadily marginalized the majority to a degree not seen in America since the Gilded Age of the late nineteenth century. Back then, 1 percent of the population controlled about half the nation's wealth; in 2024 the richest 1 percent of Americans held more than 30 percent of total U.S. net worth. Many outside the corridors of power today have lost trust in government, industry, and even science, as formerly reliable markers of merit, such as titles, degrees, brands, and pledges, have been hijacked to commodify dissent. The perpetual outrage being stoked on all sides hurts not only those who are targeted as scapegoats but also those sincerely trying to fight injustice. Many feel despair as they watch their causes distorted, their activism vilified. The resulting ruptures in our shared integrity reflect an unspoken pathology: America is suffering from a national moral injury.

Fortunately, the American Psychiatric Association has now officially recognized the gravity of moral harm. In its annual update of *The Diagnostic and Statistical Manual of Mental Disorders* (DSM), which sets the framework for clinicians and researchers to document, treat, and study mental health conditions, the APA in 2025 added *moral injury* as a recognized source of psychological harm under the existing code for "Religious or Spiritual Problem." This means that clinicians can finally document and track moral injury in medical records, and researchers can study it systematically, beyond the narrow military or religious frame, as a mainstream mental health concern.

"Moral problems," according the APA's definition, "include experiences that disrupt one's understanding of right and wrong, or sense of goodness of oneself, others or institutions." This language allows doctors and therapists to write "moral injury" or "moral distress" in a patient's medical record. Researchers can begin to track and investigate moral harm as a legitimate psychological condition. And this DSM update also will pave the way for critical discussions about the accountability of insurance companies, employers, and entire institutions for psychological damage that occurs as a result of systemic ethical violations.

Some of today's moral stressors, including racism, sexism, homophobia, and economic inequality, are, admittedly, as old as civilization. The residue of guilt, shame, distrust, and injustice they've deposited throughout society has long challenged collective moral well-being. But this pressure is now building to critical levels that are hammering our reserves of social capital.

"Social capital" is a twentieth-century term for the friendship, favor, and assistance that healthy humans have always exchanged as a matter of course in daily interaction. The tacit understanding goes something like this: *I'll scratch your back today, and you'll scratch mine another day.* This instinctive reciprocity is baked into group behavior, and it's essential both for individuals and for cultures to thrive. Without social capital, our resources shrink. We feel alone, cut off, abandoned, largely purposeless. And without a functioning *system* of social capital, society would have no way of knitting together the diverse talents and strengths of individuals to build the many types of infrastructure that large groups require. In simple terms, social capital allows us to help each other survive.

Violations that produce moral injury wreak havoc on social capital. Personal betrayal, abuse of trust, crimes of passion, violence, deception, and neglect all sow resentment and shame, to alienating effect. And the legacy of such assaults on human dignity, when passed down over generations, impacts the descendants of victims and of perpetrators alike. Ancient grievances do not fade on their own. We shadowbox their ghosts every day.

Many of our current social tensions can be traced back to harm inflicted before the Revolutionary War. Slavery and the theft of land from Indigenous people play especially enduring roles in America's collective moral trauma. The legacy of subjugation and colonialization has for centuries fueled unyielding conflict between racial groups in our communities and politics, in who gets heard and who gets power and who gets denigrated. All these "legacy threats" perpetuate blaming and shaming between the descendants, with the resulting polarization posing an ongoing challenge to our entire society's moral integrity.

The moral resentments we've inherited will continue to fester until we're willing to name them for what they are and deal as a nation with the ethical mess they've bequeathed us. This undercurrent is like a constant background hum of distress that touches us all, regardless of who we are, what faith we practice, or what specific moral principles we embrace.

That is not to say, though, that everyone is affected in the same way. Moral injury occurs when we make a choice, usually under emotional duress, that so violates our deepest values—our core moral identity—that it leaves us feeling like an *irredeemably bad person*. That depth of personal violation is what causes one's moral compass to break. And yet, we all have different moral compasses, and no two break under exactly the same circumstances.

By "different moral compasses," I mean that we all have our own ethical priorities and moral absolutes. Transgressions that some view as unforgivable will barely register for others. So, we can't make a blanket rule that all murderers, liars, and cheaters will experience moral injury. Some will, but some won't. It depends on how deeply each individual cares about the value that's been violated, how closely that value is tied to their identity, and the degree to which they believe upholding it defines them as a *good person*.

This notion of moral diversity may take some getting used to if you believe that a single set of moral principles *ought to* apply to everyone universally. That belief, known as moral absolutism, is a form of deontology, which uses ordained rules to distinguish right from wrong. The trouble is that people around the world observe all sorts of different rules, and many of them contradict each other. Researchers have found that the ethical frameworks governing laws in most societies do reflect a common set of broad moral concerns, but moral *priorities* can vary radically from one culture to the next. In some societies, where group cohesion is morally prioritized over individual rights, honor killings are considered a "good" response to the transgressive sin of adultery. In others, adultery isn't even considered a crime, but murder most definitely is, so there, honor killings are viewed as evil. As psychologist Jonathan Haidt reminds us, "Understanding the simple fact that morality differs around the world, and even within societies, is the first step toward understanding your righteous mind."

Acknowledging moral diversity without sliding into moral relativism is a tightrope that we have to walk if we're to make sense of moral injury. I am not suggesting that all moral systems are equally good for their societies, let alone for their believers. But people do tend to believe in the righteousness of their own moral codes—often passionately—even when those codes are objectively harmful to the believers themselves. Accepting moral diversity, then, does not mean blindly saluting this plethora of systems. Instead, it acknowledges that the innate mechanism of belief, *whatever* one's particular value system, has a profound and universal hold on the human psyche and soul.

Moral diversity is key to understanding that, while members of any society will experience distress when their core beliefs are violated, the underlying syndrome of moral injury is agnostic about the *objective* definition of those beliefs. What matters is not the code of conduct that's expected of you, but rather your *subjective identification* with the particular virtue that's been transgressed.

Offenses that trigger moral pain will involve violations that you personally find so odious that you're filled with disgust at having played any role in them. It's like a moral contamination that lays waste to your sense of self. If and when you reach full-blown moral injury, you'll feel irredeemable.

This feeling of hopelessness need not be permanent. The psychological and emotional damage of moral injury can be addressed with appropriate support, reflection, and therapy that lead to healing and a gradual restoration of self-worth. But the first step toward mending your soul is to recognize the true source of distress.

For many of us, religion and spirituality have shaped and reinforced our private notions of right and wrong, and we naturally turn to faith for moral solace. Religion is not always helpful in warding off moral injury, though, especially not for those who silo their morality in religion. *As long as I pray and tithe or confess in church on Sundays,* some tell themselves, *I can sideline my conscience the rest of the week.* But moral identity involves much more than devotion or religiosity. Moral choices don't stop at the church, temple, or mosque door. And when those choices go wrong, they have the power to crush one's soul.

Consider, for instance, the airplane factory workers who raised safety concerns about the planes they helped build. According to multiple court filings over more than twenty years, employees faced punishments ranging from transfers and demotions to termination if they spoke up about these structural weaknesses. The few whistleblowers who did speak out claimed management was more concerned with production speed and shareholder returns than the safety and integrity of the product. Even before two crashes of commercial airliners killed a total of 346 people between 2018 and 2019, quality manager John Barnett had warned that production priorities were leading to defective aircraft. The FAA eventually confirmed some of these claims, but Barnett's conscience would not let him rest. "It keeps me up at night," he said in 2019. "I can't sleep. It's taken a heck of a toll on me." That toll was moral injury.

In 2024, just a few months after an exit door blew out of a jetliner mid-flight, Barnett died by suicide. "I can't do this any longer," he'd written in a note found beside his body.

Barnett's suicide was not an anomaly among whistleblowers. In fact, his death was followed just a few months later by the suicide of the twenty-six-year-old AI whistleblower Suchir Balaji. In recent years, the Veterans Affairs whistleblower Christopher Kirkpatrick and the Department of Homeland Security whistleblower Philip Haney also took their own lives. The moral injury that whistleblowers carry can be treated and mitigated if it is recognized and acknowledged, but far too often these individuals suffer in silence until the crushing burden of conscience makes them feel they can't go on.

THE MAKING OF MORAL INJURY

It's essential to remember that moral distress is a natural response to situations our conscience perceives as profoundly wrong. When heeded, moral pain can prompt essential reflection, recognition of responsibility, and positive action to resolve ethical conflict, or at least to mitigate fallout. In this light, such distress can be viewed as a vital warning signal.

Moral pain escalates in three stages. Remember the chaotic feelings that Jonathan Shay's thought experiment illustrated? That initial chaos is *moral stress*, which registers a threat to your conscience and warns you to react. Help the neighbor in trouble. Tell the truth under oath. Honor promises made in good faith. Your conscience will instruct you to do whatever you must to protect the integrity of your sense of self—your moral identity. If you want to feel good about yourself, moral stress cautions, you must act in concert with your primary values. Otherwise, you'll feel bad about yourself and, thus, bad in general.

The second stage, *moral distress*, sets in when you do not or cannot resolve the dilemma in a way that satisfies your conscience. When you cannot do enough to feel good about yourself and cannot forgive yourself for what you've failed to do or done wrong; when a powerful authority prevents you from doing the right thing; or when you're faced with a "Sophie's choice" between equally immoral and damning alternatives, with no escape.

Perhaps you remember William Styron's acclaimed World War II novel or the 1982 film version of *Sophie's Choice*? In the movie, Meryl Streep played Sophie, a devoted young mother forced to make an unbearable decision: choose one of her children to go to the gas chamber, or watch both be killed by the German officer who holds them captive. Sophie has no hope of escape, no code of justice to protect her or her children. Imprisoned in a concentration camp, she has no weapons, nothing to barter with, no allies to support her, and no time to think through her decision. In terror and desperation, she sends her little girl to her death in the futile hope of saving her son. Sophie herself survives the war. She moves to America, technically free, but every second of every day her so-called choice torments her. Haunted by feelings of moral failure, shame, and violation, she finds life unendurable, and this crescendo of accumulated despair ultimately drives her to suicide.

In the aftermath of tragic events, survivors like Sophie, who escape bodily harm, are often at tremendous risk for moral injury. To understand how this can be, consider this diagram:

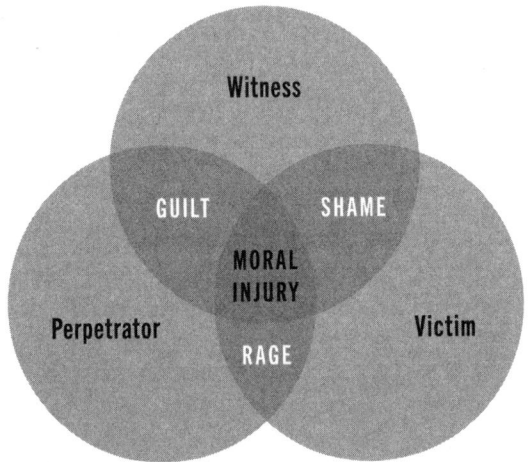

Imagine you're the victim of an immoral command, forced to perpetrate an unconscionable act and then witness the devastating consequences. You may walk away physically unharmed, but beneath the surface of your life you carry overlapping layers of guilt, shame, and rage. Even if these moral emotions are undetectable to others, they can compound over time, isolating and alienating you until they destroy your physical, psychological, and social well-being.

Victims, witnesses, and perpetrators all experience the same basic symptoms of moral injury. That's because events powerful enough to crack your moral compass will tend to make you feel both culpable and violated, as if you'd played all three roles. Whatever your objective involvement in the transgression, your conscience doesn't care about excuses or rationalizations. It doesn't care who was really at fault. It cares only that it's been nicked on your watch. So, if a transgression pierces your conscience, your conscience will blame you. The message you receive is that you *should have* figured out some way to protect your moral integrity.

Try this thought experiment: Place yourself in each of the following situations and name your feelings. Guilt? Shame? Rage? Or all three of these moral emotions?

- You teach in an overcrowded school without enough supplies, time, or bandwidth to attend to all your students, so you focus on those who need the most help . . . but those you neglect are falling behind and will probably never catch up.

- After freezing during a sexual assault in which your boss threatened to destroy your career if you screamed or fought, you report him . . . but now you're accused of "inviting" this attack because you didn't resist.

- You send your children to a school with a good safety record and excellent teachers . . . but one day, just moments after you drop them off, a troubled kid brings a gun to campus and opens fire, gravely injuring your daughter and several of her classmates.

If these examples seem too remote or extreme, then think of the emotions you feel every time you pass a car crash, an injured animal, or a stranger on the sidewalk asking for money. *I feel terrible for this poor soul, but do I stop and risk getting involved—perhaps jeopardizing my own or my companions' safety—or do I keep moving and hope someone else comes to the rescue?* Statistically, most of us choose to keep moving, especially when other witnesses are present (researchers call this the "bystander effect"). We perform similar moral gymnastics when we must choose between reporting workplace harassment and steering clear of it, between confronting friends about their addiction or tolerating it "for the sake of the friendship."

Witnessing discrimination, feeling powerless against systemic injustice, and facing ethical conflicts in business and personal relationships are all part of the moral reckoning that underscores the human condition. You're hardly alone if you make concessions to get around such tests of conscience, especially if taking a principled stand means risking your livelihood or courting physical danger. But if your dodges compromise values that are integral to your moral identity, your conscience will not forget or easily forgive. And as more and more of these incidents accrue, the guilt, shame, and anger will build, making you feel ever worse about yourself.

So, each time you rationalize not doing "the right thing"—however you personally define "right"—you're adding to your moral burden.

The critical stage of moral injury is arrived at through a graduated progression known as the crescendo effect. We'll dig into this process in chapter 5, but to get the general idea, picture your psychological self as a house poised on a system of moral fault lines, including interpersonal conflicts, workplace disputes, and more general social and political tensions. When you're feeling *good*, this house stands tall, "upright and clean" in the language of moral righteousness, with "dignity" and "integrity." Each tremor of the underlying fault lines tests this integrity, and a secure, well-balanced home that holds its moral ground can withstand many mild tremors. But even the most solid house will start to crack if the tremors are frequent and continuous, or if a major quake—like a pandemic, war, or violent crime—rocks it. Then, as your moral home loses its balance, you will start to feel *bad*, and each successive aftershock will add distress until a final crescendo of tremors knocks the house "down," shattering the integrity of its moral foundation and laying you "low." As if you'd fallen—physically, mentally, and emotionally.

The progression from good to bad, upright to fallen, has no uniform timeline. The crescendo might crest so gradually that you can't even identify why you've lost faith in yourself. Or the quake could arrive so suddenly that you feel as if you've been leveled in a single blow. In highly pressurized situations, moral injury can crescendo over a short, specific period, as it did for health workers during the pandemic. But in all these scenarios, the ultimate impact is the result of a thousand small betrayals, each compounded by the inner struggle to stay true to one's values in a world that often seems at odds with them.

The most advanced stage of moral injury is distinguished by six psychological hallmarks:

- **MORAL DISORIENTATION** makes you feel as if you don't know who you are anymore. You feel that you've lost your ethical bearings and cannot trust your own perceptions or assumptions about yourself or others. You're not functioning like normal. You're not *yourself*.

- **MORAL JUDGMENT** nevertheless dominates your thoughts. You feel profoundly wrong or wronged, preoccupied by the need to somehow correct the moral balance, to atone or make things *right*, to censure or get revenge. The impulse to judge all actions—your own and those of others—as right or wrong/good or evil can become obsessive.

- **SOCIAL DISCONNECTION** increases as distrust becomes more pervasive. This may involve isolation, alienation, or emotional withdrawal. Intimate relationships and friendships may suffer, draining social capital. This detachment can undermine work engagement, as well as social status and goodwill. The resulting loneliness and insecurity can feel like punishment or exile, even if self-inflicted.

- **DISTURBING MOODS** make it difficult to focus or function as usual. Feelings of guilt and anger may intrude during ordinary conversations and activities. Emotions can erupt out of nowhere, for no apparent reason, with incidental thoughts or actions triggering intense disgust, contempt, distrust, or shame. These moods may also prevent naturally soothing activities, like petting a dog or playing with kids.

- **SELF-HARM** invites behaviors like cutting, drinking, or drug use to numb the pain. This impulse might also extend to more subtle forms of self-sabotage, like lying or shirking duties at work or at home, which can undermine relationships and destroy trust, as well as dignity. If these enactments of rage or guilt spiral out of control, they'll worsen the symptoms of moral injury, instead of relieving them. When the pain becomes unbearable, thoughts can turn to suicide.

- **LOSS OF FAITH** occurs when it's no longer possible to see any purpose in life or redeeming qualities in oneself. Spiritual faith may hold no convincing answers. Human interactions can feel empty or false. Work loses its meaning. Such changes signal a long-term identity crisis with the power to shred the moral fabric of daily existence.

This constellation of maladies is hardly new. In fact, it's as old as the human record. When Sophocles wrote of the boy-warrior Neoptolemus, "All is disgust when one leaves his own nature and does things that misfit it," he was talking about moral injury. And in the book of Genesis, Cain's punishment for murdering his brother Abel was to wander "cursed" and "restless," bearing the "mark of Cain" so that no one would dare to kill him, thus condemning him to a long and lonely life of moral injury. But while the nature of the curse remains largely unchanged, the causes of moral injury, like all aspects of human existence, are continually evolving.

THE NEW MORAL FAULT LINES

Throughout my own life, first as the son of struggling immigrants and later in the military and as a provider of mental health services, I've observed contemporary moral injury up close. I've treated a broad spectrum of individuals whose lives were derailed by this syndrome, from impoverished farmworkers, struggling teens, and battle-scarred veterans to Wall Street traders and Silicon Valley executives. And I've concluded that the current epidemic of moral injury is escalating due to several unprecedented twenty-first-century developments, which are amplifying the risk for all of us.

I am *not* suggesting that there's more "evil" in the world today or even more "bad actors" sowing harm and disunity (though there may well be). But we do face a host of new tectonic shifts that are raising the moral threat level to heights humanity has never seen before. These include technological, environmental, and political developments for which we have no ethical playbook.

Technology

The internet is hardly not the first technological invention to test the norms of social interaction. The printing press, telegraphy, phone, radio, and television all greatly expanded the moral influence of savvy individuals and institutions, and for that reason all were controversial in their day. But the reach of online communication dwarfs any previous technology. The pervasiveness of social media, text, and email was unimaginable just a generation ago, yet it's now made everyday interactions more potentially compromising than at any other time in history.

More than five billion people use social media globally, and that number is ever increasing. We spend more than half our waking hours scrolling, posting, gaming, or working online, and data collectors mine and sell our every digital move, as well as the details of when, how, where, and with whom we connect. Complete strangers now have the means to threaten and deceive us through channels over which we have minimal control. Online predators can persuade victims to kill themselves on camera or to commit terrorist acts, for which the virtually untraceable instigators often pay no penalty. Such threats turn our everyday devices into moral hazards.

Digital technology itself, of course, is morally neutral. It can be used for socially positive, as well as negative, ends. On the plus side, social media and the internet are widely used to build online communities around mutual needs, causes, and struggles; to advance professional development and connection; to increase knowledge and understanding of complex issues and problems; to crowdsource assistance during emergencies; and to mobilize constructive movements for social change. But internet activity can also be morally corrosive, especially when users are influenced or targeted by so-called conflict entrepreneurs, including trolls, cyber stalkers, conspiracy theorists, and political extremists. The web is rife with disinformation, manipulative propaganda, personal harassment, and false accusations designed to incite moral emotions like outrage, shame, and disgust. The dark side of online interaction foments conflict and distrust, societal polarization and division, prejudice and physical violence.

Unfortunately, according to researchers who've studied the moral effects of social media, the negatives outweigh the positives—especially when use is excessive or driven by outrage rather than connection. One reason is that the internet's attention economy capitalizes on user engagement. The most reliable drivers of engagement are short bursts of content that trigger quick, strong emotional reactions, and the emotion that stokes the most viral engagement is moral outrage. Online predators and influencers who strive to grow their platforms are well aware of this formula. That's why many of them post controversial and divisive content, stripped down to base elements that arouse anger and grievance.

Much of this content includes misperceptions or outright lies about individuals or groups. Millions of ordinary web users each year are targeted for moral exploitation through virtual attacks like doxing, social cancellation, identity theft, and online stalking. Millions more are duped by online disinformation campaigns that sow doubt and discord, vilifying targeted groups and fragmenting the common ground that all healthy societies depend on. The rise in false "evidence" generated by AI only adds to the challenge of distinguishing truth from lies.

Moral outrage online often leads to the equivalent of a virtual lynch mob mentality, rendering judgment without justice for the accused or any avenue for appeal. Around the world, this pattern has incited physical violence against minority groups such as the Rohingya in Myanmar, Muslims in Sri Lanka, and anti-authoritarian activists and journalists in Cambodia and the Philippines. Such conflicts can create deep moral schisms when users become complicit in abuses they might otherwise abhor, unwittingly sharing lies that contribute to the harm of people they don't even know. Those who recognize these patterns of deception, meanwhile, may despair over their inability to prevent the damage.

Because the internet accelerates the speed and scale of moral influence beyond the range of any previous form of human communication, it is having an unprecedented and, to date, largely untested impact on the human brain and social behavior. The minimal cost of online dissemination means that content flows globally around the clock, with few barriers to access; virtually everyone with a computer or mobile device can be contacted by anonymous strangers. And who among us has the will or ability to investigate every message's veracity, much less to identify and block every unethical sender in the flurry of links, claims, and graphics that we share online? Yet without extreme online vigilance, almost any of us might find ourselves victim, witness, or perpetrator of a moral breach—possibly all, at once. As a result, moral injury is now firmly embedded in the digital arena.

The consequences ripple outward. Families fracture over ideological divides stoked by online outrage. Communities falter as trust in information sources diminishes. Individuals grapple with cognitive dissonance, questioning their own judgment. Even worse, these are the *intended* effects when bad actors pit people or groups against each other for power and profit.

Online conflict entrepreneurs include divisive media influencers who build followings by spreading sensational rumors and misinformation; political figures who exploit social or ideological fissures to fuel campaigns; corporate manipulators who stoke controversy for competitive advantage; and state-sponsored cyber agents who sow conflict to destabilize societies and disrupt political order. Because the law has few remedies for the new and proliferating forms of digital assault, many victims feel violated not only by their online assailants but by the justice system that's supposed to protect them, as well as by their own reliance on the very devices and apps that expose them to harm. This can lead to a paralyzing sense of shame, helplessness, and isolation. If we don't feel that there's anything we *can* do to change things for the better, it's impossible to know what *to* do.

Environmental Change

A collective crisis of conscience is also being fueled by unprecedented fear for the future of our planet, which researchers have termed "ecoanxiety." This fear can lead to depression, anxiety, PTSD, and even suicide—especially among young people.

In 2021, a large global study led by the English psychologist Elizabeth Marks found that nearly 60 percent of people between the ages of sixteen and twenty-five struggle with climate anxiety. More than half said they felt sad, anxious, angry, powerless, helpless, and/or guilty about the fate of the planet, and a whopping 75 percent said they found the future "frightening."

Teens who are most distressed tend to live in poorer countries in the global south, which has been hit hardest by climate disasters such as drought and flooding. But the general pessimism is universal. So is the feeling of moral betrayal—that governments and prior generations have failed to heed the warnings of climatologists. Older adults, including government and business leaders who bear the greatest ethical responsibility for greenhouse gas emissions, might complete their natural lifespans without facing the full impact of the climate crises they helped to create, but today's young people do not have the luxury of looking away. This has left them gravely demoralized.

The environmental sociologist Sarah Jaquette Ray, who's been studying a surge of ecoanxiety among her students at California State Polytechnic University, Humboldt, for nearly a decade, found that her students would "go into pretty severe depression where they weren't even leaving their rooms." She attributes this syndrome to a "cocktail of doom" that comprises shame, guilt, and anxiety over the fate of the planet. As she told NPR in 2025, "There's that complicity factor, the guilt, I don't want to have an impact, I want to refrain from my negative impact on the planet, and this kind of shame for being a human at all."

"I don't want to die," one teen told researchers. "But I don't want to live in a world that doesn't care about children and animals."

No previous society has faced the kind of existential threat that today's climate change represents. It is true that in the eight decades since the atom bomb was developed, we've all been living under a nuclear menace that includes invisible fallout and ICBMs pointed at every continent on earth, but our leaders have consistently maintained that no nuclear power would ever "press the button," because that would initiate "mutually assured destruction." Since nuclear test ban treaties have, to date, contained the threat, we might convince ourselves that these unthinkable weapons will never again be used. That's allowed the existential nuclear danger to recede from the forefront of our daily lives, out of sight and out of mind. The threat of climate change is different because it's growing exponentially, with dramatic and frightening consequences that inescapably demand our attention.

Sure, there have always been hurricanes and tornadoes and droughts, but the spike in global temperatures contributed to a more than fivefold increase in the frequency of these weather disasters between 1970 and 2019, and the numbers worsen every year. There have always been refugees during wars, but by 2050 the number of climate refugees fleeing weather-caused disasters is expected to top one billion. And while there have always been periodic famines and regional food shortages, climate change has globalized the threat to food production, inflating prices and disrupting the supply chain worldwide.

Despite countless laws, organizations, innovations, and projects dedicated to reversing global warming, the rising prospect of an unlivable planet creates countless individual moral dilemmas. As ever more catastrophic fires and storms bear down, many residents in the path of destruction must choose between saving their own lives or their neighbors', between hanging on in unsustainable locations or sacrificing their homes, between defending their own freedom or safeguarding their children. Not everyone can forgive themselves knowing their actions, from using plastic to driving gas-guzzling cars, have contributed to these disasters. But when so many of our ingrained habits contribute to the problem, how are we supposed to act in good conscience going forward?

Also, like the uncertainty around the coronavirus, uncertainty about what's "right" and "wrong" for the environment has fueled social polarization. Just when we most need to unite around our shared dependency on a healthy planet, we've been divided by fear, confusion, frustration, and feelings of betrayal, anger, and guilt—all signs of moral injury.

Political Polarization

Finally, American society is grappling with a trend toward political polarization that's been rising since the 1960s but is now more extreme than at any point since the Civil War. The divide goes beyond politics; in many quarters, the champions of the right and the left see themselves as defenders of *moral* truth and their opponents as *immoral.*

This trend isn't limited to media echo chambers. It can poison face-to-face interactions, too, as many Americans have discovered over the past decade. Shadowy operators and extremist groups, along with the politicians and celebrities they champion, have for decades been weaponizing morality as a means of gaining power and influence. The conflicts they stoke are now shaping our conversations, invading our daily decisions, and exacting a steep moral toll on our psyches.

Traditionally, Americans have been united by faith in the U.S. Constitution and Bill of Rights, our system of justice, our rights to privacy, free speech, and democracy itself. We've long believed in majority rule, without question. Few would pretend that our republic was perfect, but most preferred it over any of the alternatives. Support for our system of government has historically been equated with patriotism. We generally expected our elected representatives to pass laws that protected public health and safety for the common good.

The January 6, 2021, attack on the U.S. Capitol gave proof that those traditional assumptions no longer hold us together. Rips in the moral fabric of society have since undermined both our national unity and our traditional consensus. And the pervasive influence of disinformation spread online has accelerated those changes. Residents in red and blue states alike are inundated with messaging designed to make them feel violated by "other" racial, ethnic, religious, or political groups. Cynical operatives have politicized and polarized everything from medical advice to children's books, from gun safety to fossil fuels, from the right to vote to previously indisputable facts of American history. And they've done this largely by flooding the airwaves with moral denunciations, fear, and outright lies.

No wonder so many of us feel compelled to restore moral balance. But in the overheated cauldron of America today, even well-intentioned words and actions are often met with distrust. The turning of colleagues, friends, and relatives against each other has bred a sense of despair in many about the integrity of our country and the future of democracy itself. Distrust and despair are two core symptoms of moral injury.

When you listen to pundits and politicians insult the character of anyone who disagrees with them, how do you feel? If you feel violated, as if your sense of moral order and your faith in society's rules and protections are being threatened, you're not alone. In fact, it hardly makes any difference which side of today's issues you stand on; combustible, morally aggrieved rhetoric has become the air that we breathe. The tension it engenders runs like an electric current through our collective soul.

This tension is amplified by the daily onslaught of moral violations that we've all collectively witnessed in recent years. Unarmed Black men killed in police custody. Aid workers and journalists targeted by remote-controlled drones in conflict zones. Children abused by pedophile priests. Dedicated civil servants and corporate employees fired without cause. Millions denied vital health care due to stratospheric pricing, opaque insurance restrictions, and endless red tape. Law-abiding immigrants rounded up and denied their right to due process.

Even if we're not personally affected by these assaults, every news report serves up a fresh wave of moral outrage that spills into our inboxes. Just look at the hate-filled vitriol that targeted both Palestinians and Israelis after Hamas's 2023 attack on Israel and Israel's retaliation in Gaza. It's hard not to get pulled in.

What makes the moral injury surrounding such conflicts so contagious is the involvement of supposedly trustworthy authorities—elected officials, peace officers, clergy, judges, doctors, business leaders—who either turn a blind eye, excuse, or actively cover up grave offenses. The sheer volume of such ethical breaches can penetrate our psyches and erode our moral resilience, leaving us feeling depleted, unsafe, and uncertain even of our own code of conduct. Indeed, this tension now threatens the moral integrity of our whole society.

Disease epidemics occur when an illness spreads from a single contagious outbreak. With moral injury, one unresolved moral conflict can function like a "patient zero," triggering a cascade of consequences that ripple through families, communities, institutions, even nations, potentially afflicting multiple generations. Companies that have knowingly profited from dangerous products or policies may suffer long-term erosion of customer trust and employee morale, not to mention legal jeopardy. Countries marked by sustained moral conflicts often break into violence, with enduring geopolitical consequences. We are seeing the catastrophic price of these conflicts today in Asia and the Middle East and in the moral accusations inflaming public discourse throughout the world.

The problems before us represent an urgent call to pay closer attention to matters of conscience. The moral discomfort we're feeling is not just yours or mine alone. We all share responsibility for the changes that are reshaping our lives, our communities, and our planet. The ubiquity of these challenges, their impact on our collective moral compass, and the resulting personal and societal distress demand our immediate attention.

If we pull together, this epidemic can be mitigated. We may not yet have all the answers, but we do have effective tools to prevent, treat, and heal moral injuries. We also know that acknowledging the profound impact of these twenty-first-century challenges on our lives, both collectively and individually, is the essential first step toward restoring moral health.

CHAPTER 2

EVOLVING

The Biology of Morality

> It can hardly be disputed that the social feelings are instinctive or innate in the lower animals; and why should they not be so in man?
>
> —CHARLES DARWIN

According to the Gospel of Luke, when Jesus was asked to define what it meant to be a neighbor, he told the story of a Samaritan who came upon a man who'd been beaten by robbers and left for dead. Two others, including a priest, had passed the stranger by, but the Samaritan stopped and tended the man's wounds, then helped him to an inn and paid for him to stay there while he healed. The Samaritan, Jesus told his followers, was a neighbor because he showed the stranger mercy. And then he said, "You go, and do likewise."

Though the word "moral" doesn't appear in this parable, the story encourages two of the most universal elements of morality: compassion and kindness. It also takes as a given that there are dark, cruel forces at large in the world and within the human soul—forces of greed, evil, selfishness, and hypocrisy that represent the opposite of mercy and often get away with inflicting harm. The robbers who left their victim for dead weren't the only bearers of these dark forces; so were the priest, who embodied hypocrisy, and the other passerby who chose not to get involved. Jesus here is a voice of conscience, warning that the tension between selfishness and selflessness represents a spectrum of moral choice, and that each of us bears responsibility for the decisions we make along this spectrum.

But Jesus was hardly the first to call out this dilemma. Four centuries earlier, Plato, too, struggled to make sense of the contest between human impulses. In *The Republic* he recorded his brother Glaucon's assertion that no mortal "would be so incorruptible that he would stay on the path of justice or stay away from other people's property [if] he could take whatever he wanted from the marketplace with impunity, go into people's houses and have sex with anyone he wished, kill or release from prison anyone he wished." In other words, it's only the fear of getting caught and judged by others that stops human beings from misbehaving. That was Glaucon's conclusion around 375 BC, and in the moral psychologist Jonathan Haidt's contemporary estimation, Glaucon was right.

According to Haidt, the only way for society to control people's primal urges to behave badly—that is, selfishly, without regard for others—is "to *make sure that everyone's reputation is on the line all the time*, so that bad behavior will always bring bad consequences." This conclusion speaks to the twinned facts that the self-centered impulses we typically deem bad date back to our origins as human animals, and that moral intuitions around goodness evolved later, to promote social cooperation and group loyalty *in spite of* the human brain's tendency to make selfish choices. As the French sociologist Émile Durkheim wrote in 1893, "What is moral is everything that is a source of solidarity, everything that forces man to . . . regulate his actions by something other than . . . his own egoism."

In Latin, the word "conscience" means "to know together." The brain processes we call conscience, then, developed to link our social sense of belonging to the moral knowledge that "bad" behavior would make us feel unacceptable and "good" behavior would help us feel socially connected.

In fact, behavior that feels morally good can generally improve not just our social status but also our physical health, mental clarity, and even longevity. Studies show that moral elevation—the pleasure we feel when witnessing acts of virtue, such as kindness, generosity, and forgiveness—can reduce stress and anxiety. Moral wellness also leads to healthier habits like regular exercise and better nutrition. The practice of seeking forgiveness, in particular, alleviates guilt and shame, fosters emotional healing, promotes resilience in the face of conflict, and can play an important role in healing moral injury. On a deeper level, the two-way experience of forgiveness restores social trust, repairs relationships, and renews each participant's sense of purpose, which, in turn, has been shown to reduce inflammation, strengthen the immune system, and support healthier aging.

The power of conscience varies widely, of course, from one individual to the next. That's how we wound up with Good Samaritans at one end of the moral spectrum and unrepentant thieves at the other. But biblical and philosophical interpretations aside, where does the core conflict between ego and morality come from *biologically*, and why is it so persistent? These questions are central to our exploration of moral injury because the pain we experience when we succumb to "bad behavior" and lose faith in our own "goodness" is both emotional and physical.

THE THREE R'S

The Latin term *moralis*, coined by Cicero back in the first century BC, means "proper behavior of a person in society." Most of the values and practices that cultures throughout history have considered morally "proper" serve the greater good by moderating individual self-interest through respect for others in community. They remind group members of their interdependence—that each of us relies on our neighbors, and that fellow humans need to be able to count on each other for reciprocal protection.

Think of the pillars of morality, then, as the three R's: respect, relationship, and reciprocity. As the Three Musketeers would say, "One for all, and all for one." The group cannot survive without individual members, and individuals cannot survive without their group. This mutual need is the underlying premise of morality.

"Ethics," a term sometimes used interchangeably with "morals," more accurately refers to the philosophical rules, laws, and cultural standards that societies construct to guide the moral behavior of their members. If morality encompasses the values and principles we *feel* to be right and true, then ethics serve as the external guardrails that govern and *reinforce* those feelings.

All societies have ethical systems that reflect prevailing notions of the common good while discouraging divisive or alienating conduct. Most promote behavior that unites the group, like volunteer work and charity, while condemning offenses like rape, robbery, and murder, which threaten societal trust and stability. "Do unto others as you would have others do unto you" has been a golden rule around the globe at least since ancient Egypt because it's an easily understood reminder to keep egoism in check, and because that check generally benefits society.

But ethical systems more broadly span everything from food choices and sexual norms to sacred rituals and business transactions, and the differences between them can be vast. Humans don't come close to agreeing on all the specifics of right and wrong. We don't even agree on standards for the three R's. Among Hindus, for instance, it's a sign of deep respect to touch the feet of an elder. But in most Middle Eastern cultures, where the feet are considered impure, touching them would be read as a grave insult.

Moral values vary between individuals, geographic regions, ethnic groups, class cultures, and faith traditions, not to mention political extremes. When these values collide at the macro level, as they have done throughout history in religious and civil wars, they can lead to incalculable bloodshed—the exact opposite of the outcome you'd expect if all groups shared a uniform code of respect, relationship, and reciprocity.

Clearly, this force we're calling morality is more complex than a simple parable. And that complexity helps to explain why moral injury casts such a long shadow over the human psyche. If moral beliefs and behavior were easy to understand and reconcile, they wouldn't cause us such anguish. But how to explain the *core* contradiction? Is morality a force for brotherly love? Or is it an excuse to wage war? It can't be both! Or can it?

To answer these questions, we need to look beyond the granular differences in moral beliefs and consider the *universal* purpose of morality, which is to help people form and maintain the cooperative relationships that their *immediate groups* need for survival.

From the beginning of human history, our species has relied on social partnership to find, kill, and gather food, to procreate and raise children, to fight predators and secure territory, and to endure natural catastrophes. Growing out of this need for social cooperation, morality evolved to promote group cohesion. In this sense, within one's group, morality is inherently "prosocial." But the catch, which we'll explore more closely in chapter 3, is that group survival historically has also involved competition *between* groups. So, if the evolutionary job of morality was to secure the group, it is also needed to strengthen group defenses. As a result, the moral director we all carry inside our brains—conscience—evolved to serve the dual purpose of bonding us *together* with fellow members of our own tribe while simultaneously uniting us *against* outsiders.

This prosocial paradox goes a long way to explaining how humans got into the business of warfare, an activity that blurs the line between right and wrong and good and evil in ways that are almost guaranteed to produce moral injury. Even in seemingly minor skirmishes, loyalty to one's group can lead to impulsive, brutal, and hateful violations of the moral rights of anyone identified, accused, or mistaken as an enemy.

Not only does this paradox undermine the concept of universal human rights, but it also creates moral schisms *within* groups. What happens when friends are condemned and punished for crimes they didn't commit? Or when trusted leaders abuse or cheat other community members? Or when the majority persecutes a minority, forcing everyone in the group to take sides against friends and neighbors?

Repeatedly throughout history, societies have ruptured when group members pin their identity to positions on one side of a moral issue, and then vilify those on the other. Such struggles can cause group loyalty to generate personal anger and remorse—a crash of conscience that often results in moral injury.

Conscience, it would seem, is a complicated taskmaster with a lot of contradictory demands and physiological clout. Philosophers and scientists have spent centuries trying to figure out where this internal mechanism came from and how it became so powerful. Now, thanks to evolutionary biologists working in tandem with neuroscientists, we are beginning to glean some answers.

According to a growing body of research, the brain systems that produce the effect of conscience weave together two types of information processing:

- **Intuition** reflects the moral code that we've internalized through genetic instinct, cultural conditioning, and personal experience. Moral intuition continuously monitors our circumstances and flashes emotions that subconsciously signal whether incoming information is in sync with our moral code or not; whether it feels right or wrong.

- **Reason** employs conscious thought to translate intuition into rational perceptions, explanations, choices, and decisions that can be acted upon—or overridden if one intuition collides with another. For example, if a lie is needed to protect a friend from danger, the rational mind might overrule the moral intuition that lying is wrong. In that case, reason judges that the moral duty to defend the friend trumps the moral objection to lying.

In *Conscience: The Origins of Moral Intuition*, the neurophilosopher Patricia Churchland describes intuition and reason, respectively, as *"feelings* that urge us in a general direction, and *judgment* that shapes the urge into a specific action." This sequence produces sensations throughout the body, starting literally as "gut feelings," which then prompt the brain to think through moral reactions to ethical dilemmas.

If, for instance, you're someone who instinctively feels that stealing is wrong, your gut will prick your conscience whenever the opportunity to steal arises. But what if a medical emergency causes you to lose your job and use up your savings, and your children are now going hungry? Then, when you see a chance to shoplift a loaf of bread, your heart will race and your palms become sweaty as intuition duels with reason, one moral instinct fighting the other as you struggle to decide what to do. The experience of physical discomfort telegraphs the emotional turmoil of moral conflict.

"That voice of conscience that we hear when we consider violating a norm," Churchland writes, "is our reward system sending out a 'negative value' signal. Our conviction that we are justified in a choice does not come from some hypothetical 'pure reason' unconnected to the physical brain. It depends on what our brains have internalized as an appropriate norm—on what our reward system assigns value to, and on what constraints dominate the situation."

Intuition, then, warns us emphatically that we'll feel bad if we make the morally wrong decision. If, for whatever reason, we go ahead and do the wrong thing anyway, the dual processes of conscience will react both with bodily sensations of pain and with the mental anguish of confusion and distress. The same "negative value" signal that's designed to keep us in line with our conscience also initiates pain that can develop into moral injury when we betray the standards that our brains value most highly.

MORAL INSTINCT

Moral intuition is deeply rooted in instincts that date back to our origins as a species. In the primeval tundra, even the most rugged individualists couldn't survive, much less reproduce, on their own. Loners would die out, while those who stuck together learned that cooperation led to both longer life and strength in numbers. Natural selection then promoted social connection by passing on genetic traits that fostered collaboration. This evolutionary patterning encoded in our brains the prosocial moral instincts required to support human connectedness.

But moral evolution was not a quick or uniform process. It faced significant legacy challenges in the traits and tendencies that the human brain retained from earlier stages of evolution, especially the primitive, self-centered, and defensive instincts that predated the limbic system's focus on social and emotional attachment.

Species like reptiles, which preceded the evolution of mammals, had no need of prosocial instinct because they were designed to be loners. Unlike humans, the reptile kingdom's snakes and lizards are equipped for independence at birth. They don't need parental nurturing or instruction to survive; instead, their innate brain circuitry guides them to forage alone, to detect, hunt, and kill their prey, and to compete for mates. They have sex drives but no capacity for affection. And since they have little to do with their offspring beyond laying eggs, they have no need for maternal instinct. When faced with opportunity or threat, they'll fight, flee, or freeze but rarely assist one another. As a result, they have a strong capacity for aggression and few of the collaborative instincts that we associate with social behavior. Cold-blooded emotionally as well as physically, reptiles are pre-moral.

You might have heard the term "reptilian brain" in connection with the triune brain model proposed in the 1960s by the neuroscientist Paul MacLean. His theory was that vestiges of earlier evolutionary stages of brain development remain nested in the modern human brain. MacLean suggested that the oldest regions of the brain, including the brain stem and cerebellum, formed a "reptilian complex" responsible for primitive instincts like aggression. More recent research has debunked MacLean's notion of dated brain regions with specific controls. Today's neuroscientists have found that evolutionary changes are both more widespread and more dynamic, threading genetically throughout the cerebrum, brain stem, and cerebellum. But that doesn't mean we've left reptilian instinct behind. Quite the opposite.

As Patricia Churchland explains, "All animals must have the basic circuitry for self-care, or they will fail to survive long enough to reproduce." In other words, a certain amount of instinctive selfishness is necessary, given the world's unpredictable hostilities, even for creatures who are socially connected.

Biological adaptation, then, has taken the human animal's original self-care circuitry and tweaked it "to yield something rather new that happens to be advantageous in the struggle to survive. A few genes get altered or duplicated, with the upshot that an old function gets a new look and a new application." The old reptilian impulses thus become intertwined with newer adaptations. And instincts like the fight-flight-freeze response are woven into and around moral intuitions like tend and befriend, which evolved after mammals started raising their young.

"In the evolution of the mammalian brain," Churchland writes, "feelings of pleasure and pain supporting self-survival were supplemented and repurposed to motivate affiliative behavior. Self-love extended into a related but new sphere: other-love."

Quite simply, mammals couldn't afford to be as self-centered as reptiles. Unlike snake and lizard babies, whales and cats and chimpanzees are born helpless. If their parents didn't protect, feed, and teach them, their species would die out. The mammalian brain therefore grew to foster bonding, cooperation, and trust. And as these instincts took root, other attachments began to form, not just between parents and offspring, but also between mates and other family members, distant kin, and eventually unrelated group members. By-products of this evolution include compassion, empathy, a sense of fairness, and love.

Researchers have identified these qualities in mammals ranging from apes and elephants to dolphins and even rats. If given equal access to two boxes—one containing chocolate and another containing a fellow rat in distress—research rats will choose to free the suffering animal before helping themselves to the candy. In the wild, dolphins will heroically "carry" their injured comrades to safety by swimming directly underneath them, sometimes for hours. And elephants routinely help each other care for their young. They protect members of the herd that are injured or disabled, and they cry out to warn distant elephants of dangers such as swarms of bees or human hunters. They also grieve for their dead.

Such behavior doesn't occur solely through instinct. Emotion and thought, concern and commitment, too, are involved. Our primate cousins, including chimps and bonobos, make conscious choices each time they voluntarily share food with each other. Chimps have been known to drown while trying to save their fallen companions in zoo moats. And rhesus monkeys in research experiments will starve rather than pull on a chain that would bring them food but hurt another monkey. All these compassionate choices have counterparts in human behavior that we label "moral." As Churchland explains, "Attachment begets caring; caring begets conscience."

Our earliest hominid ancestors, who lived in small kinship groups, had a primal sense of morality. They cared for mates and offspring and shared food on a limited basis, but their earlier, more selfish instincts still dominated. They didn't share equally, and their default was to help themselves first. That only began to change some 250,000 years ago, when Neanderthals and the first *Homo sapiens* formed larger, more interdependent clans.

According to the anthropologist Christopher Boehm, when these early tribes hunted large game together,

> they had to start really punishing alpha males and holding them down. . . . you cannot have alpha males if you are going to have a hunting team that shares the meat fairly evenhandedly, so that the entire team stays nourished. . . . That set up a selection pressure in the sense that, if you couldn't control your alpha tendencies, you were going to get killed or run out of the group. . . . Self-control became an important feature for individuals who were reproductively successful. And self-control translates into conscience.

Early human collaborators developed self-control with the help of a new cognitive function that the developmental and comparative psychologist Michael Tomasello calls "second-personal morality." In order for humans to size each other up as prospective allies, their brains learned to envision future "you" scenarios. Can *you* be trusted? Will *you* pitch in and be fair? Would *we* work well as a team? This ability to imagine and assess another's capacity for cooperation helped our ancestors develop standards for respect, relationship, and reciprocity and to apply these moral standards not only to others but also to themselves.

According to Tomasello, "When everyone in a group began to share a common understanding of how things were supposed to be done, and then felt a flash of negativity when any individual violated those expectations, the first moral matrix was born." That flash of negativity was the pinprick of self-controlling conscience that got encoded in our genes. And since, over time, this flash would be threaded with guilt, shame, remorse, and fear, it could also be viewed as the first spark of moral injury.

The more that individuals used second-personal morality as a yardstick to judge each other, the more they began to care about their own moral standing in the eyes of others. Contributions to the common good now became a measure of status and self-worth, as well as a source of social capital that could be exchanged through the process that evolutionary biologists call reciprocal altruism: *I'll help your family build your hut; you'll help mine tend our children.*

On the flip side, failure to measure up morally led to social pain. *You came late to the hunt and stole all the game for yourself, so from now on you hunt alone.* The ultimate moral enforcer really was that *everyone's reputation was on the line all the time.*

"A 'we is greater than me' morality emerged," Tomasello explains. "During a collaboration, the joint 'we' operated beyond the selfish individual level to regulate the actions of the collaborative partners 'I' and 'you.'" As the two identities of "I" and "we" intertwined, the human brain internalized the shame and guilt of group betrayal so that hurting one's friends felt like hurting oneself. At the same time, the brain encoded a natural preference for kind, generous, and considerate conduct that promoted the group sense of "we."

In the early '00s at Yale University's Infant Cognition Center, the developmental psychologist Karen Wynn proved that this human preference for respect, relationship, and reciprocity is on full display in babies just a few weeks after birth. Picture a cozy, sunlit nursery with a group of wide-eyed five-month-olds seated on their parents' laps in front of a puppet theater. Onstage, a cheerful puppet struggles to open a brightly colored box. The audience of babies watch intently, their little faces reflecting curiosity as a second puppet comes along, offering the first a helping hand. The infants smile and coo. But then the story takes a twist when a third puppet appears and rudely slams the box shut, hindering the other two puppets' efforts. The babies flinch in alarm.

After the show, Dr. Wynn and her research team offered each infant the chance to play with the puppets. In a moment of pure, unspoken judgment, almost every baby reached for the helper puppet and rejected the mean one. It was as if these infants, in their silent wisdom, were voting for a world where aid is given freely and bullying is discouraged.

Karen Wynn's broader studies revealed that infants' innate preference for cooperation is not unique to specific cultures or environments. In fact, it appears to be a universal element of normal human morality. This means that a core sense of justice and compassion is wired into the very fabric of our being. It's no evolutionary accident that such instincts promote social collaboration and group stability.

But what is the chemistry behind these prosocial instincts? What are the internal mechanisms that prompt babies to reach for the "good" puppets and reject the "bad" ones? What is happening *neurologically* when toddlers smile at characters that Mr. Rogers called "the helpers"?

The scientific study of moral neuroscience is some thirty years old—still in its own infancy. We don't yet fully understand how the brain processes moral judgment and reactions, but researchers have traced some of the neural circuitry involved in conscience. We know that moral processing occurs primarily in the cortex, a brain structure unique to mammals.

Imagine the cortex as an orchestra with special sections for moral judgment, empathy, and emotions like resentment and guilt. The prefrontal cortex controls our ability to judge what's right and what's wrong. The anterior cingulate cortex, the empathy section, helps us read and resonate with the emotions of others. And acts of kindness—like puppets helping each other—prompt the pituitary gland to release harmonic waves of oxytocin, the feel-good "love hormone" that helps bond us to romantic partners, babies, family, and friends. Thanks to this orchestration, our default settings cause most of us to feel good and right when we hold the gate open for a neighbor or give a stranded friend a lift home. Volunteering at our kids' school can ignite the same glow of oxytocin-fueled pleasure as if we'd won the lottery.

Witnessing or participating in cruelty, on the other hand, normally causes the amygdala, the brain's emotional processing center for fear and aggression, to sound a neural drumroll of alarm that triggers a cacophony of dissonant stress hormones. These are the chemical culprits behind the mental and physical pain that accompanies moral injury.

While originally linked to primal behavior like aggression, the amygdala has somewhat counterintuitively evolved—over millions of years—to serve as a hub for wide-scale emotional processing. It still detects threats and triggers fight-flight-freeze responses, but intricate links to the prefrontal cortex and anterior cingulate also enable this small, almond-shaped structure to blend emotional reactions with social cognition. Its complex signals coordinate survival instincts with social responses, making the amygdala paradoxically essential both for self-defense and for group cohesion and cooperation.

When babies feel "bad" in the presence of cruelty, they're experiencing the amygdala's warning that social harmony is in trouble. This powerful response evolved to foster community cohesion and cooperation and to discourage actions that could disrupt social order. Moral discomfort and distress, then, are nature's prompts to stop and *do something* to restore fairness, justice, and social balance—to resolve the social menace of conflict. Viewed from this idealized perspective, the pain that fuels moral injury is as necessary and beneficial as good conscience; both help reinforce a well-connected society.

MORAL FOUNDATIONS THEORY

In 2004 the social psychologists Jonathan Haidt, Craig Joseph, and Jesse Graham distilled the available wealth of evolutionary and neuroscientific research on morality across cultures to create a blueprint of moral instinct, which they called moral foundations theory. The core concept of this theory is that morals evolved to help humans manage specific "adaptive challenges" that they faced as a species.

These challenges included raising and protecting children from harm; forming reciprocal partnerships; joining forces for defense against predators and competitors; organizing groups for efficiency and security; and maintaining social stability by discouraging bullies. The ethical virtues that humans have embraced to meet these challenges, according to this theory, represent the six moral foundations:

1. **Caring, kindness for dependents (to support family nurturing).** The natural need to protect vulnerable group members stokes feelings of

compassion, nurturance, and sometimes even a visceral protective response to suffering—especially when a child or other vulnerable individual is endangered.

2. **Fairness, justice in relationship (to promote cooperative partnership).** Sensitivity to unfairness and cheating is the emotional basis for reciprocity in gift giving. It's why humans generally strive for trade balance in relationships and social and economic exchanges.

3. **Loyalty, self-sacrifice for one's group (to boost defense coalitions).** Allegiance and fidelity to one's group, even at a personal cost, produces high levels of team bonding. This in turn raises a common sense of collective identity, which can be weaponized against outside groups that pose a threat.

4. **Respect, honor for authority (to maintain social order).** Individual willingness to follow leaders, to defer to traditions, and to respect hierarchy facilitates group order and cohesion, even as it permits authority figures to silence dissent or skepticism.

5. **Purity, self-control (to prevent disease).** Disgust is a biological response to dirty or tainted physical hazards, but it also can drive a quest for moral purity in social conduct and an aversion to behavior that one's group deems degrading or ethically "unnatural."

6. **Liberty in solidarity (to protect group strength and dignity).** Instinctive resistance to bullying and oppression reflects the threat that domineering individuals (like those early human alpha males) pose to the common good. Our moral aversion to tyrants who overpower and disregard the needs of the group helps us stabilize and defend society.

These moral concerns vary in degree from person to person and culture to culture. And the list is not fixed or comprehensive; researchers continue to study other virtues that may be foundational around the world. But these six foundations have been tested and found to be global, which suggests that they're encoded, to varying degrees, in the human brain, whether we're aware of them or not.

We'll revisit moral foundations theory in later chapters and take a closer look at the cultural and individual factors that determine which virtues matter more—or less—to each of us. But it's important to state up front that moral signals are not always clear. Even within the same culture, not everyone receives or interprets them the same way. Also, they often conflict with each other, as when a father's moral commitment to care for his daughter collides with his loyalty to a country that demands he fight in a war far away from her.

Unfortunately, not every moral conflict has a satisfactory remedy. No matter how hard our conscience struggles, it cannot eliminate all tension, either between competing virtues or between self-control and selfishness. "One of the greatest truths in psychology," Haidt writes, "is that the mind is divided into parts that sometimes conflict. To be human is to feel pulled in different directions, and to marvel—sometimes in horror—at your inability to control your own actions." That feeling of horror is the neural protest that catalyzes moral injury.

Throughout history this horror has involved violence. As the late Dutch primatologist Frans de Waal found while documenting the fierce and unrelenting competition among male chimpanzees, survival of the fittest often means fighting. And group survival often means fighting other groups. All of which makes war another inescapable fact of human evolution.

Archaeological evidence suggests that humans have been engaging in warfare for at least 800,000 years. In 2010, anthropologists in Spain reported finding the bones of eleven early humans, eight of them children, who had been killed—and eaten—by their Paleolithic foes. Some Stone Age cave paintings show hunters pierced by arrows. And as tribes became more territorial, they often launched raids on each other for scarce resources. To survive such attacks, combatants needed a strong residual dose of selfishness—and tribal protectiveness—to compel them to fight back.

Thus, competitive impulses remained in our brains even as the neural rewards for collaboration multiplied. And moral systems designed to cohere group loyalty for "us" intertwined with aggressive impulses that discouraged trust of outsiders—"them."

"Love for one's family members," Churchland explains, "is a colossal neurobiological and psychological fact" that helps to secure and strengthen our sense of belonging. But exclusivity is wired into the intimacy of love. We may share affection with friends, distant relatives, and neighbors, but we rarely care as deeply or feel as much trust for people we don't know well. In evolutionary terms, this makes sense, since strangers might turn out to be enemies: them.

But this us-versus-them division yields a set of moral impulses that objectively contradict each other. While most humans work hard to be virtuous and cooperative with people they view as members in good standing of their own "us" group, they tend to be suspicious of "others" who don't share or honor their collective identity. Unfortunately, cruel, even barbaric treatment of targeted "others" is common, because moral wariness can ignite a catalytic release of dopamine in the brains of "us" members, which in turn can fuel and reward open hostility.

The amygdala is like the brain's alarm system; it processes emotions such as fear and anger and prepares you to fight back whenever you sense a threat. It signals the adrenal glands to release a rush of adrenaline for energy, and areas like the nucleus accumbens and the ventral tegmental to release dopamine and other "feel good" chemicals to bolster defensive action by making aggression feel pleasurable. This two-pronged response, which both initiates aggression and rewards it, helps to explain why some fighters take pleasure in brutalizing their foes.

Perversely, this hostility high can also strengthen group bonds between "us" members. Patricia Churchland describes the moral whiplash of group aggression with unsparing candor:

> If our sociality motivates caring for others, it is also true that we are given to hate. We humans regularly derive pleasure from hating those we consider outsiders. We tend to find hating energizing. When things go awry in our lives, we can be perked up by hating and blaming outsiders or misfits. Hating those we regard as strangers may strengthen the bonds within our inner circle, which itself can make us feel elated. Our self-esteem soars as we tell each other how superior we are to those miserable wretches in the other group.

The late war correspondent Michael Herr spent two years in the 1960s documenting the human experience of combat among American troops in Vietnam. Initially, Herr thought his role as witness would insulate him from the darkest psychological effects of moral conflict—including aggression toward the enemy. "I really believed that there was a space between myself and what I was watching," he told an interviewer in 1989, "that I was on the clean side of a line and not a participant. But after a couple of months—certainly by the time of the Tet offensive—I saw my position all too clearly."

During the Tet offensive, Herr found himself firing a machine gun in defense of his life. Though the choice was a matter of survival, the experience of taking up a weapon dramatically changed his moral perspective. As he told another interviewer for the Dutch documentary *First Kill*, about the psychology of war, "Our collective unconscious is where the real shit is going on. If you're not conscious of it, it will express itself in really awful ways—in violent action, primitive."

Herr was talking about hostility highs that included "survivor's exultation" and also the base thrill of killing, an adrenaline rush that other vets in the documentary compared to the exhilaration of sex. This force field of violence, which Herr situated in the collective unconscious, was a source of moral anguish for him after he returned to civilian life, especially when Americans who'd never been to war refused to acknowledge it.

"They never explored their own violence," Herr said. "They would like to pretend that they haven't got those capacities, that they are not violent people . . . [but] saying that it's not there doesn't make it go away."

Both neuroscience and humanity's history of warfare generally support Herr's view of instinctive aggression, but that's not to say that everyone harbors the same dark tendencies in equal measures. For all the genetic patterns that unite us as humans, each of us is nevertheless unique in personality, physiology, and moral circuitry. Some people are easily aroused by group outrage and fear, which fuels hostility. Others are quiet loners who instinctively withdraw from conflict. Few of us go looking for violence, but that doesn't immunize us from causing harm. Extreme circumstances might push almost any of us to extreme behavior.

Human thought and behavior can also be conditioned by structural anomalies in the brain or by changes in neural circuitry resulting from injury, illness, medication, or substance use. In some cases, physiological factors can distort or disable the moral mechanisms of empathy and conscience. The most extreme and problematic example of this structural abnormality is psychopathy.

Even though they make up just about 1 percent of the general population, psychopaths have an outsized impact on society. They account for more than one-fifth of the prison population and are fifteen to twenty-five times more likely than non-psychopaths to commit serious crimes, such as murder, rape, arson, and identity theft. Studies of virtual behavior have found that psychopathy is also by far the most common driver of trolling, cyber stalking, doxing, and other antisocial activity online.

Psychopaths generally understand the objective rules of right and wrong, but they feel no personal investment in moral behavior, no need to "be good," no fear of "being bad." When convicted of crimes, they typically express no compassion, empathy, guilt, shame, embarrassment, or remorse. Yet they test the moral fiber of virtually everyone they encounter, both by preying on victims and by luring accomplices and unwitting associates into ethical breaches that often lead *them* to moral injury.

The causes of psychopathy include abnormalities in the amygdala and ventral medial prefrontal cortex—unsurprisingly, a system that is directly involved in moral decision-making. These anomalies, according to Patricia Churchland, result in

> a lack of feelings of guilt or remorse, the absence of significant bonding with others, and a lack of compassion or empathy even for those in the family who have shown them great affection. Psychopaths are narcissistic and are pathological liars, showing no sense of embarrassment or shame when caught flat out in a barefaced lie. They are without a moral compass.

There is a degree of emotional variation here. Some prisoners who are diagnosed as psychopaths may be unable to answer questions like

Is murder an immoral act, or just unconventional behavior? Or, *What does guilt feel like?* But others, like the serial killer Ted Bundy, are cold-bloodedly rational, fully aware of the difference between ethical and criminal behavior. They simply have no compunctions about acting immorally or manipulating others, and no inclination to control their own amoral impulses. Because they're impervious to social rejection, they are also immune to moral injury.

Unfortunately, psychopathic ruthlessness can be an effective tool for power. According to the forensic psychologist Robert D. Hare, high-functioning "successful psychopaths" can be charming and socially skilled enough to manipulate others in arenas like politics, business, and the military. When Hare and his team tested 203 participants in corporate management development programs, they found that 3 percent of these rising executives had psychopathic traits. And the rate of psychopathy rises with corporate success, since CEOs are often rewarded for being tough, calm under pressure, decisive, and fearless—all qualities that come naturally to psychopaths.

In a *Forbes* article titled "Psychopaths Who Lead Us," leadership expert Gautam Mukunda zeroed in on Al Dunlap, the late CEO of Scott Paper and Sunbeam, and Elizabeth Holmes, the biotech founder of Theranos. According to Mukunda, Dunlap "so reveled in firing people that he dubbed himself 'Chainsaw Al' and titled his autobiography *Mean Business* (the double meaning was intentional)." Elizabeth Holmes was sentenced to more than eleven years in prison after being convicted of cranking her company's valuation up to $9 billion by lying about its blood-testing technology.

The tragedy of Theranos's chief scientist, Ian Gibbons, illustrates the ways that such corporate heads can become instruments of moral injury for others. A seasoned and accomplished British scientist, Gibbons was one of Holmes's first hires, and for years he oversaw the company's research, which he believed had promise. But he also felt that the technology wasn't safe or reliable when Holmes began marketing it. Afraid of repercussions, Gibbons hesitated to speak out. But he also feared that patients who were using the technology could be impacted. He tried to warn Holmes, and he told his colleagues that the technology didn't work. Finally, under increasing pressure to testify, he died by suicide.

The moral hazards can be even greater when psychopaths rise in government. Heinrich Himmler, who devised and oversaw Germany's concentration camps under Hitler, lacked empathy, was manipulative and cunning, and treated his victims with sadistic brutality. He is widely considered to have been a psychopath. And while the atrocities committed by Nazi leaders during the Holocaust represent an extreme example, it's worth remembering that more than 800,000 SS personnel executed Himmler's commands. Statistically, it's unlikely that all those SS members, too, were psychopaths, yet somehow they performed the moral jiujitsu required to override their conscience as they murdered and brutalized innocent civilians. This is what I mean by the outsized danger that psychopaths pose to the moral health of everyone else in society.

For all that human evolution has done to prime us as moral beings, moral choices continue to vex our species. Ethical dilemmas are rarely as clear or simple to sort out as we'd like. And social conflicts that test our good conscience often defy our rational control. Just like our ancient forebears, we must still contend with the dark forces of others, as well as with our own conflicting instincts.

This moral mess has always posed a challenge for society. Early farmers needed to trust each other as they worked together to feed their communities, but they also had to guard against those who would try to shirk their duties or cheat the others. Early societies needed soldiers whose adrenaline in combat would turn them into killing machines, but they also needed to convert these killing machines into peaceful civilians when they returned home. For groups to survive, leaders had to come up with ethical systems and practices that leveled the moral playing field, dealt with deficits in conscience, and prevented social harm while still motivating individuals to become violent when necessary to defend the group. These ethical balancing acts have varied dramatically in different civilizations over time, playing their own integral role in the evolution of morality.

CHAPTER 3

CIVILIZING

The Power of Moral Communities

If civilization is to survive she must rediscover the moral and spiritual ends for living.

—MARTIN LUTHER KING JR.

Whenever I travel back to my parents' homeland, I'm reminded of the central role that *familismo*—the primacy of family and community ties—plays in Mexico's culture, especially in small towns and villages, which have been less influenced than cities by modern American-style values. Personal struggle in traditional Mexican society is a family affair, which can make challenges both easier and harder to resolve. On the one hand, you have moral support in meeting difficulties and coping with ethical dilemmas; you're not alone. On the other, if you bring shame or dishonor to your family, you have a lot of people besides yourself to answer to. To make things right, you might need to sacrifice some personal goals to restore harmony and balance across multiple relationships, because those relationships constitute the moral fabric of life in tightly knit cultures.

Immigrants coming to America from traditional societies like my family's often bring their sociocentric values with them. This can offer the advantage of strong social support. But it can also set up a culture clash for those who try to assimilate. In the United States, moral virtue tends to hinge on individual integrity and responsibility. Most Americans are taught to exalt personal rights, even if those rights violate group expectations, traditions, or beliefs. They're also judged on their own merits and decisions. Turning to family for help or advice can be viewed in America as a sign of weakness, even as cheating, since performance here is considered a personal, rather than family, responsibility. By the same token, moral lapses are often treated—and internalized—as individual failings, not group problems.

How did our cultures come to have such different approaches to morality? As I dug into that question, I realized the answer is as complex as the history of morality itself.

Scientists often study genetics and culture as if these systems had little to do with each other, but in fact the same genes that shape human behavior necessarily influence human philosophy, religion, and politics—and vice versa. There's a constant ebb and flow between our biological instincts and the decisions we make socially and morally, and this tide spills across generations and societies. As a result, many of the cultural designs that originally reflected our ancestors' genetic tendencies are still conditioning our own moral compasses. And societal changes we make today may influence adaptations of moral instinct—and moral injury—in our grandchildren. Culture and biology are thus engaged in a kind of coevolution.

THE EVOLUTION OF ETHICS

This adaptive circuit, from biological instinct to cultural influence and back again, has been training moral behavior ever since the first murmurs of the human family, but the guidelines and expectations we now call ethics are a little more recent. Anthropologists believe that groups began formalizing rules of social conduct some 200,000 years ago, when small closely knit bands first expanded into geographically dispersed tribes. At that point, kinsmen needed new ways to secure tribal identity and loyalty over long distances, to maintain trust bonds despite separation, and to distinguish friendly strangers from potential enemies.

Those societal challenges prompted leaders to start building ethical structures that included community rituals and shared traditions. Elaborate headdresses weren't just fashion statements; like team hats or jerseys, they helped tribal members recognize each other from afar. So did verbal chants and scarring or body painting with symbolic insignia. Ceremonial rites of passage, gift exchanges, and dietary rules also helped secure the group's internal sense of tribal identity—and distinction from other tribes. Conformity helped keep the group together and therefore needed to be encouraged. That's where morality came in.

To make the new rules and habits stick, chiefs enlisted the power of social reputation. They directed tribal members to reward "good" compliant conduct with approval while reacting to "bad" deviant behavior with revulsion. Leaders might instruct the group to shun or attack members who rebelled, showering outcasts with the moral disgust they otherwise reserved for enemies. In this way, collective social instincts became intertwined with the preservation of group identity. Moral correctness was bound to a sense of shared belonging and security; moral independence summoned fears of being shunned. And the same ethical systems devised to strengthen and secure group bonds also served to discourage and punish not only criminal behavior but also diversity and dissent. The resulting threat of social rejection gradually became encoded in moral instinct and, through that process, also contributed to the pain of moral injury.

With the development of farming some twelve thousand years ago, geographic and ethnic distinctions were rolled into the ethical systems separating tribes and nations. If competition for territory and resources led to war, these differences could be turned into rallying cries that energized fighters to protect "us" by dehumanizing the enemy as "them": *Fight for our land! Our people! Our way of life, against theirs! It's our moral duty to defeat them!*

Note that the earliest moral cries did *not* invoke religion. You might be surprised to learn that religion originally had little to do with morality. Early tribes had plenty of sacred rituals, but their gods tended to be disinterested in human interactions. These shamanic deities, like the god *Cher eezi*, still worshipped by the small ethnic Tuva group in Siberia, were primarily responsible for the natural world, weather, protection of the land and harvests. The Tuva do make ceremonial offerings to *Cher eezi*, whose name means "spirit of the world," but for moral harmony they rely on familial bonds and secular traditions of sharing and reciprocity, rather than the instruction or oversight of any supernatural authority.

According to the social psychologist Ara Norenzayan, religions only began to mind human morality with the rise of great civilizations, like Egypt and Mesopotamia. It was the need to unify and control vast populations that caused leaders to invent the moral enforcement mechanism that Norenzayan calls the Big God.

Unlike *Cher eezi*, Big Gods acquired ever more powerful and omniscient reputations as their followers multiplied and dispersed. The ancient Egyptian sky god Horus, for example, was often depicted as a keen-eyed falcon, vigilant and all-seeing, his piercing gaze promising divine surveillance of followers' moral conduct across a territory that stretched from modern-day Syria all the way to Sudan and Libya. Buddha's serene eyes, likewise, are said to see in four directions with an omnipresent awareness that transcends geographic boundaries. So, too, is the God of the Abrahamic religions generally described as omnipotent and omniscient, watching and judging every soul from heaven above. As Hebrews 4:13 of the New Testament explains, "Nothing in all creation is hidden from God's sight. Everything is uncovered and laid bare before the eyes of him to whom we must give account."

Once Big Gods became all knowing, or so their priests told followers, they could monitor minds and hearts and pass moral judgment on human behavior 24/7, anywhere and everywhere. This turned Big Gods into supersized consciences, able to shame, guilt, frighten, and reward believers into following whatever ethical strictures their high priests prioritized. In other words, they served as proxies for human authorities who couldn't be everywhere at once and so relied on the "fear of God" to compel widespread loyalty and compliance.

In the First Babylonian Dynasty, the Code of Hammurabi, one of the earliest and most complete sets of recorded laws, was inscribed on a stone stele and placed in a public space for all to see, in part "to bring about the rule of righteousness in the land, to destroy the wicked and the evil-doers; so that the strong should not harm the weak." But what secured this ethical code was belief that Babylon's Big God Marduk watched over the city to ensure that justice was served. Fear of divine retribution from Marduk gave the laws unassailable authority, which not even King Hammurabi could command on his own.

The spiritualization of morality allowed ancient civilizations like Babylon to impose group cohesion and cultural norms and traditions, even as their populations diversified. When total strangers worshipped the same god, they could be called upon to make common cause and work together as if they belonged to one family. They were more likely to trust and accept each other. And they could more easily be riled up to form alliances as "us" against "others," including heretics and anyone who worshipped different Big Gods.

The Egyptian pharaoh Ramses II, who claimed authority directly from deities like Ra and Osiris, invoked the Big God Amun to inspire his troops and justify his campaign during the Battle of Kadesh in 1274 BC. The Greek city-states united under the banner of the Big God Zeus to defend their homeland against invaders during the Persian Wars in the fifth century BC. And the Roman Empire's subsequent expansion was often justified through the divine mandate of Jupiter, the Big God king who was believed to favor Rome's conquests and bring order to the world. But the Big Gods weren't limited to the Western world. During China's Zhou dynasty, from 1046 BC, the emperor claimed to be the Son of Heaven, appointed by the celestial deities to maintain harmony between the heavens and earth through the rule and expansion of empire. Even after the Zhou dynasty finally fell in 256 BC, that notion of divine mandate continued to secure imperial power in China for another two thousand years.

This pattern spread across civilizations, one savvy ruler after another enlisting Big Gods to help simultaneously maintain civil order within their own kingdoms and justify their empire building by inciting holy wars against others. *Good for us*, kings and priests messaged relentlessly through their Big Gods, but *bad for them*. This signaling worked like magic, as Jonathan Haidt explains, because "sacredness [as well as morality generally] binds people together, and then blinds them to the arbitrariness of the practice." Blinds them, in other words, to the fundamental fact that "they" are just as human as "we" are.

Unfortunately for the troops who fought their holy wars, Big Gods offered little comfort once the storm of combat was underway. And by conflating faith-based morality with incitement to assault, torture, and murder on the battlefield, the political maestros of the all-seeing gods compelled soldiers to pay a horrific personal price. After the adrenaline and dopamine rush of aggression wore off, warriors had to face savaged corpses, grievously wounded teammates, and devastated innocents, and they couldn't always deny or overlook the victims' humanity or their own moral complicity in the carnage.

Homer chronicled the moral penalty of war in *The Odyssey* by tracking the changes in Odysseus's character after he'd led his Greek troops to victory against the Trojans. The simple truth is that Odysseus lost his moral compass on the voyage home. In the struggle to sedate his own trauma from the war, he multiplied the moral injury many times over among the very men he claimed to love, honor, and lead—his "us." He became selfish and callous, squandering most of their lives through his indulgence and recklessness in adventures with Cyclops, Calypso, the Sirens, and the Lotus-Eaters, until finally he wound up shipwrecked and alone, at the mercy of the very gods who had sent him into battle in the first place. What Homer was trying to show through Odysseus was that, in ancient times as today, moral injury posed a real problem for society by stripping war veterans of their ability to function as productive citizens.

To address this problem, the same religious authorities who designed the Big Gods invented special rites to purge troubled souls of their sins. In Rome, soldiers made ceremonial sacrifices known as *lustratio* while passing beneath a special beam with their heads covered in a ritual of purification. In ancient Athens, combat veterans performed *katharsis* by witnessing tragic plays to expiate moral transgressions and clarify their minds and hearts. In the medieval Christian church, purification took the form of penance, which was adjusted up or down, according to the weight of transgression. Knights returning from the Crusades would undertake pilgrimages, fasts, or other acts of self-sacrifice to atone for the bloodshed and atrocities committed during their campaigns. The church maintained that such rituals would cleanse warriors' souls and restore their moral standing both in the eyes of God and in their communities. If only it were that simple.

Such rites highlight religion's long and troubling history as both instigator and mitigator of moral injury. Religious performances of atonement and purification often had less to do with relieving individual suffering than they did with protecting those in power. Priests and kings were not themselves deities, after all, but mortals who embodied the same moral contradictions as any other members of our species; their moral compasses often skewed to selfishness. And they grew adept at weaponizing sacred morality's tendency to bind and blind anyone who might threaten their command. If binding and blinding weren't sufficient, they would excommunicate.

In medieval Europe, for example, the Catholic Church claimed a divine mandate to safeguard society's moral and spiritual purity by conducting inquisitions, but the church leaders' true objective was to exterminate competing "heretical" faiths and beliefs and consolidate power under Catholic monarchs. For seven hundred years, then, the church prosecuted "moral crimes" that commingled civil offenses, such as rape and tax fraud, with religious blasphemy and heresy, including the "crime" of being Jewish or Muslim. All under the guise of righteousness, the condemned were tortured and exiled or executed, with a total death toll that's estimated to have run into the millions.

But the dead and physically maimed weren't the only casualties of the inquisitions. Church tribunals also inflicted deep psychological and spiritual wounds on countless individuals who were coerced into giving false witness, brutalizing prisoners, or passively witnessing atrocities. The ripple effect of institutionalized moral injury often begins with leaders using "higher purpose" or divine authority to justify orders they know to be wrong; it then extends to those who become victims or instruments of injustice out of obedience to these authorities—whom they've been taught to trust or fear. The trauma doesn't stop there, though. It radiates outward, even affecting subsequent generations who inherit the resulting psychological and spiritual wounds through family or community hostilities and dysfunction. Over time, the struggle to reconcile personal values with a legacy of guilt, shame, rage, and injustice becomes a collective scar. The evolution of moral injury is closely tied to this intergenerational fallout, especially after major historical depredations.

Remember that morality is both socially constructed and historically situated. Personal conscience and collective conscience coevolve with the help of cultural influences, including commerce and religion. Through the centuries, theological leaders have constructed elaborate ethical scaffolds to support their preferred economic power structures, and these frameworks have molded moral sensibilities to reflect and accommodate the resulting social order. By binding believers to "sacred" hierarchies of power and group identity while blinding them to intrinsic injustices within these systems, religious doctrine could also ease the personal discomfort of ethical compromise. In other words, doctrine has often invoked religious reasons to persuade believers to "trust in God," even when that trust violates their own moral intuitions.

For centuries, Christian claims of divine will provided conquerors and defenders of slavery with reassurance that the subjugation of their fellow human beings was justified, or at least permissible, within a sacred "tradition." But the religious dogma that supported the decimation of Native Americans, enslavement of kidnapped Africans and their descendants, and related forms of oppression didn't only rationalize actions; in many cases it actively reshaped the moral capacities of individuals to such a degree that their conscience no longer triggered disgust at those actions. This spared them the moral emotions of guilt, shame, and remorse that they'd have felt had they not been blinded to the simple fact that Indigenous and enslaved people deserved to be treated not as "them" but as full human beings. Morality's tendency to bind and blind whole groups of believers then allowed white European and American clergy to perpetuate schemes like the Indian Removal Act of 1830 and the Fugitive Slave Act of 1793 while handily shielding slaveholders and settlers on stolen Indian land from the inconvenient obstacle of moral injury.

This spiritual protection did not extend, however, to slaves, Native Americans, or their descendants. As the nineteenth-century abolition and later Indigenous rights movements grew in competing corners of theology and society, ordinary citizens' moral blinders began to fall, and the tilt of moral reputation began to shift. The result, as the historian Jon Meacham writes, is a battle for "the soul of America" that ignited the Civil War, raged through Reconstruction, Jim Crow, and the civil rights movement, and continues to tear us apart today.

Each new generation of Americans must grapple anew with the repercussions of our country's seminal moral trauma. Centuries after the last slaves were freed, the fight for justice, forgiveness, and atonement continues. It's no accident that faith leaders often find themselves at the forefront. In 2018, for instance, the Catholic sisters of the Religious of the Sacred Heart in Louisiana created a reparations fund to finance scholarships for Black students. Other multimillion-dollar reparations funds were announced by Virginia Theological Seminary and Princeton Theological Seminary and several Episcopal dioceses. In 2021 the Jesuit Conference of Canada and the United States pledged $100 million in reparations.

All of those churches had histories of endorsing and participating in the institution of slavery—vivid evidence that religion's influence on ethical development and social cohesion is a double-edged sword that can lead to both oppression and virtue.

CIVIL SOCIETY

For all their power, the Big Gods never did secure an exclusive hold on the ethics governing society. Early philosophers also studied virtue and vice, and their efforts yielded ethical frameworks that could operate free from divine oversight. Confucius emphasized the importance of *ren* (benevolence) and *li* (proper conduct), teaching that a harmonious society depended on the moral integrity of each individual. Socrates pursued the concept of *eudaimonia* (flourishing/happiness), arguing that living a virtuous life was essential to achieving true fulfillment. Later Stoics, such as Marcus Aurelius, believed in a universal reason (*logos*) that governed the cosmos and human behavior.

As a general rule, these philosophers all taught that virtue was the highest good and that individuals should live in accordance with nature and reason. In their various languages and examples, all emphasized respect, relationship, and reciprocity.

Then, in the eighteenth century, with the Spanish Inquisition waning, European scientists, philosophers, and intellectuals began to openly question religion's stranglehold on ethics. Societies with trustworthy systems of secular law and justice acknowledged the benefits of separating church and state. And the Enlightenment ushered in an age of secular moral contemplation that challenged the supremacy of both monarchy and religion.

Visionaries like John Locke and Immanuel Kant emphasized reason, personal accountability, and the universality of moral principles such as reciprocal fairness, duty within relationship, and respect for human dignity. Locke cast life, liberty, and property as fundamental human rights, deriving moral principles from rational thought and human nature rather than divine command. Kant's categorical imperative, which posits that one should act only according to maxims that can be universally applied, provided a rational basis for ethics that focused on duty and the inherent dignity of all individuals.

The Enlightenment brought forth a vision of society governed by a legal framework that promoted justice and collective well-being—free from the heavy hand of religious doctrine. This secular vision encouraged individuals to honor their own moral beliefs without fear of divine retribution or ecclesiastical punishment. One could now be morally good without praying or, indeed, believing in any Big God.

Even as morality moved away from spirituality, though, the spirit of morality was still collective. The core goal of secular ethics, consistent with moral instinct, was to help humans help each other. It's just that the three R's—respect, relationship, and reciprocity—no longer required divine oversight. In a sense, this tilt away from theological authority restored humanity's original preset (though it now seemed revolutionary): the implicit understanding that people are responsible for their own moral conduct, whether or not there's a deity watching.

These "radical" notions paved the way for the American and French Revolutions and the drafting of the U.S. Constitution. America's Founding Fathers, influenced by Enlightenment principles, explicitly separated church and state in the First Amendment so that laws would be based on reason and fairness, rather than religious doctrine. In the French Revolution, the cry for "Liberté, égalité, fraternité!" sought to dismantle the deep-rooted power of the Catholic Church over French society. Shedding religious control was seen as essential for liberty and justice to flow to all; citizens must be free to follow their own moral convictions without theological coercion.

But the increasingly secular societies that grew out of the Enlightenment now required a judicial representation of human conscience that was at least as effective as a Big God. Not only did this legal surrogate need to curb immoral behavior; it also had to mitigate moral injury by restoring ethical balance, healing the wounds inflicted by wrongdoing, and upholding the dignity of every individual. As the philosopher John Rawls observed, by ensuring fairness and respecting individuals, a just society *prevents* moral harm.

Laws, courts, and enforcement authorities, then, needed both to promote honest and responsible behavior and to remedy damage done by criminals and bullies. The new legal systems had to persuade citizens that their moral grievances would be heard impartially and that justice would be meted without fear or favor. And as the weight of religious conformity lifted, modern ethics also had to grapple with a whole new cultural ideal: individualism.

THE RISE OF INDIVIDUALISM

If you're American or European, what I'm about to reveal may surprise you, but the truth is that individualism is WEIRD. This acronym, coined by the cultural psychologists Joe Henrich, Steve Heine, and Ara Norenzayan, stands for Western, Educated, Industrialized, Rich, and Democratic, and it's meant to signal that WEIRD societies contain "the least representative populations one could find for generalizing about humans." That's because the vast majority of cultures around the world have always been—and still are—*sociocentric*, rather than *individualistic*.

As in my grandparents' Mexican village, people in traditional societies assign moral privilege to the needs of family groups and sacred institutions, not to individual freedom. Their ethics favor what's good for the group, even at the expense of personal or private rights, and people typically feel the most moral distress if they believe they've let down their family or community. Moral goodness, too, is linked to group values and responsibilities, rather than personal ambitions. For example, an employee ordered by his company to relocate from his hometown to a distant city might feel anguish over abandoning his community for the sake of his career. Likewise, his obedience to an unrelated boss could be viewed by his family as a moral betrayal. More than a personal wound, such conflicts reflect the fact that moral integrity in sociocentric cultures hinges on the preservation of group harmony and honor. Conscience is collective, not individual.

Citizens of WEIRD societies often act as if individual rights are universally sacrosanct, but for many in non-WEIRD cultures the concept of individual rights doesn't even compute. Henrich and his team found that members of sociocentric cultures literally *perceive* the world differently than Western individualists do.

This distinction has to do with the different ways the brain processes objective information. One approach, called holistic thought, views a given scene in its entirety, with individual objects registering only in relationship to each other and to the big picture. The other approach, analytic thought, focuses instead on each object as a whole unto itself, as if detached from the big picture.

Henrich's research team tested different cultures' processing approaches by presenting people with an array of miscellaneous objects and asking them to sort the objects into subgroups. They found that Chinese participants typically connected items that somehow worked together, like pencils with notebooks, or sky with sunshine. American participants, on the other hand, grouped items according to rules about their individual properties, like notebooks with magazines (because both were forms of books). The team concluded that Westerners tend to be analytic when sizing up a situation, paying more attention to abstract rules and the traits of individual objects than to the relationship or interaction *between* objects. People from Asian, African, or Middle Eastern cultures, in contrast, tend to focus on the potential for cooperative interaction. Bottom line, we in the West see a world populated by separate and distinct objects, individuals, concerns, and issues. Elsewhere, people see the world as a system of interpersonal roles and relationships serving a cooperative purpose. In Africa, this system is reflected in the core moral philosophy of *ubuntu*, which generally translates to mean "I am because we are."

So, where did this great divide between WEIRD and non-WEIRD come from? The Enlightenment paved the way. But the American and French Revolutions, with their celebration of freedom and equality, radically demoted the principle of *inter*dependence that had governed moral behavior for 99 percent of human history. In 1776, the promise of life, liberty, and the pursuit of happiness enshrined in America's Declaration of Independence celebrated the rights of individuals—not states, religions, families, or communities—to determine their own destiny. Emerson, Thoreau, and Whitman wrote lyric odes to this new ideal of American self-reliance, which, in the words of Alexis de Tocqueville, "disposes each citizen to isolate himself from the mass of his fellows and withdraw into the circle of family and friends; with this little society formed to his taste, he gladly leaves the greater society to look after itself."

The land of the free and the home of the brave thus set a new precedent for social order, and the chains of moral obligation to the group fell away, to be replaced by a system that the sociologist Émile Durkheim dubbed "the cult of the individual."

Right from the start, the cult of individuality stressed freedom over connection, competition over collaboration. But the arrival of the Industrial Revolution in the early nineteenth century accelerated this shift in ways that few of the original revolutionaries could have imagined.

Until that moment, most people in both the New and the Old Worlds lived and worked in small communities that still generally adhered to cooperative traditions, with everyone's personal roles and identities closely intertwined. The village miller bought wheat from local farmers and turned it into flour for the town baker, who sold bread to both the miller and the farmers. Whole towns worshipped and socialized together. They gathered to build each other's houses and expected their children to grow up, marry each other, and take over the family businesses, following the global pattern of interdependence passed down over generations and tied to community. Morality was still intertwined with group acceptance and inclusion.

As long as horses were the primary means of transportation, few people challenged this status quo or moved far from their birthplace. Even those who did emigrate tended to settle down at their destination and replicate the same system of community life they'd grown up with. Appealing as the idea of individual freedom might sound, the practical logistics of society didn't permit just anyone to venture off in search of personal fortune.

Industrial mechanization changed that. Suddenly tools were produced in city factories instead of by the local blacksmith. Fabric was spun in textile mills instead of at home on looms. Trips that used to take weeks by horse now took only a day or two by train. And family reputations and social ties were no longer prerequisites for jobs that paid a steady salary. Assembly work in the city could provide more economic opportunity than could many family shops and farms.

Young American and European workers in the late nineteenth century, just like rural workers in China and India a century later, began to flock from farms to urban areas in search of those promising industrial jobs. Suddenly generations within families were separated by long distances. Small towns and villages shrank. And the spirit of interdependence began to wither. This produced what Durkheim called "a spontaneous weakening of the old social structure."

There have been moments, to be sure, when this weakening reversed itself. As Robert Putnam pointed out in *Bowling Alone: The Collapse and Revival of American Community*, "The story of social capital in America during the past 125 years turns out to look like an inverted U-curve." While the country was almost as fragmented in 1900 as it would again be at the end of the twentieth century, the threat of fascism during World War II unified the nation around the shared goal of defeating a mortal enemy. But America's wealth and power gaps began to widen precipitously with the Reagan Revolution of the 1980s, and many of those who've since been left behind feel morally betrayed by the effects of individualism.

For the first time in nearly three centuries, the generation coming of age today cannot expect to do as well economically as their grandparents. Nearly 40 percent of millennials are saddled with student debt that will follow them for decades, compared with only about 18 percent of their parents who had student debt at their age. And the racial wealth gap hasn't closed, either. In 2021, household wealth for Black and Hispanic families was more than 80 percent lower than for white families.

The greatest moral alienation is occurring at the bottom of the income ladder, where economic resentments are fueling social and racial hostility, political conspiracies, and hate groups. Distrust between class and ethnic clusters is rampant, and isolation, fear, and outrage—symptoms of moral injury—are all on the rise.

TODAY'S DIGITAL DIVISIONS

In many ways, the advent of digital technology has accelerated these trends. That's not to say that technology itself has agency; our apps and devices are largely inert until we interact with them. Tech's effect—positive or negative—depends largely on the mindset and uses we humans apply to it. But the speed and scale of online communication, including access to information and opinions, make it an unprecedented conduit for influence over our values and behavior.

When approached with positive intention and a sense of personal responsibility, the web can amplify human connections, foster collaboration, and provide a platform for expansive knowledge and cooperation.

Digital tools like Zoom, Gmail, and Slack have been used to organize environmental campaigns to fight climate change, to bring literacy and mental health support programs to rural and underserved areas, to raise global health awareness, and to crowdsource information and assistance during public emergencies. But over the past thirty years, digital technology has played an undeniably mixed role in the moral evolution of society. One reason is that human behavior online can easily sidestep the ethical norms that have governed social behavior for millennia.

Humans aren't built to "go it alone." Our brains are wired for direct face-to-face contact and reciprocity, for physical company, intimacy, touch, laughter, and emotional support. We thus evolved to function within a limited social geography of people we actually know or at least have met in the flesh. But now, in just a couple of decades, virtual communication has challenged our social equipment to connect with a potentially limitless number of strangers anywhere in the world—all at once and all while being simultaneously alone behind our screens.

There's little room in this virtual setup for the moral intuitions that we'd normally rely on as social safeguards. Screens don't allow us to see the twitching foot or smell the fear that we might if we sat physically with each other in the same room. That amounts to a moral handicap, which we all carry online, so that every time we interact onscreen, images can be misread or manipulated to mislead.

It's difficult to be completely authentic online, even when you want to be. And many bad actors don't want to be; instead, they take advantage of digital shielding to serve their own self-interests, which often involve predatory and divisive engagement with unsuspecting users. Some online insults and deceptions are too subtle or personal for platforms to even detect, but they still can do huge moral damage. And virtual lies, threats, theft, assault, and intimidation can be weaponized at scales that are too large to police and too invasive for most people to avoid. Much predatory behavior online can be traced to conflict entrepreneurs with psychopathic and antisocial tendencies, but trolls and cyber stalkers are assisted by the screening effect that's built into all digital "connection."

Our moral instincts are also co-opted online by the ranking and recommendation systems that tech platforms set to drive virtual engagement. Algorithms learn user preferences and deliver the content most likely to get clicks, hold attention, and go viral, even if that content may be deceptive or harmful. They capitalize, in other words, on social contagion. And no human emotion is more contagious than moral outrage.

Rooted in the primitive moral instinct to protect one's family and friends from imminent physical threat, outrage is stoked by stories that portray members of other groups as menacing. Such stories tighten loyalty and identification with one's own "endangered" group while arousing surprise and disgust that inflames hostile aggression toward the Other. This mental lynch mob effect has had catastrophic consequences, especially for marginalized groups, throughout history, but online content today exposes us to more moral outrage than we've ever experienced before—than print media, TV, and radio combined.

Research on the relationship between digital technology and morality suggests that social media often accelerates moral outrage. That's because hate speech and lies about moral infractions ignite far more readily and frequently online than complex facts or stories of inclusivity and acceptance. And the more hate speech proliferates, the more it is accepted; researchers have found that people who get most of their news through digital media consider hate speech normal, not morally bad. This, in turn, makes them think it's socially acceptable to discriminate and persecute, even to entertain violence against the targets of the online hatred they consume.

The most dangerous deceptions are often preposterous conspiracy theories. Remember the viral "Pizzagate" claim that led one true believer to shoot up a pizza restaurant because of online lies that it was the center of a pedophile ring? The gunman honestly believed he was a crusader for moral good because the hoax had hijacked his moral instinct and judgment. The increasing frequency of incidents like this demonstrates that the spread of moral outrage as clickbait isn't just fragmenting society; it's endangering all of us.

On an individual level, some of these hazards can be avoided by balancing our daily use of technology with social connection in real life. When we spend all our working hours alone doing gig jobs or staring at a screen; when our primary forms of diversion isolate us instead of bringing us together; when we have our most meaningful conversations reduced to sounds and images on a handheld device—we frustrate our basic instinct to connect with others through physical presence.

We need physical interaction to develop empathy, and we need empathy to remind us why and how it's important to treat each other right. Moral respect, relationship, and reciprocity require practice, and we don't get that practice when we're reduced to little boxes on a screen, so it's vital that we balance our online hours with offline time spent in person among friends and colleagues.

Not everyone will find it easy to strike this balance. Many people have jobs that are entirely online. Others spend most of their social life online; some have practically no social life *off-line*. And the rise of AI is only likely to complicate matters. While most people today use conversational AI assistants as practical tools without issue, new studies are showing that heavy use—especially when AI is used as a substitute for emotional connection—can be linked to increased loneliness and withdrawal from real-world social interaction. If chatbot design and business models don't evolve responsibly, this new technology may wind up exploiting users' emotional needs instead of supporting their mental well-being.

In extreme cases, without regular human connection, the limbic brain systems that foster intimacy and nurturing can fall into disuse, and the older "reptilian" instincts may show up as selfishness, aggression, and distrust. Loneliness typically unleashes these old defensive instincts. So do the senses of grievance, envy, and resentment that a steady diet of online outrage and hate speech often breeds.

We saw these symptoms emerge on a mass scale during the COVID pandemic, when widespread months-long lockdowns prohibited millions from engaging in *any* direct personal contact. On the one hand, screens were a social lifesaver, because we relied on them to sustain work and personal relationships. On the other, rates of social isolation doubled between 2019 and 2020, and although they dropped after 2022, they've yet to return to pre-pandemic levels. The amount of time young people between ages fifteen and twenty-four spend socializing in person has dropped shockingly by nearly 70 percent since 2003.

All this means that it's more important than ever for civic and business leaders to prioritize human interaction and social well-being in schools, town centers, and workplace cultures. The need is so great that the U.S. surgeon general, Dr. Vivek Murthy, in 2022 issued a Framework for Workplace Mental Health and Well-Being to help executives reorient workplace culture away from demoralizing practices, including excessive screen time and cutthroat contests for promotion, to more humane, interdependent, and morally sustainable standards. We need buy-in from corporations, including big tech, to rise to 100 percent.

Let's be honest: If safety were truly a high priority, tech products would look radically different. Daily time limits would be built into screens to moderate daily usage. Apps used by kids would lock after a certain hour. Features that feed social comparison—likes, follower counts, popularity rankings—wouldn't exist. Content moderation teams and systems would use lower precision thresholds, tracking false positives to catch the dangerous or borderline harmful content that can't be unseen. External volunteer experts, not internal teams, would decide which content should be removed. Tech companies should also be doing research with public institutions to identify and implement best practices, particularly for promoting children's health and well-being.

Unfortunately, all these decisions come with economic trade-offs for many of the platforms. Slower growth. Less engagement. More friction and more risk of regulation. That moral dilemma is built into the online system. External pressure, including regulation and public outrage, often does push tech companies to act. This is not generally a pivot toward integrity, however, but a maneuver for survival. Once again, the fear of getting caught and judged by others is what stops human beings from behaving—and leading their companies—in ways that society deems immoral.

Civilization is a human creation, and we all play a role in shaping society's collective conscience. We can choose to challenge the digital divide that's isolating and polarizing us. We can decide to reconnect across class and race lines instead of drifting ever farther apart. And we can also recalibrate our own moral compasses and nurture our kids in ways that strengthen their sense of right and wrong. For evolution and culture are only part of the story of moral injury. Conscience is also the product of personal growth. And that aspect of morality is uniquely our own.

CHAPTER 4

SOCIALIZING

The Nature and Nurture of Moral Identity

About morals, I know only that what is moral is what you feel good after, and what is immoral is what you feel bad after.

—Ernest Hemingway

I was ten when I had my first panic attack. It happened one warm August afternoon in Guerneville, California, as I lay on the couch in our mobile home watching a telenovela with my mom. Just moments before, I'd been enjoying this rare moment of calm. I loved my mother and was grateful whenever depression didn't drag her under, because usually she was the one who thought she was going to die. Most mornings I'd wake to her moaning, "¡Lo que dios quiera!" Whatever God wants. My parents were devout Catholics, and they slept beneath a giant crucifix—it must have been four feet high—on the wall above their bed. It seemed to me that God himself was hovering over us, ready to strike us down, and that's why my mom would plead with him not to.

But on this day, out of nowhere, I was the one in mortal terror. Beginning with a quivering in my stomach that spread to my limbs and face, a sense of imminent doom sent my heart racing. My breath caught in my throat as if I were being smothered. I gasped for air, suddenly drenched in sweat, and felt the trailer crashing in around me.

My mom switched off the TV and folded me into her arms as I shook, sobbing.

"¿Qué tienes, hijo?" she asked, bewildered.

"I feel like I'm going to die," I told her in Spanish. "When the sun goes down today, it won't ever come back up."

"No," she said. "No." She rocked me back and forth. "Look, *mijo*. The sun comes up every morning and has for, oh, many years. It's not going to stop tonight. Tell yourself that, all right? You've got to think realistic, *mijito*."

Gradually, I stopped gasping. My pulse slowed to normal, and I managed to think, to reason with myself. My mom was talking sense. The sun would come back up tomorrow. Sure.

I felt better. For now. But, of course, I wasn't panicking about the sun. Not, at least, the sun up in the sky.

My mother was *my* sun, and from a young age it had fallen to me to be her guardian and caretaker. For years, I knelt by her bedside as she wept. I struggled to comfort her. I tried to make her laugh, but she only told me she loved me and then cried more.

By the time I was eight years old, I was taking my mom by county bus to the Santa Rosa Medical Center, translating for her at psychiatric visits. I learned that when her father was eighteen, he'd shot a man in a bar. Later, my grandfather was shot in retribution, leaving him with a permanent limp. Demanding discipline and respect, my *abuelo* routinely beat his eleven children—six sons and five daughters—for any reason, or no reason at all, as they clung to each other. Using the butt of his prized Smith & Wesson .45-caliber pistol, he also delivered blows to my grandmother for walking too slow, calling her a "turtle." When she was seven months pregnant, he kicked her out of the house, forcing her to remain outside all night in a severe thunderstorm while my mother and her siblings helplessly crouched at the window and cried.

My mother, Herminia, escaped in her teens by fleeing north, but her journey to the United States as an undocumented immigrant left her battered by new horrors. One of the coyotes leading her group raped another woman. Later, she was detained with a rifle pointed at her head. Herminia was spared physically, but she would never shed the moral torment of her own paralysis as her companion screamed and pleaded for help. The rapist held both their lives in his hands. If my mother had tried to stop him, she'd have died, yet how could she forgive herself?

Life in the United States brought only more isolation, depression, and anxiety after Herminia married my dad, "Nacho," whose father, too, had savaged his wife and children. On really bad days, Grandpa Pancho would make my dad and his brothers lick chicken shit smeared on the backs of the hogs they tended. Once, as my dad stood, helpless, my sociopathic grandfather hanged my uncle briefly from a tree for saying he was tired. To escape, my father made the trek from his village near Cotija to the United States through a feces-filled sewage tunnel connecting Tijuana to San Diego. Like Herminia, he considered himself a moral failure—unable to stand up for himself or his siblings, unable to trust or keep his family safe. He also saw his father's abuse as a betrayal of love, which made him angry and aggressive himself. Unlike my mom, Nacho took out his anger on his son.

My dad never raised a hand to my mother, but he beat me regularly until I was a teenager. His fury seemed bottomless. Anytime he thought I was misbehaving or disrespectful, out would come the belt, and the cramped space of our trailer gave me nowhere to hide. My enduring childhood memory is of that worn leather strip whipping across my legs and butt as he swung me around by the arm. As Nacho exerted himself, his eyes would widen and his breath got heavier. I knew his body and mind were going to dark places only he could remember. But he was visiting them upon me in ways I could never forget.

My father's treatment felt like a profound wrong that I was powerless as a kid to combat, and that combination of moral injustice and helplessness left me angry and distrustful. I couldn't see the cyclical nature of this abuse, the tortured "gift" of it handed down from one generation to the next. Instead, I blamed myself. How could I respect myself if I couldn't stand up for myself? How could I even show my face? Why couldn't I be good enough to satisfy my dad? Why was I so weak?

Morally battered and bruised both inside and out, I convinced myself that these lashings were justified. They meant I was a shitty son. I ought to bring home better grades and ease my mother's mind. I would never measure up to the white boys who ruled my school. As the inner voice of recrimination continued, I became socially withdrawn and lonely, blaming myself for feeling so terrible. When one of my high school teachers told me I wouldn't amount to anything, I, of course, believed him. Everything wrong with my life had to be my fault. Moral distress feeds on itself.

For years, I kept having panic attacks. Sometimes I thought they were heart attacks, which, metaphorically, they were. Having failed the people I loved most—including myself—I did feel as if my heart had broken. What was actually spinning out of control, though, was my conscience—my moral compass. Not knowing where else to turn for safety or trust, I found solace in music, especially Prince, and in the vast wonder of nature and the ocean. But I still didn't know where I belonged or who my people were.

Disoriented and confused, I felt as if I'd lost connection with myself. I didn't know how to act. I didn't know how to *be*. And this caused a terrifying existential panic and sadness. There were times, in my father's presence, when I couldn't distinguish right from wrong.

I couldn't understand it then, of course, but the pain I experienced as a boy was my body's cumulative response to moral trauma. Being subjected to so much inexplicable cruelty had sent my amygdala into overdrive, its neural drumroll of alarm pounding me with stress hormones like cortisol and glutamate, which amplified the pain. Meanwhile, a mounting sense of betrayal, rejection, disgust, and shame caused my feel-good neurotransmitter—dopamine—to dive. Serotonin, my mood stabilizer, also took a hit. The crescendo effect of moral injury was in full swing.

This chemical chaos also triggered my panic attacks. That's because the brain's amygdala reacts to emotional overload—including feelings of shame, disgust, and hopelessness—by activating the fight-or-flight response and releasing a barrage of stress hormones. A constant state of heightened stress will flood your body and mind, making you feel on edge all the time. Eventually, this can lead to panic attacks.

Had I known at the time that stress hormones can cause this chemical chain reaction, it might have made those attacks less frightening. But even without the neurological explanation, I could *feel* that something was slipping, causing me to lose my inner bearings. What I couldn't yet understand was the connection between this imbalance and my moral identity.

CONSCIENCE AS IDENTITY'S COMPASS

We've now seen how natural selection supported the genetic evolution of morality as a kind of social glue for humanity, and how cultural evolution continues to dovetail with genetic evolution to shape the moral foundations of society. But how do we as individuals develop the unique moral compass that guides us *personally* between right and wrong? And what explains the broad spectrum of moral orientations, even within strictly controlling cultures? How can one boy beaten by his patriarchal father grow up to become resolutely nonviolent, while another thinks it's his moral duty to repeat his father's example?

The short answer is that personal conscience is a product of both evolution *and* individual experience—the same nature-nurture factors that forge our personality and physical health. These influences, which encompass innate temperament, religious upbringing, socioeconomic status, and family dynamics, are so variable that no two moral compasses can be identical. Our moral identities are unique because they reflect social experiences, personality traits, and responsibilities that are entirely our own.

According to moral foundations theory, most of us do value the same six basic virtues—caring, fairness, loyalty, respect, purity, and liberty—*but* we value them in different (sometimes radically different) ratios. One person's top moral priority might be respect for authority, so being a law-abiding citizen becomes the ultimate litmus test for moral goodness. For another, the ultimate definition of goodness might hinge on protecting loved ones, which could justify almost anything—even lawbreaking—if necessary to keep family safe and well. Most people prize multiple values, of course, but not all values matter to everyone to the same degree. Moral integrity appears different in different people because it's defined not by 100 percent adherence to *all* moral values but by the alignment of one's own personal moral *priorities*.

Before we delve into this variability, let's take a moment to consider *why* moral integrity has so much power over us—not only in directing our actions but also in determining our mental and emotional well-being. It's the loss of moral integrity, remember—due to transgressions so subjectively indefensible that your very sense of self feels contaminated—that triggers moral injury. The linkage between conscience and identity helps to explain why this loss is so devastating.

Think of conscience as the mind's referee in the ongoing match between self-centered desire, fear, and aggression, on one side, and social-centered empathy, stability, and moral values, on the other. As

Patricia Churchland explains, "We do not cease to care about ourselves just because we are also bonded to others. We all contend with the fact that self-care and other-care typically abide together in what is often a delicate balance." The brain's reward system manages this balance through the coding of pleasure and pain into signals. These signals then direct thought and behavior to fulfill essential self-centered needs *and* to cooperate with others. "Between them, the circuitry supporting sociality and self-care, and the circuitry for internalizing social norms, create what we call conscience."

Like a tennis ref, conscience's job is to mediate conflicts and relieve tension between the two sides of identity, which we'll call self and social. But unlike refs, whose calls are fixed to a single moment, conscience weighs in continuously, before, during, and after each conflict. A momentary flash of social judgment might warn a child not to heed self's call to steal a chocolate bar when the kindly shopkeeper turns his back, but that flash won't end there; it will continue, perhaps even gaining potency as social remorse years later, especially if the child selfishly goes ahead and pockets the candy. For the ref's power lies not only in the transient *cognitive* pressure that conscience exerts at the time we make a moral choice but also in the lingering *emotional* pull of conscience after the fact. This potent combination gives conscience tremendous sway in defining the self by molding social intuitions and, simultaneously, by integrating the two sides within a single coherent *moral identity*.

If the child's conscience decides it's seriously bad to steal a candy bar, then she may end up feeling like a bad *person* if she steals it anyway. She can make social excuses. Maybe some bully put her up to it. Maybe she gave the chocolate to her hungry brother. Maybe she traded it for cash to help her broke mother. But the inner ref knows the truth and holds the ultimate moral scales. If the child has betrayed her core moral identity and continues to do so, she'll eventually believe her self to be rotten. Why else, she might ask, would she act like this?

This is the same logic that convinced me I was bad for not standing up to my father or protecting my mother. Conscience doesn't consider factors like age or power imbalances; it only pushes us to do what feels *personally right*—to act in sync with our moral identity. Psychologists refer to this alignment as congruence.

When your actions align with your moral compass, the chemistry of conscience rewards you with positive sensations of dignity and comfort. You experience a sense of integrity, of being right with yourself. That's congruence. But when your choices clash with your moral compass, your neural system responds with feelings of unease, and the lack of congruence can lead to profound inner turmoil. Conscience sounds this alarm whenever it senses imbalance between your actions and your values; if the warning goes off on a regular basis, the resulting instability will threaten your moral identity.

Let's say you identify as kindhearted, and your conscience prioritizes concern for others. Your body will release the feel-good brain chemicals oxytocin, dopamine, and endorphins whenever you witness or participate in acts of generosity. This feedback loop reinforces the Golden Rule in action. If you volunteer every week at the local food bank, the congruence of your values with this conduct will give you a morale boost; your sense of moral integrity will help you feel secure in who you are, what you're worth, and your reputation as an "upstanding" citizen. This consistency will bolster and protect your conscience.

What's more, others will see you in the same light. Studies show that individuals who act with moral integrity tend to be viewed as more trustworthy. And, since trust is a form of social capital—for example, we're most likely to help and support the friends and colleagues we know we can count on to help and support *us*—people with moral integrity also have stronger personal and professional relationships.

Secure human relationships being one of the first lines of defense against moral injury, this makes moral integrity vital to our physical and mental health. Regular doses of shared virtue—especially compassion, generosity, and trust—all help build our well-being and resilience to illness and stress.

By contrast, the mere contemplation of choices that we find morally odious will trigger the chemistry of disgust. Ever wonder why people refer to antisocial acts like rape, murder, or arson as sickening, vile, foul, or nauseating? It's because many of the same centers of the brain that register moral disapproval also process the feelings of physical revulsion we experience when confronted with rotting flesh or polluted water. The insula, in the frontal region of the brain, for example, evaluates taste and smells for signs of contamination in food, and it also processes moral information for signs of untrustworthy people or unfair behavior. Whenever it detects danger, the insula will trigger disgust, a sensation that's the same whether the threat is spoiled milk or a blatant liar—or oneself.

Researchers associate this systemic overlap with the "Macbeth effect" (Shakespeare's Lady Macbeth, remember, cried, "Out, damned spot! out, I say!" imagining bloodstains on her own hand after urging her husband to murder the king). Studies have found that people who've just washed their hands will become more puritanical about issues like pornography and drug use. Subjects are also more likely to select cleaning products if offered a choice of household gifts immediately after they've written about moral transgressions.

Another region of the brain that links gut feelings to moral reactions is the ventromedial prefrontal cortex, behind the bridge of the nose. The neuroscientist Antonio Damasio has found that patients with brain damage in this region have *no* gut feelings about right or wrong decisions. They'll understand their choices rationally, but because they lack any sense of disgust about the consequences of their choices, they have little inhibition to steer them away from immoral behavior. By contrast, Damasio says, a healthy, functioning ventromedial prefrontal cortex will make the prospect of a major transgression, like murdering one's parents, so repulsive that most people can't even bear to contemplate it.

Witnessing or participating in a cruel or unjust act may also prompt your brain to release stress hormones, triggering an impulse to fight, flee, or freeze, as if you were personally threatened. There's a core logic to this reaction, since threat is present in many, if not most, morally compromising situations. What if, like my mother, you hear a friend screaming for her life? Her screams mean you could be in danger, too, especially if you get involved. So the impulse to flee or freeze makes sense. But the resulting conflict between your moral desire to help your friend and your sense of self-preservation can leave you feeling both disgusted by your moral failure and just plain *wrong*, in the sense of not being true to your identity.

Empathy is the secret agent that enables a healthy conscience to align thoughts and social behavior with moral identity. That's because empathy allows us to vicariously share other people's experiences, to anticipate their expectations and needs, and to process how our choices affect them and how they view us. Through empathy, we can physically feel the impact of our actions on others, and that helps us internalize the moral consequences of our decisions. These consequences empathetically *become* us.

Scientists first began to understand empathy in the 1990s when they discovered mirror neurons, those magical brain cells that allow us to read each other's faces and body language and intuit what's going on inside the people around us. Whenever we "ape" each other—"Monkey see, monkey do"—we're activating mirror neurons. This process allows us to learn from each other. It's also the reason yawning and laughter are socially contagious. Mirror neurons stimulate the empathy that allows us to share each other's fatigue and joy, to imagine ourselves *inside* the experience of others.

As a social agent, empathy completes the loop of human connection and reciprocity by activating our brain's reward systems whenever we help or receive positive attention from others. This makes it feel not just morally but also *physically* good to share the experience of being human, and this feeling of mutual goodness promotes trust, intimacy, and connection. It also helps shield us from serious damage when we're morally injured. If we have strong coping mechanisms and supportive relationships and can quickly rekindle empathy, reconciliation, and forgiveness, we're likely to recover more quickly even from traumatic betrayals.

By contrast, without any empathy, our experience of the social world would deteriorate. The threads that bind our sense of self in relationship with others would fray, shredding the emotional fabric of our moral selves. Then, having lost the very foundation of conscience, we'd navigate the social world as psychopaths do, without noticing or caring deeply what others feel. While we might still recognize social norms intellectually, our actions would lack regard for others' needs, respect, or opinions. We'd behave as if only our own desires mattered.

You might think that a force as powerful as empathy would dominate our thoughts. Yet most of the time it operates below the surface, like software that we barely notice until and unless it sets off the alarm of conscience. Imagine that you're a responsible, law-abiding driver, calmly cruising through your neighborhood, when suddenly the driver ahead of you speeds up to run a red light, narrowly missing a pedestrian who's just stepped off the curb. You're not involved, yet stress hormones nevertheless pump through your body like flashing sirens. They cause your heart to race, your pulse to quicken, your skin to break a sweat. Witnessing the violation triggers this distress not because you're directly threatened but because you can't help empathizing with both the pedestrian and the driver—as if you shared *their* respective physical and moral danger. Your body reacts as though it were preparing to respond *for* them. This jab of empathetic distress puts your conscience on alert.

Now imagine that *you* ran that light, possibly even hitting the pedestrian. Believing yourself to be the *agent* of harm would amplify the empathetic impact because you feel responsible, suddenly, for doing "wrong" instead of "right" (presumably, your normal way of being). You tell yourself you could have prevented the accident but you didn't. Instead, you made a grave mistake that caused something bad to occur to an innocent person, with whom you empathize, and this, in turn, will likely make you feel much worse than you would as a mere witness.

The degree of understanding with which you made the wrong choice—your *moral agency*—can play a pivotal role in your suffering. If you didn't realize the light was turning, didn't see the pedestrian, didn't hurt them badly, or couldn't stop in time because you were being tailgated, all those mitigating factors might lessen your remorse, leaving you primarily with regret. Still, the effects of empathy would mark you, forcing you to mentally and emotionally replay the impact from both sides, as both the striker and the stricken, with guilt, shock, and moral betrayal rolling through you like an avalanche of empathetic distress. For some time after the accident, your blood pressure might rise, your conscience going into overdrive, relentlessly signaling you to do whatever you must to regain your moral equilibrium, to reconcile your actions with your values by righting the wrong in any way you can. The more complicit you feel in causing harm and the more your moral identity prioritizes law, order, and the care of others, the more urgently you're likely to feel the need to atone.

THE NATURE OF MORAL ORIENTATION

When your moral identity is in balance, your thoughts and deeds align with your sense of morality to give you the dignity you need to feel socially secure. But when your moral balance is off, you can feel wrong in your own skin, as if you were not *yourself*. The rabbinical philosopher Jonathan Sacks explained the connection this way: "Morality and dignity go hand in hand. Lose one, and we will lose the other."

Moral identity is also inextricably intertwined with social identity. Researchers put this linkage to the test in 2015 by comparing relatives' impressions of two very different groups of dementia patients: One had lost memory to Alzheimer's disease, but their personalities were unchanged; the other could recall their lives but had lost their sense of honesty, compassion, and inhibition due to frontotemporal dementia, which causes changes in the ventromedial prefrontal cortex. Though the Alzheimer's patients might not be able to tell you who they were, their behavior still reflected the same moral values and instincts they'd had all their lives, and their relatives still saw them as the same people. Not so with the other group, who viewed themselves as they always had but now indiscriminately lied, cheated, and acted out sexually as never before. *Their* relatives said their loss of moral control had turned them into entirely different people—"Not the same." What this means is that moral consistency matters more than memory in defining who we are to each other. Loss of moral integrity can devastate the ability to make and maintain social connections.

But what defines who we are morally to *ourselves*? That question brings us back to the variability of moral identity and the role that nurture—personal experience—plays in shaping conscience.

―――

Many years ago, I had a patient named Dee who came to me with her inner life in turmoil. She'd built a successful career as a trader on

Wall Street, but in midlife she developed serious doubts about her vocation. Her restless nights and surges of self-directed anger warned of moral injury.

Dee had grown up in the shadow of her father, a legendary trader much admired for his uncanny ability to turn market volatility into profit. He drilled into Dee the belief that the only real measure of success was winning and that she should follow his lead. But even as she mastered the expected business skills—calculating exposures, managing risk, taking positions—Dee had the nagging sense that she'd sold herself out. Some of her biggest wins came from shorting companies on the brink of collapse or from betting against currencies in ways that magnified other people's losses. Unable to decide what was right or wrong, she felt as if she'd lost her ethical bearings—or had never found them in the first place.

What Dee was hearing was the call of her conscience. Not the example, lessons, and expectations of her father, which had dominated her for as long as she could remember, but the pulse of her own temperament—the moral instincts and intuitions she was born with. For this innate circuitry is a core component of moral identity, and when it's thwarted or misshapen by others, by events, or by our own neglect, we are likely to feel unmoored.

Dee's childhood had been a mosaic of high expectations and cognitive dissonance. Her mother, a dedicated yoga instructor and Manhattan homemaker, taught her daughter the virtues of caring, compassion, and fairness. She warned Dee about *wetiko*, a Native American term for selfishness, which she used to describe the rampant greed and destructiveness she saw all around her in high society. Yet she never criticized her husband's pursuit of wealth or the moral emphasis he placed on authority and personal liberty. Instead, Dee's mother encouraged her husband as he built his financial empire, and she enjoyed the material benefits of his success.

The disparities between her parents' conflicting messages and their behavior left Dee frustrated. Personally, she admired her mother's stated values and felt most at home in creative and caring pursuits—writing poetry, graphic design, and occasional volunteering at local shelters. In her youth, these activities were her escape, her way to connect with a deeper sense of purpose and harmony. But she also wanted to please her father, who derided Dee's interests as frivolous, not "serious" or "useful" like a career in finance. Dee excelled in school, not out of any interest in business, but out of a desperate desire to gain her father's approval.

As she grew older, Dee began to see her work in trading through the lens of the destructive forces her mother had warned her about. Yet she also recognized that her mother had supported her husband's career and values, even as she encouraged Dee to question them. These colliding realizations filled Dee with profound guilt and regret—not because her father's values were inherently wrong, but because they weren't her own. Dee came to view herself not just as someone in the wrong profession but as a sellout—actively participating in a system that clashed with the principles she personally held most dear. This internal conflict deepened over time, culminating in a moral identity crisis that forced her, through therapy, to confront and reconcile the dissonance between her chosen path and the person she wanted to be. Only then could she chart a new course.

My own childhood was, like Dee's, a puzzle of contradictory moral lessons. After solemn Sundays praying at church, my father, Nacho, would take me to the mall, where he bought me the latest Air Jordans and Ralph Lauren polo shirts not as fashion statements but as tokens of assimilation. In his silent, sardonic way, Nacho was messaging, "Look white, feel right." Some days, he'd also surprise me with a trip to the beach, where we carefully handled shore crabs to avoid hurting them. But back home, his eyes would suddenly narrow. He'd accuse me of some minor youthful transgression and pull out his belt. Then everything descended into chaos.

While Dee's instinctive nature pushed her to seek harmony by pleasing her father at her own expense, mine leaned more toward self-preservation. I learned to gauge the barometer of my dad's moods so I could bend without completely breaking, and I vowed *not* to follow his example. Instead, I held tight to the kernel of dignity that was all my own.

The need to make sense of my childhood wound up propelling me toward a vocation in psychology, where I discovered how much power parents can have over their kids' moral development. I learned, for example, that betrayal by a loved one in authority is both a hallmark of child abuse and a significant trigger for moral injury. For if we can't trust those who raise us, how can we feel safe? How can we trust ourselves to form or sustain relationships, raise our own children, hold jobs, or plan for the future? How can we learn right from wrong?

My professional training also taught me, though, that the *core* of identity lies within our own innate nature—our DNA. As we grow up, our genetically primed instincts respond to our experiences and surroundings, "nature" interacting with "nurture" in ways that orient our moral compass. This orientation provides essential direction for our moral identity. If we try to ignore or override it, our conscience will protest. Like Dee, we'll feel wrong, inauthentic, not *ourselves*.

As I grew up, liberty from oppression—from bullying—emerged as a cardinal virtue in my personal moral code. In many ways, this innate value saved and strengthened me as I eventually stood up to my father, left home, and became a psychologist. My social, professional, and emotional identity gradually fell into sync with my moral identity, and that gave me a welcome sense of personal integrity.

Dee, on the other hand, had steadily lost her sense of integrity as she searched in vain for a compromise between her own core values—caring and fairness—and the priority her father placed on authority and daring. Her pain was the emotional equivalent of being a square peg pounded for decades into a round hole. Moral injury occurred not because her father's values were objectively wrong for everyone but because they were *subjectively* wrong for Dee.

Fortunately, people are capable of reflection and change. Just as moral injury can result from experiences that misshape one's sense of self, healing and growth can come from confronting those influences and cultivating a morally authentic way forward. After reaching her crossroads, Dee worked on redirecting her personal and professional choices until, eventually, they supported her own true moral identity instead of undermining it.

Most of us as children absorbed ethical rules of right and wrong from our families, schools, spiritual elders, and cultural traditions. Legacies of belief and habit, as well as moral grievances handed down over centuries, went into those lessons—so much so that many people equate being morally upright with obedience to such teachings. Authority figures and preachers throughout history have encouraged this notion, as if individuals couldn't possibly have any moral values without ideological instruction. Others maintain that right and wrong behavior is universally self-evident. "I know it when I see it," as the U.S. Supreme Court justice Potter Stewart wrote in 1964 of hard-core pornography. But the truth is, we can't all see morality the same way, much less through the same lens.

Even in societies with rigidly uniform codes of ethics, you'll find wide variations in the values that individuals hold as absolutes. There are unrepentant alcoholics in the most abstemiously conservative circles of Islam, and strict disciplinarians among America's "freest" libertarians. One devout Christian might have no moral compunction about corporal punishment but consider lying to be an unforgivable transgression, while another might view child endangerment as the only true sin. Such variations reflect moral compasses set to many different true norths.

"Moral orientation" is a term I've coined to describe the gravitational pull of conscience toward the specific virtues that dominate one's moral identity. A few examples: Mother Teresa built her moral identity around caring, kindness, and self-sacrifice; Martin Luther King oriented his life toward fairness, justice, and liberty from oppression; General George Patton prized courage, leadership, and personal honor. Such priorities forge a unique true north for each of us. Whether we're conscious of our settings or not, they nudge us toward certain choices and actions while tugging us away from others.

The concept of orientation is important in the context of moral injury because, as I mentioned earlier, this type of trauma is agnostic about *which* values you care about; what determines moral pain is *how much* you care about the specific value that's been violated. If you accept that everybody lies from time to time, then you're unlikely to feel too distressed when your boss boasts about cheating on his taxes. If you believe that complete honesty is nonnegotiable in marriage, however, you'd probably feel morally devastated to learn that your spouse has kept a secret bank account hidden from you for years. The more you care about the underlying value, and the more personal the relationship that's affected, the more the transgression will hurt. When your highest priority, your true north, is violated in a major way by you or someone close to you, that's when you're at greatest risk for moral injury.

Self-knowledge can provide a protective buffer. Moral injury is most likely to land as an insurmountable shock if you've never considered how much your beliefs matter to you or which ones truly matter the most. Betrayals during childhood and adolescence can be especially traumatic because that's when moral identity is still in flux. But once you've assessed your moral orientation and identified your true north, you can avoid some of the whipsaw of surprise and take steps to protect your moral integrity before harm occurs.

Temperament

I was just beginning to contend with my own moral injury when I realized that no one-size-fits-all spiritual or ethical prescription for this pain can ever work for everyone. That's because moral orientation is like a tapestry of unique instincts, strengths, and vulnerabilities. Many of the underlying threads are woven by DNA. How we experience empathy and disgust, for example, and whether we're innately fearful or impulsive, cautious or sociable, introverted or extroverted. These are all expressions of temperament, which we colloquially refer to as our "nature." And they have a profound effect on our moral orientation.

You can see genetic traits of temperament even in newborns. Some infants watch faces up close with open curiosity, while others flinch and turn away to escape intense scrutiny. Some stare with patient concentration at the mobile above their crib, while others are easily distracted by new sounds or sights. Even one's relative need for rules and order is evident from birth. And these core characteristics don't change much with age. Instead, they lurk like default settings, stealthily guiding children's responses to the experiences and people who nurture—or fail to nurture—them as they grow.

Psychologists tend to saddle the core traits of temperament with clinical labels that can sound misleadingly pathological. I've devised a more neutral terminology for our purposes here, but the underlying science is the same. These basic traits, like the six moral foundations, belong to everyone, but they appear with such widely varying set points that we each wind up with our own unique temperament.

Your DNA determines whether your set point is high, medium, or low for each trait. Those settings, in turn, influence your thoughts, feelings, behavior, and interactions. They color your personality, and they orient your moral identity.

Here, then, are four key traits of temperament:

- **Adventurousness**, regulated in the brain by dopamine levels, determines how eager we are for new experiences. Highly adventurous people are not necessarily more curious than others, but they tend to be more impulsive, more tempted by novelty. On the flip side, people who have low setpoints for this trait gravitate to familiar patterns of behavior and belief and can be resistant to change.

- **Self-protectiveness**, governed by serotonin levels in the brain, makes us wary of other people. If you're highly self-protective, you may come across as shy, allergic to social judgment and conflict. People who have low setpoints for this trait, on the other hand, can seem socially fearless and uninhibited.

- **Agreeableness**, regulated by the neurotransmitter norepinephrine, makes us eager to please others. Highly agreeable people are strongly motivated by the need to belong. They can be very devoted friends but may also be gullible and sensitive to rejection. By contrast, people at the low end of the spectrum for this trait may come across as aloof or indifferent.

- **Perseverance**, a core aspect of conscientiousness, is influenced by neurotransmitters like glutamate and serotonin, which help us push through setbacks or fatigue. Those high in perseverance tend to be stubborn, with a strong drive to complete tasks, often coupled with a careful, detail-oriented approach. In contrast, those with a lower set point for perseverance may struggle with impatience, become easily frustrated, and avoid long-term challenges.

Moral balance—where conscience situates us in the daily tug-of-war between self-interest and social cooperation—is intimately tied to these traits and their collective impact on our core personality. Fortunately, most of us are born with temperamental set points somewhere in the mid-zone. This allows us to bond in healthy ways with our parents and families and, as we grow, to make friends and learn at school, find work, and form fulfilling relationships as adults. More broadly, a balanced temperament helps us navigate conflict and recover from moral distress so we can function as productive members of society.

But many of us do have certain traits with a high or low set point. That's why you may think of some of your friends as natural "people pleasers" and others as "loners" or "iconoclasts." Such temperamental variety makes humans interesting and useful to each other. It reflects the evolution of countless different skills and specialties that our species needs to build and maintain complex societies. Alas, this variety can also lead to conflict.

Imagine the pressure you'd feel if your gregarious boss insisted you attend a gala business opening, ignoring the fact that you're a born introvert prone to anxiety in large groups. Or if you tried to please your adventurous spouse by joining his cycling expedition, only to quit the first day because you're easily frustrated. Normal temperamental differences might account for such conflicts, but they can still lead to heartache, misunderstanding, and moral finger-pointing.

Character

Fortunately, we all have a second set of traits that serve as temperamental arbiters. These *character* traits, which manage our instincts and fine-tune our moral compasses as we mature, can help us weather conflict.

One extraordinary example of character strength is Malala Yousafzai, who began life in Pakistan's Swat valley in 1997. Malala's father, a local teacher, taught his young daughter that education was her key to independence and personal dignity, and with high levels of perseverance and adventurousness Malala excelled at her studies. But when she was eleven, the Taliban seized control of her town and forbade girls to attend school. The family fled the area so she could continue her education, and Malala revealed her low set points for self-protectiveness and agreeableness by becoming a defiant blogger, appearing in international television newscasts to defend her right to an education—and to think for herself.

Then, when Malala was fifteen, a man boarded her school bus and shot her in the head to silence her. He only succeeded in making her more famous, though. After she recovered from the surgery that saved her life, Malala leaned into her gregarious nature to become an activist for girls' education. Pakistan passed its first Right to Education bill, backed by a $10 million fund in her honor. She wrote books and graduated from Oxford. She earned the Nobel Peace Prize.

Temperament alone cannot account for Malala's courage or grit. Early on, she also possessed qualities of character far beyond her years.

Unlike temperament, character is not fixed at birth but develops with age and experience. That's why we typically associate a person's maturity and moral integrity with development of the three principal character traits:

- **Self-directedness** gives us focus, confidence, and a strong sense of personal investment in our goals. With high levels of self-directedness, we take initiative and feel personally and morally responsible for our actions, reducing the risk of moral injury by aligning our actions with our values. Imagine the levels of self-directedness that Malala required to defy the Taliban and begin blogging about girls' education as a preteen.

- **Cooperativeness** makes us accountable and responsive to the people around us. Empathy, tolerance, and compassion guide the moral principles of highly cooperative people, fostering supportive relationships that mitigate the impact of moral transgressions. Malala might have begun her quest to further her own education, but even before her attack she was working to help others as well as herself. As for her attacker, she told the press, "That boy who shot me, I can't imagine hurting him even with a needle. I believe in peace. I believe in mercy."

- **Self-transcendence** allows us to access awe and wonder, the sense that we're part of a larger universe. It's a core component of spiritual faith and creativity. High levels of self-transcendence can ease suffering and help us gain humility, perspective, and forgiveness in the wake of moral injury, providing a pathway to healing and resilience. Malala demonstrated self-transcendence by approaching her medical care with fascination and curiosity, rather than fear and anger, after she was shot. And she summoned it again at the United Nations when she addressed a youth assembly at age sixteen, declaring, "One child, one teacher, one book, one pen can change the world."

It's no accident that ethical codes across all religions and cultures promote character traits as the building blocks of moral goodness. By modulating temperamental tendencies such as fearfulness, obstinacy, and impulsiveness, mature character can ease our reactions to conflict. Another way of looking at this: Character greases the wheels of temperament so communities can function.

Teachers and leaders also lean into character development because these traits can be cultivated. Like temperament, they are rooted in our DNA, but unlike temperament, character builds through the lifelong process of moral learning. This is one critical area where "nurture" plays at least as important a role as "nature" in the sculpting of moral identity.

THE NURTURE OF MORAL IDENTITY

It's worth remembering that 75 percent of the human brain's growth occurs between birth and age twenty-five. In the first year alone, the brain doubles to three-quarters of its adult volume. Experience during this formative period dovetails with genetics to orient intellectual, emotional, and moral development.

How we're cared for, whether we're cuddled or breastfed, comforted or traumatized, what we're given to eat and play with, how people touch and talk to us, whether they respond quickly, slowly, or not at all to our needs—all such experience in the first years of life can influence our ability to regulate our own needs, care for others, and rise above selfish desires and frustrations. A nurturing, supportive childhood helps strengthen the prosocial neural networks and stress resiliency we need to mature in character and build moral health. Abusive or indifferent parenting, on the other hand, can thwart this healthy brain "revision," leaving a child more anxious, insecure, and distrustful, and thus more vulnerable to moral confusion and distress.

The ability and will to empathize are central to all of this. Babies learn empathy from family members who mirror their smiles and affection, who pick them up when they cry, intuiting and responding to their needs. Kids learn to trust and empathize later with the help of close friends, teachers, and other role models who care about them. With a healthy social support network, children normally develop the three R's of morality as a matter of course: the ability to respect other people's feelings, to relate to their needs, and to understand that normal interaction involves mutual give-and-take—reciprocity.

But it's important to remember, the same neural system that teaches kids to empathize with the familiar people who constitute "us" can also bias them against "others." Empathy initially binds children to their closest relations, typically family and friends. This closeness fosters trust, care, and cooperation within their inner circle, but it can discourage connection with people outside that circle.

Especially when children grow up in homogeneous communities where neighbors have the same racial, ethnic, religious, economic, and educational background, their capacity for empathy may be limited by these boundaries. They'll naturally learn to trust and care for people who look and act in ways they're taught to view as "good," but they can also come to *distrust* as "bad" anyone who behaves or appears differently, especially when protective elders teach them to be suspicious of outsiders. When a child believes that loyalty to her own group *requires* her to reject all others, she'll face a moral quandary every time she interacts with someone who appears different. Without encouragement and exposure to diverse perspectives, the initial bias that empathy cultivates in such uniform communities can be formidable.

This double edge can also cause distress in close relationships, since "us" group members who defy authority or breach expected norms in tightly controlled communities can be "othered," too. Rebels and freethinkers may get the cold shoulder from friends for a few days, or they may be cast out by family or community altogether. For most people, this kind of social rejection is so hurtful that it's been likened to torture. To be shunned is to be flooded with fear and social pain—registered in the amygdala, anterior cingulate cortex, insula, and medial prefrontal cortex—that can be every bit as intense as physical pain. Worse, this pain readily recurs when triggered by memory, which makes it a key ingredient of long-term moral injury.

Strict, tightly knit societies long ago adopted excommunication as a form of severe punishment for transgressions that, in the eyes of authorities, threatened group unity. Many ultraorthodox religions, for example, still shun those who marry outside the faith. In such communities, empathy runs deep for those who heed group customs, laws, and expectations, but these ethical systems can also blind group members to the basic humanity of anyone who fails to conform—even when the nonconformists are loved ones.

Fortunately, moral blindness is not insurmountable. Empathy has the potential to loosen social bindings as we mature, and our capacity to connect with others can grow not only to include members of different groups but also to bridge cultural divides. This broader empathy flourishes with active learning and exposure to diverse perspectives that push against the initial biases of early childhood. In families that demonstrate compassion and concern for people from different racial, ethnic, and status groups, kids' capacity for empathy opens outward. Schools can play a critical role here, too, by encouraging cooperative learning with inclusive teams of students from diverse backgrounds, as well as restorative justice approaches that impartially listen to all sides of student conflicts before administering discipline. What starts as a human instinct rooted in close bonds can thus become a universal, human-centered value that supports broader social experience and cooperation.

When it comes to judging ourselves, however, the tension between "us" and "other" can be trickier to resolve, for *attribution bias* kicks in when we betray our own conscience. Attribution bias is the tendency to blame a person's behavior solely on their character, without regard for other factors or circumstances. When we've been seriously wronged, this tendency can produce a snap judgment that tells us the person who hurt us must be evil to the core—a "punk," a "bully," a "monster," a "thug." It's difficult to alter this perception, even if we later discover that the accused is innocent or never meant to hurt anyone; the conflation of blame with identity shatters empathy, rendering compassion and forgiveness inaccessible. For that reason, attribution bias is particularly destructive when we blame ourselves. It makes us feel unworthy, unforgivable: Other. When morally injured, this is how we can wind up judging ourselves to be irredeemably *bad*.

My wife, Alison, noticed signs of attribution bias in our older daughter one ordinary afternoon when Lauren was nine. Fortunately, Alison saw right away that Lauren was upset. She was sitting at the kitchen table as she usually did after school, but today instead of immersing herself in her latest vibrant art project, Lauren just stared out the window. She appeared on the verge of tears.

Alison sat down and gently asked what was wrong. Not a demand, but an offering of comfort and wisdom. And Lauren's pain spilled out in a tumble of words. One of her classmates had unfairly belittled another girl, and Lauren hadn't stuck up for her friend. She felt guilty, ashamed, confused, and powerless.

"Why do I feel so bad if I didn't do anything wrong?" she asked, brow furrowed, grappling with the moral weight of witnessing injustice and not intervening, in painful violation of her own moral priorities: caring and fairness.

Alison took our daughter's hands and spoke of the conscience that would guide her through life's quandaries. "It's right there, inside you, honey," Alison said. "Just stop for a sec and listen. Hear it? Your conscience is like a compass. It points toward the right path when you're faced with tough choices. It tells you what's right, even when that's hard to do."

Eventually, Lauren turned to her art supplies and began a series of heartfelt, handmade cards, each adorned with vibrant colors and thoughtful words. The first card was for her friend who had been belittled; it was filled with words of kindness and support, reaffirming the girl's worth and strength. Other cards were for the rest of their classmates, gently reminding them of the power of words and the importance of standing up for one another.

The next day, Lauren asked her teacher for a few minutes in class to share this project. With bravery she hadn't known she possessed, she stood in front of her peers and spoke from the heart about empathy, kindness, and the impact their actions and words had on others. She handed out the cards, including one for the girl who had been unkind, with a simple message of peace and an olive branch of friendship.

Lauren's act didn't just resolve the immediate conflict; it brought the class together, turning "us" and "other" into a whole team of "us." Her peers began to open up, sharing their own experiences and feelings, fostering a new atmosphere of understanding and support. Lauren's moral quandary, and her creative response to it, had become a pivotal learning moment for all involved, teaching the whole class about compassion, mutual respect, and the importance of standing up for what's right. She had lifted everyone's morale and healed the rifts, unifying the group.

For Lauren herself, this incident galvanized her moral identity. It taught her the importance of honoring her values, even when that's difficult and the outcome isn't certain. It helped her gain confidence and reinforced her natural inclination toward kindness, shaping her into a more compassionate, resilient, and conscientious person. The experience highlighted her ability to turn personal pain into creative and positive action, fostering a sense of agency and purpose, for which she's now known at school and in the community.

Sadly, of course, not everyone grows up with nurturing families and healthy surroundings. Kids who are routinely deprived or neglected may have trouble developing the empathy they need for moral health. These deficits are especially profound among those who are socially isolated, traumatized, or abused as children. And some individuals, of which psychopaths are the most extreme example, are born with genetic predispositions or neurological anomalies that impair their capacity for empathy and compassion. Many additional conditions—arising from congenital vulnerabilities and/or environmental damage—can lead to personality disorders.

Personality disorders are like psychological lenses that warp empathy and distort social perception, creating fragmented reflections of reality that hinder genuine connection. We generally think of these conditions by their labels, which include narcissistic, histrionic, avoidant, borderline, and obsessive-compulsive personality disorders. While distinct from each other in many ways, all these conditions upset the normal balance of reciprocity in human relationships. They restrict tolerance for emotional distress, making it difficult to accurately read the intentions and reactions of others. They distort self-awareness and can savage mutual trust. Personality disorders can also encourage the kind of reckless, deceptive, or selfish behavior that produces moral injury.

According to the National Institute of Mental Health, around 9 percent of U.S. adults have a personality disorder, though this is likely an undercount, since many are never diagnosed. In terms of moral injury, the most problematic of these conditions is antisocial personality disorder (ASPD), which affects less than 4 percent of the general population—and mostly men.

The terms "antisocial personality disorder," "psychopathy," and "sociopathy" are often used interchangeably. That's because, while sociopathy stems primarily from traumatic experience in early life and psychopathy has stronger genetic roots, both produce traits also associated with ASPD: casual cruelty, manipulation, deceit, grandiosity, and impulsive criminality, all without any remorse. People diagnosed with ASPD have so little capacity for empathy that they will hurt others without experiencing guilt or moral conflict. They're effectively immune to moral injury, both because they lack moral sensitivity and because they see no connection between their moral conduct and their identity. Even if they have a lifelong reputation for lying, cheating, disrespecting, and physically harming others, people with ASPD may nevertheless consider themselves unimpeachable. They might actually take pride in the pain they inflict.

People with severe personality disorders of any kind can inflict a disproportionate amount of moral harm. That's why we must heed the warnings of our better instincts when we witness or experience trauma committed by perpetrators who show zero empathy or regret for causing pain. However, most of us go through life without ever personally encountering anyone whose moral compass is so deviant that they're truly dangerous. It's easy to call someone a psychopath or narcissist when we don't understand their moral orientation, but we'd generally be better served by learning to understand and respect the broad variety of *normal* moral orientations that constitute our ethical landscape—so long as we recognize that there's no place on this spectrum for the dangerous mindset of those who willingly inflict cruelty on others.

THE SPECTRUM OF MORAL IDENTITY

By the time we reach adulthood, the combined effects of temperament and character, nature and nurture, have forged a particular moral identity for each of us. As Dee discovered, this sense of self plays a major role in our choices throughout life, not only determining our vulnerability for moral injury but also pointing us toward certain social groups and partners, vocations, hobbies, and dreams. It can influence our ambitions and expectations, direct our basic assumptions about right and wrong, and guide our everyday negotiations with people whose values conflict with our own.

The possible range of moral identity spans three broad orientations, each reflecting different character and value priorities—different true norths. These orientations generally correspond to social roles that have evolved over millennia to help groups stay connected, organized, and protected. Few of us fall neatly into a single zone, and many straddle more than one. But in most cases, one orientation dominates our moral judgment and responses, even if others add their push and pull.

In 2004 the psychologists Lawrence Walker and Karl Hennig identified heroic archetypes for the three orientations. They dubbed these moral models the "just," the "brave," and the "caring":

- **The just** are self-directed idealists who place principle above other moral values. Justice warriors like Atticus Finch in *To Kill a Mockingbird* and Nelson Mandela exemplify this group. The objective rules of righteousness they embrace can take priority even over personal needs. The just might, for example, think it more important to be faithful to a law or code they deem righteous than to the people closest to them. This moral model reflects a temperament with high levels of perseverance aimed at a true north of perfection and singular moral ideals. Being principled matters more to them than being agreeable or respectful.

- **The brave** are self-transcendent risk-takers who prize courage, problem-solving, and self-sacrifice. Brave icons include military heroes like Audie Murphy, the most decorated American soldier of World War II, as well as business iconoclasts like Steve Jobs and awe-inspiring daredevils like Philippe Petit, who walked a tightrope between New York's Twin Towers in 1974. Risk-takers' temperaments include high set points for adventurousness and low set points for self-protectiveness. Yearning to lead and inspire, the brave set their moral compass to a true north of unprecedented accomplishment and freedom, even if that can sometimes make them morally insensitive to the needs and vulnerabilities of others.

- **The caring** are cooperative harmonists who orient their moral decisions primarily around compassion and social connection. Florence Nightingale, who volunteered to tend wounded soldiers during the Crimean War, was an icon of caring. So was Bill Wilson, who co-founded Alcoholics Anonymous. The caring are typically warm and attentive, empathetic and thoughtful, with temperaments high in agreeableness. Helping others is paramount because it serves their core need to belong, but they may also be so trusting and eager to befriend that they fall prey to deception or manipulation. The priority the caring place on human connection can make them especially vulnerable to moral injury when faced with injustice, cruelty, or social strife.

It's important to recognize that moral orientation need not be rigid or fixed. It can adapt in response to experience. The brave and the just can become more caring, and vice versa. Many athletes exemplify this growth, dedicating their early years to competition, but later turning to more cooperative roles. The legendary Muhammad Ali managed to span all three orientations, fighting his way to the title of world's greatest boxer, while also becoming a peace activist and humanitarian goodwill ambassador. Such flexibility is not merely healthy but, as I've discovered through my reconciliation with my father, it can hold an important key to recovery from moral injury.

Long before he used it on me, my dad, Nacho, had learned a brutal language of courage from his own father. A Mexican kid who ran from a dusty home in Mexico so he wouldn't end up killing the man who savagely whipped him and his siblings, Nacho crossed the U.S. border with callused hands and a storm he had no words for. He worked six, sometimes seven, days a week and raised me to abide by his strict terms: be respectful, be useful, keep up. When overcome by fear and rage, as he often was, he let the belt speak for him.

The belt told me that Nacho had proven himself to be a brave man by enduring his own father's blows, and so, he believed, I must do the same. In this distorted legacy, courage was measured by how much hurt could be tolerated—and inflicted—in the name of duty. Honor meant protecting and keeping the family warm and fed at all costs, but one of the costs was trauma. What my father saw as sacrifice left a trail of moral destruction.

When I learned as an adult to name moral injury, the chaos of my childhood became a reality I could hold. Identifying this pain didn't excuse the harm; my father remained responsible for his actions, just as his father had been. But it created a context for the damage. And that allowed me to acknowledge the truth and stop pretending that nothing was wrong. I finally took stock of the guilt and shame, the permanent flinch I carried, and I privately vowed that one day I'd muster enough bravery to face everything I'd fled.

I was twenty when my father made a similar vow. Unbeknownst to me, he'd started seeing a therapist who encouraged him to tell his whole life story out loud. As Nacho later explained to me, "When those things happen and you feel like you can't talk about it, it eats you alive." Still, it was so traumatic to remember his childhood, "I figured I'd record it all at the same time because I couldn't do it more than once." So, he set up a camcorder on the construction site of a house he was building and just began talking to the camera. Afterward, he gave me the tapes.

The video was four hours long. I couldn't watch the whole thing in one sitting. It was too raw. But the image of my dad alone in that construction site—just studs and sunlit dust—served as a powerful metaphor for the process of change that he was undergoing. As the sound clicked on, Nacho began to describe the nightmares of his childhood. One time his dad lashed him so severely that his mom had to apply warm compresses to his back for almost a month before the wounds scarred over. The whippings and terror chased her, too, and Nacho tried to protect her, but his father's cruelty was relentless. Forced to choose between violence and escape, my dad chose flight. And then he revisited his childhood traumas on me.

As the tape played out, Nacho pled for forgiveness. He struggled to maintain his composure but couldn't hold back his tears. He may not have been eloquent but, for the first time in my life, he showed me that he was brave enough to give voice to his conscience and to admit he was fully human.

My father needed to tell the truth so he could place the blame where it belonged. He needed to make amends that would require more courage than he'd ever shown when wielding his belt. The documentary was only a start, but it served as a powerful launchpad for the process of reconciliation that continues to this day.

I realized I had to step up, too. Our family had a history of walking out on each other after fights or tough conversations and then not talking to each other for months. My dad and I both had to learn to stay in the room, to trust each other to work things through, not expecting a cure but making a vow to staunch our relational wound before we passed it to yet another generation. This meant that when we attempted understanding and missed, we'd see the conflict through, fighting clean and ending the battle before sleep.

It was messy, often painful. We failed often *and* made progress. Sometimes conversations boiled over, and my grievances pushed me to flee, but we both managed to break that pattern. Even if we couldn't resolve everything between us, we'd end the discussion together. That became our mutual practice of repair.

Ultimately, I forgave Nacho, not to erase the past but to stop letting it own our future. I also stopped thinking of him as a monster. Monsters don't change. Men sometimes do. And once I stopped calling my dad a monster, he couldn't hide behind that mask.

He genuinely wanted to change. He proved this by showing up, by listening, by staying open. And by sitting with me in the pain instead of looking away. Through all this he modeled a new kind of bravery composed of discipline, loyalty, and fearless honesty, but with care and justice liberally threaded through it. This new model, I believe, reflects my dad's true moral character.

Now living next door to me, Nacho is a father who often says less than he feels. He will likely wrestle his ghosts as long as he's alive. But he wants to be better and, more often than not, he is. He pours tenderness into his grandkids and his beloved old deaf chihuahua. He's always there if we need him. And I've learned to translate his new language of courage without abandoning myself.

One of the problematic beliefs that was transmitted to my father as a child involved what psychologists call *moral licensing*. The idea here is that righteousness earns credits, which allow you to then break the rules. It's like a dieter who's been "good" all day feeling entitled to "cheat" by eating chocolate cake for dinner. But moral licensing can cloak deeply unethical, even criminal, behavior in the language of moral virtue. A husband, for example, might tell himself that because he's a "good" provider, he can reward himself by beating or cheating on his wife—without any moral stain on his character. A CEO who's built a company renowned for its ethical practices might feel he's earned the right to ignore his own rules around sexual harassment. Moral licensing also allows some people to justify conduct like corporal punishment by telling themselves it serves a "greater good," teaches a "lesson," or deters someone else's "bad" behavior. This free pass offers no relief, though, for the victims of these transgressions.

And when a sense of moral permission is combined with a rigid moral orientation, people can act in ways that invite potentially disastrous consequences. "Once any person, book, or principle is declared sacred," Jonathan Haidt reminds us, "then devotees can no longer question it or think clearly about it." This tunnel vision can lead not only to multigenerational ripple effects like those that affected my family but also to unintended personal consequences. A few examples:

- Reena Virk was a fourteen-year-old girl of Indian descent who desperately wanted to belong, though her white Vancouver classmates shunned her. Though normally respectful of others, Reena tried to gain social approval by imitating the way one group of girls double-crossed each other. Her harmonist instincts blinded her to the danger that her actions had unleashed. A tragic trail of reactions then led to Reena's murder.

- John Chau was a young, self-appointed missionary who felt God had called him to bring Christianity to an uncontacted and historically hostile tribe in India's remote Andaman Islands in 2018. Chau's uncompromising idealism blinded him to abundant evidence that the island tribe did not want anything to do with outsiders. Believing he knew better, he did not respect their wishes. Even after he was met with arrows on his first try, he approached the island again. On this second attempt, he was killed.

- Lance Armstrong was hailed as an international icon of bravery after winning the Tour de France seven consecutive times and beating advanced testicular cancer. Yet his determination to excel evidently blinded him to the rules of fair play. He wound up at the center of a doping scandal that cost him his titles and terminated his cycling career.

These cautionary tales show just how important it is to be consistent and careful in minding your moral compass. They also demonstrate the risk of allowing personal identity to become *hyperconnected* to a rigid definition of moral superiority. This combination can turn the moral compass from a useful guide into a shield that actually blocks moral judgment.

Psychologically, this pattern taps into "moral narcissism," or the use of moral certainty to elevate oneself above doubt, consequence, or critique. The resulting overidentification with an almost singular moral frame often flatters the self as exceptional, chosen, or righteous. There's no "moral injury" in the conventional sense because there's no internal crisis, just external and potentially fatal fallout. But the pain that radiates from such moral rigidity can certainly result in moral injury for others.

What we're talking about here is the shadow side of righteousness. Moral certainty can feel like clarity, but if that certainty is unchecked by humility, it can cause real harm, as well as distortion of one's underlying moral purpose. To prevent such hubris, we need to be able to step outside our moral convictions and ask questions like *What am I missing? Whom am I harming? What part of me needs this to be true?* If we are truly to act in good conscience, we must respect both the power of our own true north and its moral hazards.

To explore just how profoundly moral orientation controls our thoughts and decisions, one compelling study from Germany, published in 2011, monitored the brains of subjects whose moral orientations leaned toward the brave, grouped as *individualists*, and another group identified as *collectivists*, whose orientations were more aligned with the caring. All the subjects were asked to examine pairs of abstract words and decide which word in each pair most appealed to them. The words included terms like "power," "autonomy," "tradition," and "community"—each reflecting the values of one group or the other, but not both. In some pairs the value difference between the two words was strong. "Assist" and "duel," for example, had nearly opposite meanings. But in other pairs, the value difference was ambiguous. "Swords" and "racing," for instance, both reflect competitive interaction, and "wedding" and "charity" both hint at cooperation. This moral ambiguity led to frustration when participants had to choose between words that both had the same underlying value. As it turned out, the two groups—individualists and collectivists—processed that moral frustration in startlingly different ways.

As subjects chose the word in each pair that most appealed to them, functional magnetic resonance imaging recorded their brain activity. This revealed that the collectivists employed three different cortical regions of the brain to make their decisions. They balanced and weighed each choice from a variety of perspectives. The individualists, however, relied primarily on a single subcortical structure that included the amygdala—the same region that sorts fear and aggression. According to the study's authors, "The strategy of the individualists might be interpreted as a 'fight-and-flight' strategy. They did not try to weigh each decision in each possible way as the collectivists did, but aimed at detecting the social relevance, and consecutively, the possible menace of the decision with regard to their own social status."

What this means is that our moral orientations literally determine how we think, and we do *not* all think alike or even with the same brain mechanisms. From political grievances to uproars on Nextdoor.com and simmering resentments in the classroom or office, many of the moral wounds we experience in daily life can be traced to stalemates between people with very different true norths. Each group might think their moral compass is best for everybody. They might mistakenly assume that everyone shares their orientation (which can aggravate both their righteousness and their confusion when others violate their supposedly common code). They might try to impose their orientation through force, legislation, or religion, in the belief that society would work better if everyone's conscience guided them to the same true north. But humans simply aren't wired that way.

This complexity has special ramifications for parents and teachers as they steer children's moral development. Kids need to learn that society is a mixed bag of personalities and moral priorities. They need guidance to figure out which of their own basic instincts to honor and which must be adjusted in order to get along with others. And they need practice in tolerance to discover not only that civility and respect can help resolve moral conflicts but also that acceptance can produce valuable lessons in compromise, which will raise their moral resilience.

Unfortunately, many young people don't receive that sort of thoughtful guidance. As a result, they can end up conforming to social cues and demands without considering their own needs or questioning the larger context. Especially online, they may adopt personas that bear little resemblance to their true moral identity. They may do what's expected because they feel socially pressured or because it doesn't occur to them to consult—or respect—their own moral compass. Psychologists call this "moral masquerading," and it's especially common among those who feel either adrift or coerced to conform.

Tara Westover traced this syndrome in her memoir *Educated*. As a child, Westover had believed what her parents taught her, that her goal in life was to be an obedient, family-oriented Mormon—a caring harmonist. But when she reached her teens, her true, self-transcendent nature began to assert itself. Westover felt morally torn between her family's demands and her own moral compass. Finally, she had to break away to honor her true north. Though she lacked any formal childhood education, her innate bravery ultimately led her to a doctorate in history from Cambridge and a career in academia.

Westover's journey, like Dee's, illustrates the cognitive dissonance that results from moral masquerading. A natural-born risk-taker can't be forced to become a hard-core harmonist, or vice versa. Whether conscious or unwitting, when we pretend to embrace a moral orientation that's alien to our instincts, we'll eventually realize we're betraying our conscience. The resulting loss of morale can feel like a personal crisis—one that demands sometimes painful sacrifices to restore personal integrity. Otherwise, if the masquerade becomes an ingrained pattern of behavior or lifestyle, the underlying lie will eventually cause one's moral compass to crater.

Unique new pressures, including the acceleration of technology, the collapse of trusted institutions, and the spread of disinformation have made both moral masquerading and moral injury more prevalent in the twenty-first century. But if we recognize and respect the natural orientation of our moral compass, this insight can still serve as a guardrail for integrity. It can also help us better understand each other while managing conflicts and mitigating the crescendo effect that leads to moral injury.

CHAPTER 5

HURTING

Moral Injury's Crescendo Effect

We are spinning our own fates, good or evil, and never to be undone.
Every smallest stroke of virtue or of vice leaves its never so little scar.
... Nothing we ever do is, in strict scientific literalness, wiped out.

—WILLIAM JAMES

As a requirement of his job, the state corrections director presided over a grueling schedule of executions, plus mock executions performed as rehearsals. He personally witnessed and initiated so many deaths that he was haunted by them even years after he'd retired. Then, in an attempt to mitigate some of the moral trauma experienced by the many layers of prison staff who continue to participate in executions, he joined other officials in calling for a reduction in the pace of executions. But a judge rebuffed their calls for reform, telling them to "suck it up."

Meanwhile, in Florida, a nurse in a major urban neonatal ICU (NICU) worked tirelessly to save tiny babies struggling for life. Each victory buoyed her spirits, but each failure drained her. Then, about a decade into her nursing career, she began caring for a premature infant whose biological family had given up on his chances of survival, effectively abandoning the newborn to the hospital staff. The nurse fell in love with this baby boy and planned to adopt him. But around his first birthday, the child died. The baby's biological family then reentered the picture, blaming the nurse, even banning her from the child's funeral. Shattered, the nurse quit the NICU, then left nursing altogether.

Across the Atlantic, in a small town in England, the owner of the local postal counter started noticing shortfalls in her receipts. She wasn't unduly alarmed at first, but the mysterious errors continued for years, and instead of investigating evidence of their own computer malfunction, the British Post Office demanded the sub-postmistress pay the rising balance in her books. The pressure mounted when the PO sued her for theft. She knew she was innocent, and the case was eventually thrown out of court, but not before the cumulative pressure and shame became so unbearable that she attempted suicide.

I tell these stories to remind you that moral injury rarely develops in a single blow. It is possible for one catastrophic event, such as marital betrayal, to abruptly shatter an otherwise secure and cohesive life. But it's much more common for moral distress to build up gradually over the span of months or years, until it reaches a tipping point, when the sense of irredeemable badness in the world and in oneself becomes pervasive. That crescendo of hopelessness signals the arrival of full-blown moral injury.

After studying this gradual cresting pattern among NICU nurses and doctors at the UVA School of Nursing, Professors Elizabeth Epstein and Ann Hamric in 2009 dubbed the progression from moral distress to moral injury "the crescendo effect."

FROM STRESS TO SUFFERING

"Crescendo" is an apt term for moral injury, for just as the crescendo of a symphony is loud, intense, emotionally rousing—and the sum of all that came before it—so does acute moral injury create a kind of sensory surround sound that makes it impossible to focus on anything but the sensations of mind and body. The essential difference, of course, is that a symphonic crescendo is anticipated and exhilarating, while moral injury is involuntary and debilitating.

The pain that causes this suffering is rooted in the two moral emotions we feel when our deepest sense of right and wrong is threatened: indignant anger and guilt. Indignant anger typically arises when we experience an insult directed at us personally or at the family or group we most identify with. It's a natural response to the violation of our core human need for dignity, to be treated with fairness and respect, as the good person we believe ourselves to be. On the other hand, if *we're* the ones who act unjustly, our natural reaction tends to be guilt. This inner-directed pain reflects a sense of responsibility, both for betraying our own moral integrity and for causing harm to others.

Anger and guilt may feel like antithetical emotions, one thrusting outward and the other aimed inward, yet we often struggle with both simultaneously, and that emotional conflict creates its own disturbing force field. Collision of the two feelings upsets moral identity, locking the opposing impulses in a painful standoff. Attempts to suppress anger only amplify guilt, and vice versa. This trapped tension can raise a kind of panic and elevate moral distress.

As an example, we might become irate at a family member who steals from us, even as we blame ourselves for not foreseeing the danger and preventing the theft. Such internal tension is especially common among witnesses of crimes who don't actively intervene. Bystanders may feel both anger at the violation and guilt for "allowing it to happen." The conflict is heightened if the witness knows the victim and is personally affected by the crime's repercussions. That intimate connection raises feelings of responsibility, intensifying self-indictment.

Moral emotions evolved in humans to protect social stability by incentivizing cooperation and collaboration. As such, they're designed to serve as wake-up calls, telling us a moral breach has occurred that must be resolved. Their universality can plainly be seen in any kindergarten playground where a child takes his playmate's toy without asking. Often, the other child's indignant anger will prompt her to confront him. If the boy sees that his actions have upset the girl, he might feel a quiver of guilt.

If the children's teacher seizes this opportunity to help them empathize with each other's feelings and learn to cooperate, the kids could gain a valuable lesson about respect, relationship, and reciprocity. That's the ideal moral scenario. Alas, when we don't empathize and resolve our differences, the primary moral emotions can trigger an eruption of secondary feelings, including shame, blame, remorse, contempt, disgust, sadness, and regret.

Not only does this emotional cascade make it harder to resolve the triggering conflict, but it can also infect longer-term social judgment, relationships, and self-esteem. That's because the chain reaction produces lingering biochemical traces, called moral residue, which include stress hormones like cortisol and adrenaline, alertness chemicals like norepinephrine, and even immune molecules called cytokines, released when the brain perceives danger. When we experience unresolved moral conflict, especially the kind that stirs up shame, guilt, or betrayal, our bodies can't "just move on." These chemicals stick around in our nervous system, and as they build up over time, they can dysregulate our emotions, distort memory, weaken our ability to make objective decisions, and warp our perceptions of identity and relationship.

Think of this residue as smoke. Your conscience produces some of this "smoke" every time it's distressed. Over time, the residue builds up, and if enough accumulates, it will impede your thoughts, behavior, and interactions in ways that can eventually cause moral injury.

Here's an example of an event that might well produce moral residue: You recommend your colleague for a big promotion, which he deservedly receives, but a few weeks later he's terminated in a massive cost-cutting purge of all "probationary" hires. If you hadn't put him up for promotion, he'd still have his job—as you do. Now your friend and his wife are losing medical coverage for their disabled child, and they may lose their house as well. As for you, your immediate reactions of panic and fear for their well-being are surpassed only by your avalanche of guilt. Brain regions such as the anterior cingulate cortex and medial prefrontal cortex will fire up, triggering a domino effect of emotional reactions involving empathy, remorse, anger, and shame. At the same time, the right side of the amygdala engages the stress response, releasing hormones like cortisol and adrenaline to prepare the body for a threat—even though the threat is emotional rather than physical.

Once the initial shock is over, the first wave of guilt will gradually subside. Let's say your colleague finds a new job and assures you the purge was not your fault. Time and life roll on. You try to tell yourself, What's done is done. But this is the point at which your moral orientation makes all the difference. If your conscience is intensely caring, you could get stuck on the now past transgression. You might worry that your colleague's career is permanently damaged. Maybe you ruminate on your culpability in endangering him. That could lead to feelings of self-contempt and remorse. Perhaps you also berate yourself for not "letting go" of what happened. Why are you making this about *you*, anyway? Is this just your ego talking, because you made a mistake? Why, you might wonder, don't you feel like your normal *self*?

These thoughts might sound and feel like an unhealthy obsession with self-importance, but self-importance is concerned with *credit* for being right, while moral injury is about failing to *do* what's right. One involves a damaged image, the other deeper damage to the apparatus of judgment, decision-making, and integrity. It's damage to integrity that causes true identity distress.

As long as this moral disorientation persists, the secondary emotions will keep smoldering, producing embers of moral residue. Prolonged stress will affect the prefrontal cortex and hippocampus, the command centers for decision-making, memory, and emotional regulation. As neurotransmitters, including norepinephrine and dopamine, misfire, you'll grow more anxious and prone to depression. Over time, this biochemical storm can weaken your immune system, ramp up inflammation, and disrupt sleep.

This, then, is the essence of moral residue: lingering chemical aftereffects that disrupt the psyche, causing emotional turbulence and impaired decision-making long after the inciting event has passed. When moral conflict goes unresolved, these chemical traces embed themselves in the body the way smoke clings to fabric.

Not all moral stress produces the same kind of residue, though. Agency—the amount of control you felt you had over your choices during the inciting incident—can make a big difference. Think of this as the difference between a self-inflicted wound and an aggravated assault. The more your active choices contributed to the transgression, the more likely you are to feel guilt, shame, self-contempt, and other *inner-directed* moral emotions. Your moral residue over time might take the form of corrosive self-blame and self-distrust. If, on the other hand, you had little agency over the events that caused harm, you'll more likely feel resentment, helplessness, betrayal, and *other-directed* moral emotions. In this case, your moral residue might lead to chronic feelings of powerlessness, anger, and distrust of others.

―――

In 2017, my wife, also an Air Force veteran and board-certified, licensed psychologist, and I confronted the greatest moral challenge of our lives—one that threatened to shatter our sense of agency and emotional equilibrium. That June our second daughter, Liliana, was born a beautiful, dark-haired, green-eyed, seemingly healthy little girl. Two weeks later, I noticed her left leg shaking.

The diagnosis was devastating: CDKL5 deficiency disorder, a rare genetic disorder caused by mutations in the *CDKL5* gene. The most common symptoms include "early-onset, difficult-to-control seizures and neurodevelopmental impairment that affects cognitive, motor, speech, and visual function."

Behind the dry language was a child's lost future: Liliana would never climb on a swing, blow bubbles in the backyard, or learn to read. She would never dress herself, feed herself, go to sleepovers, let loose in college, or find a career she enjoyed. She was destined to endure frequent epileptic seizures and would be dependent on others for the rest of her days. Our family's life, as we knew it, had ended.

Parental anguish isn't usually talked about in terms of moral injury. Little if any research has been conducted on the phenomenon. Yet, based on my experience with Liliana and conversations with other parents of special-needs children, I am convinced that such soul-wrenching challenges are as likely as battle trauma to cause moral injury.

I didn't just feel forsaken by the universe when we received Lily's diagnosis; it was as if every conceivable higher power had betrayed us, leaving us cornered in an unjust world. Coupled with this was the nagging feeling that my wife, Alison, and I were somehow culpable. The weight of self-blame was compounded when we learned that Lily's *CDKL5* mutation was de novo, spontaneously occurring during her development. Even with the knowledge that it wasn't inherited, we couldn't shake off the harrowing thought that some unknown fault of our own might have contributed to our beloved daughter's suffering.

"Why us?" I asked, over and over. "Are we really so bad that we deserve this?" Overwhelmed by exhaustion, despair, rage, and the endless loop of "why" and "fuck you, universe," I often felt we must indeed have done something to deserve this.

But gradually we began to realize something else: that every sleepless night, every scream and tear shed, and also every smile Lily flashed was an invitation to derive meaning from our shared pain and adversity. I'd guided countless patients to uncover slivers of gratitude even in the direst of circumstances. Now it was my turn.

Eventually, slowly, the question of agency shifted. "Why *not* us?" I whispered.

What if this journey with Lily was not a random act of a cruel universe but a call to transcend? To evolve.

Not punishment for being bad, but a signal of the *goodness* we held inside.

I understood then that our challenges with Lily weren't just hardships; they were life's profound lessons encapsulated in a being so pure. This wasn't about being special but about recognizing that within immense challenge lies immense growth. Lily wasn't just our daughter; she was our guiding light, illuminating a unique path of insight and profound love that frankly no other human could.

Make no mistake, I was furious at God for Lily's suffering. Hers is a grave condition, and, barring a miracle of gene therapy, she will have it for the rest of her life. But Alison and I have supportive families, dedicated doctors, and the resources to get Lily the best care imaginable and to be the best possible mother and father to both our children. There is so much to be thankful for.

Intentionally turning away from despair, we focused instead on the goodness in doctors who worked tirelessly to reduce our daughter's seizures, in compassionate family, friends, colleagues, and neighbors. I began to volunteer in our community as a way to heal and experience forgiveness. And we all found a deeper joy and gratitude in even simple acts of reconnection, like shared meals and walks and reunions with dear friends and family.

As many mental health professionals, philosophers, and religious leaders have stressed, it's easy to be grateful when life is good. In the wake of a terrible loss, trauma, or betrayal, feelings of anger—even rage—are to be expected. And there's nothing wrong about that. But anger doesn't negate the healing power of gratitude. We can experience both at the same time. And alongside anger and gratitude, we can find forgiveness, meaning, a sense of purpose, and an understanding that each new challenge is an invitation to deepen our wellspring of love and moral resilience.

Agency adds a complex layer of moral response that dwells in self-perception, in the tension between reality and belief and between values and behavior, especially when circumstances strip us of meaningful options. The centrality of identity is one factor that makes moral distress so lasting and deeply impactful; it's a struggle not only with external forces but with our own defining sense of power, goodness, and self.

MORAL CHALLENGES SET THE STAGE

But what happens to the corrections director whose job forces him to witness execution after execution and whose moral warnings and distress are repeatedly demeaned? What becomes of the NICU nurse whose best efforts keep failing the infants in her care and who's attacked for even trying to save them? Or the sub-postmistress who's done nothing wrong yet is persecuted for years by the country she loves and serves? Beyond those examples, consider the first responders, social media content moderators, crisis counselors, and countless other professionals on the front lines of moral conflict who pile up anger and guilt every day on the job. Not to mention the children raised in climates of continuous domestic abuse who grow up blaming themselves.

In all these cases, moral residue from one conflict will spill into the next. And each time those individuals' protests are ignored, twisted, or berated, their trust in the universe will break a little more. They may come to doubt their own moral compass, even to regard it as dangerous. If the gaslighting persists, any attempt to heal can feel like trying to stitch a wound while it's being cut. With each new crisis of conscience, the cumulative level of distress rises, until the emotional fallout reaches a crescendo that's simply intolerable.

None of this occurs in a vacuum. The stage is set by the level of *moral challenge* in one's everyday surroundings. Much as people with asthma are likely to feel sicker in areas with bad air pollution, people who live in a climate of violent hostility and social distrust are more likely to experience moral distress than those whose neighbors generally get along and support each other. That's because an atmosphere thick with accusation and divisive grievances can make it difficult to resolve personal conflicts or recover the moral stability needed to halt the crescendo effect.

Now, a certain amount of moral stress is both normal and necessary. As the psychologist Brett Litz points out, "Moral challenges are statistically ubiquitous parts of the human condition." Everyday disagreements can lead to constructive debate and innovation. They help us figure out the best way to conduct ourselves at work, to raise our children, to resolve disputes with friends and neighbors. They teach us to compromise when problems offer only no-win solutions. They offer practice in forgiving each other and ourselves when ethical lines are bent.

Constructive moral dilemmas give us valuable practice in cognitive dissonance—the psychological discomfort of holding irreconcilable values or beliefs. Cognitive dissonance ignites what Litz calls "moral frustration," a feeling of inner turmoil caused by "either incredulity about the state of things or displeasure about personal behavior." But that frustration is not all bad. Moral health requires us to be able to tolerate a certain amount of cognitive dissonance and to manage feelings of moral frustration. Learning to get along with people who hold different beliefs and to resolve the everyday moral challenges that arise out of these differences is essential for emotional maturity.

But the ethical challenges we face today are raising the emotional and existential stakes in ways that cannot be easily managed or even fully grasped. Take the climate crisis, for example. How could past generations have allowed this to happen, many ask with indignation, and why aren't our current leaders doing more to stop it? Then, too, there's guilt as we wonder how much our own use of fossil fuels and carbon chemicals has contributed to the problem. These low-grade moral emotions may be fleeting and easy to ignore so long as we're not directly affected by a climate disaster or by personal disputes around the issue. But what if you have to evacuate several times a year because of unprecedented fires or hurricanes? What if your neighbors shame you for driving a gas-guzzling car? What if your mother dies of heatstroke on the hottest day in history? Then the moral challenges start to feel like imminent threats. Cognitive dissonance rises. And moral frustration spikes.

Our society's individualistic bias only adds to the psychological pressure. "Environmental problems are often framed as up to us as individuals to solve," the environmental sociologist Sarah Jaquette Ray explains. This can cause us to feel as if we were solely responsible. Some concerned citizens enter a constant state of hypervigilance until they realize that "climate change, unlike a bill getting passed, is an ongoing kind of long term, many generations problem to solve. And if they're going to approach it like a sprint rather than a marathon, they will burn out really quick." That realization can then cause a whiplash of despair and futility. "This negative feeling of, I can't fix the whole problem because I'm so small, makes us not even want to solve a little part of it.... That cognitive dissonance makes it very difficult to really face into what we need to do to solve it, and much easier to just say, I throw my hands up."

Then, Ray says, activists who are still in that hypervigilant fix-it state of mind will accuse their despairing allies of being part of the problem.

Similar polarizing patterns are repeating across society as issues from sexuality to marriage, health care to education, civil rights to democracy spark ever new and increasingly intractable moral conflicts. We're affected not only by personal choices and interactions with friends and neighbors but also by information we consume through the media. Virtual screens present little protection. In fact, science tells us that similar neural activity occurs in our brains when we're thinking about moral conflicts *in theory* as when we're trying to solve these dilemmas *in practice*. This suggests that societal polarization could be taxing us mentally and emotionally, even if our daily lives appear to be uneventful.

The political scientist Robert Putnam, who traced the weakening of America's social fabric in *Bowling Alone*, points to routine "transaction costs" produced by generalized social distrust as we train ourselves to keep our doors locked, our guard up, our suspicions sharp. As interactive social creatures, humans require a morally cohesive ecosystem to feel secure. Even the privileged few who think they've got everything under control will fare poorly if they can't trust the people around them. That's because constant vigilance is exhausting.

"A well-connected individual in a poorly connected society," Putnam explains, "is not as productive as a well-connected individual in a well-connected society." In other words, we would *all* do well to respect and honor that African principle of *ubuntu*: "I am because we are." Unfortunately, many of the most widely accepted U.S. norms push us in the opposite direction.

Instead of encouraging people of every moral orientation to pull together, America's myth of rugged individualism exalts a level of personal autonomy that's both unattainable and destructive for the vast majority of the population. Rather than teaching us to rely on each other, as everyone must when times are tough, the ethos of individualism scolds us to "pull ourselves up by our bootstraps." When we feel lost and disillusioned, the fable of free will shames us for not having the grit to "tough it out" alone. As a result, we often lose social capital when we need it most. Then, with our sense of belonging in jeopardy, we wrestle with the primal fear of being cast out by the very people our natural instincts tell us to rely on. It's no exaggeration to say that America's fetish of self-sufficiency heightens the threat of isolation, loneliness, and depression for all of us. These conditions turn everyday moral challenges into triggers for the crescendo effect.

In 1992, a large majority of American adults cited "breakdown of community" and "selfishness" as serious problems for the country. In 1996, fully half said Americans were becoming less trustworthy, and 80 percent said we were becoming "less civil" to each other. Three years later, two-thirds said moral values were in decline and that "society was focused more on the individual than the community." By 2022, these concerns were exploding, with 87 percent of those polled by Gallup rating Americans' moral values as fair or poor. Lack of "consideration for others" led the concerns, followed by racism. And 78 percent of those polled said moral values were still getting worse.

Not surprisingly, political partisanship has widened America's moral fault lines. That same 2022 poll found that Republicans were nearly as likely to view lack of religion as a moral failure as they were lack of consideration of others. But only 4 percent of Republicans prioritized racism as a major moral problem, compared with 10 percent of Democrats and 8 percent of independents. These results may reflect even broader traditional-individualistic moral biases: Conservatives tend to value in-group loyalty, deference to authority, and the purity of group identity, while liberals care more about personal liberty, dignity, and justice for those both inside and outside their own group.

These differences should be bridgeable. Partisans on all sides agree that morality is fundamentally about not causing harm. It's just that the harm that most concerns conservatives involves their group identity, while liberals prioritize individual rights. In a pluralistic society, both group rights and individual rights need to be respected and protected. That's been the inherent moral dilemma facing America since the founding of the republic; much of our Constitution is dedicated to balancing these two sets of rights. But we've now reached an inflection point that's turned this core challenge into a national crisis.

With partisans routinely attacking each other's moral decency, honesty, and integrity, supporting policies that punish and exile othered groups and even threatening or delivering violence against the "other side," we are now in uncharted territory. As America's collective conscience warps, it's splintering the very definition of ethical behavior and pitting our individual moral compasses against each other. Unable to pull together as a society, we are pulling apart, turning against the very notion of common ground.

What's worse, this cycle is self-perpetuating. "Honesty, civic engagement, and social trust are mutually reinforcing," Putnam explains. "Conversely, the civically disengaged believe themselves to be surrounded by miscreants and feel less constrained to be honest themselves. The causal arrows among civic involvement, reciprocity, honesty, and social trust are as tangled as well-tossed spaghetti." In this situation, it's fair to say that everyone feels morally distressed. Acknowledging this distress as individuals can be a first step toward mending personal conflicts before they converge to form an impassable quagmire.

MORAL COMPROMISES ACCELERATE CONFLICT

America's long march toward individualism is not the only reason why polarization is intensifying now. Trained over millennia by average levels of moral frustration, our psyches long ago developed internal shortcuts to ease decision-making and protect our conscience when faced with ethically ambiguous situations. But under the bombardment of modern moral challenges, these instinctual dodges can and often do—paradoxically—accelerate conflict.

Attribution Bias

One innate moral compromise involves *attribution bias*. As mentioned in the last chapter, this bias inclines us to equate behavior with character, so that bad behavior is interpreted as a sign of moral badness, regardless of extenuating circumstances. Attribution bias elevates our sense of self and belonging when we believe we're acting virtuously, and it warns against trusting someone whose behavior suggests they may not be trustworthy. But it can also serve as a kind of emotional insulation against conscientious objection. If someone has done something wrong, this moral bias assures us, then they must be bad people who deserve to be rounded up and kept safely away from "good" society. Whatever is done to them, *they must have it coming*.

Attribution bias dates back to a time when everyone lived in close communities, where people knew each other personally and so were better equipped to make snap judgments about character, even in the absence of objective evidence. Early on, if a boy was caught stealing a neighbor's horse, everyone in town knew this boy's family, how he treated other kids, and whether this was his first or fifteenth offense. People, in other words, had *context* for their biases.

The mechanism is ill-suited to vast societies where diverse groups live side by side with little idea of each other's customs or circumstances. In modern history, attribution bias has fostered rushes to judgment against anyone who acts or appears different from the majority—including many who are innocent of any crime at all. It enables persecutors, like vigilantes and spectators at public lynchings a century ago, to convince themselves and other members of their group that the accused "must be" guilty. In this way, attribution bias stokes discrimination, as well as extrajudicial violence, while sparing both perpetrators and witnesses from the moral residue of shame, remorse, and regret that would otherwise follow such cruelty. Then, freed from the crescendo effect, the persecutors can go on with their daily lives psychologically unscathed. This was the moral bypass that enabled hate-mongers like Hitler, as well as hate groups like the Ku Klux Klan, to subvert the consciences of their supporters, including judges and lawmakers, even as the death toll of their innocent victims rose into the millions.

The damage from such moral blindness is not limited to immediate victims. All of society pays a steep price for attribution bias. Those who are indirectly persecuted feel cursed. Social cohesion shatters.

The moral stakes grow increasingly insidious when attribution bias is triggered by remote and ambiguous grievances involving people the accusers don't know well, if at all. Today, thanks to social media, persecution can be completely anonymous and the resulting injustice vicious, violent, and devastating. One prominent web designer, for example, was doxxed after casually endorsing online comment moderation. First an anonymous post appeared on her blog: "I hope someone slits your throat." Then others piled on. Doctored sexual images started popping up on different platforms used by her peers. One gave out her home address. Another suggested a lynching. The posts vilified the designer without giving her any chance to identify her persecutors or to defend herself. The death threats drove her to cancel public appearances and shut down her blog. Police told her there was nothing they could do.

Today's politicians and theocrats weaponize collective attribution bias, as their predecessors have throughout history. It's a tool with the power to divide and conquer on a mass scale. Every time they accuse whole ethnic groups or nations of moral violations, such as stealing, cheating, lying, or worse, they're cynically priming their followers to feel threatened and wronged by the target groups—even if their followers have never had any actual dealings with the accused. Attribution bias then kicks in, and the followers often turn en masse, treating members of the targeted groups as enemies and collectively dehumanizing them. During Reconstruction and Jim Crow, this pattern resulted in the lynching of more than sixty-five hundred Black Americans. Today the same forces that fueled those crimes are resurgent. In 2024 the Southern Poverty Law Center identified more than 110 active organizations and militias that support white nationalism. The tactics of these groups have ranged from assassination plots on elected officials, to the doxing and swatting of journalists and poll workers, to cold-blooded murders. All aided and abetted by attribution bias.

Othering has also catalyzed wars, including the latest conflagration in Israel. First attribution bias emboldened Islamic Jihad and Hamas assailants to kill or kidnap more than fourteen hundred Israelis on October 7, 2023. Then it compelled Israelis to justify retaliatory bombing and starvation that killed more than sixty thousand Palestinians in Gaza by mid-2025. As long as each group views all people on the other side as "animals," they feel no compunction about murdering, maiming, or torturing these strangers. Such moral conflict becomes self-perpetuating.

Moral Decoupling

Another protective mechanism that contributes to the fracturing of collective values is, paradoxically, the opposite of attribution bias. *Moral decoupling* allows us to "hate the sin but *love* the sinner" by separating close social ties from our feelings about our loved ones' behavior. The literary world was recently rocked by an extreme example of moral decoupling after evidence surfaced that the late

Nobel Prize winner Alice Munro had stood by her second husband even after learning he'd sexually molested her young daughter for many years. Munro refused either to defend her daughter or to divorce her husband, instead claiming that she'd been "told too late" and loved him too much to leave him—as if *he* (not her daughter) were central to Munro's identity, so therefore her daughter's victimization was immaterial to her.

Moral decoupling allowed Munro to preserve her sense of herself as a good person despite her emotional identification with a predatory husband. Furthermore, by acknowledging the abuse without forgiving him, she could psychologically absolve herself of betraying her daughter. None of this absolved her in the minds of others, of course, especially not her daughter's, but *internally* it would have muted her conscience enough that she didn't have to sacrifice her primary relationship to keep her moral identity intact.

For all the shock waves triggered by the revelations about Munro, moral decoupling is far more common than most of us want to admit. As Claire Dederer writes in *Monsters: A Fan's Dilemma*, "We don't always love who or what we're supposed to love . . . John Lennon beat his wife; T. S. Eliot was an anti-Semite; Lou Reed has been accused of abuse, racism, and anti-Semitism." Such transgressions may be well known, even proven in court, yet millions manage to minimize them, holding tight to their identification with the music or poetry or art or genius of the transgressors in spite of their sins.

To understand how this works, imagine that you belong to the congregation of a charismatic pastor who's personally gone out of his way to help your family. You consider him a true friend and moral mentor, his sermons have made you a better person, and his church is the hub of your social life. This gives the pastor *primacy* in your identity; you wouldn't feel like yourself without him. But then the news breaks that your pastor has been embezzling church funds for decades to support his gambling habit. You condemn these crimes, but your natural inclination is to preserve your own moral stability, and that means defending the faith you've placed in this man, as well as the linkage between him and your own identity. So you choose to believe him when he asks for forgiveness and promises he'll never steal another dime, and you remain in his congregation, "hating the sin, but loving the sinner."

Moral decoupling gives us an off-ramp when we want to escape ethical conflict. It allows us to justify continued support for politicians who've been convicted of felonies; to work for billionaire CEOs who mistreat staff and cheat on their taxes; to admire celebrities who've spewed racist or homophobic remarks and been filmed battering their girlfriends. It also protects our self-identification as "good people," even if we do occasionally ignore those in need or neglect to tip the waiter.

Proportion plays an important role in these compromises, of course. When we discount bad actions "in the grand scheme of things," it can feel like rearranging furniture to minimize an ugly chair for the sake of the overall effect. That may be an effective ploy if we have only one chair to hide, and everyone we know isn't hiding the identical chair, but when moral decoupling becomes a way of life for millions of people across society, such attempts at deception fall flat. The ugliness becomes inescapable, the attempts to ignore it as ludicrous as claims by the courtiers in Hans Christian Andersen's classic folktale "The Emperor's New Clothes" that the nude emperor wasn't really naked.

Widespread self-deception and denial allow moral damage to rise until finally it cannot be ignored. Then, as we saw after the #MeToo movement exposed the true scale of sexual abuse across society, at least some transgressors will be forced to account. But this whole sordid cycle shreds social trust and intensifies the conditions that spread moral pain.

THREE PATHS TO MORAL INJURY

Psychologists have only recently begun to study the etiology of moral injury, so there's little agreement on the crescendo effect's "typical" course. But the research does suggest three general pathways. All three involve events that threaten a person's deeply held values, producing moral residue and disorienting moral identity. What varies are the timelines, patterns, and subjective intensities of those events.

The Slow Drip of Moral Distress

One path to moral injury begins with a relatively minor dilemma that produces moral *distress*—a degree of pain more personally destabilizing than everyday moral challenges but less debilitating than full-blown moral trauma.

In 1999, when the British Post Office began accusing local sub-postmasters of stealing money from accounts that, in fact, were corrupted by the PO's own computer malfunctions, the sub-postmasters generally felt distressed—indignant, hurt, and frustrated—but they clung to their identification as loyal upright British citizens who firmly believed their PO and government would never betray them.

Only as the drip, drip, drip of moral distress continued over more than twenty years—as the British government persisted in gaslighting these individuals, demanding their life savings and livelihoods, and unjustly sending several sub-postmasters to jail—did the moral residue rise to such critical levels that identities shattered. At that point, some of these innocent victims broke down and attempted suicide (at least thirteen succeeded). Others fought the debilitating effects of moral injury by banding together to sue the Post Office. Their case was taken up by members of Parliament and was publicized through the television series *Mr. Bates vs. the Post Office*. In 2024 legislation was passed to exonerate and compensate the wrongfully convicted postmasters, but as of June 2025 thousands of claims still remained unpaid. And so the moral residue around this transgression continues to accumulate.

Dilemmas like the sub-postmasters' are vivid, immediate, and painful, but their initial ambiguity can allow them to fly under our emotional radar, so we fail to recognize them as dangerous. Sometimes there's no objective way to tell who's "right" or "wrong" or what's right to do, who's to blame, or even who the true victims are. Such situations generally don't appear to involve life-and-death stakes, at least not at first. Yet they nevertheless threaten morale—the balance between values and experience that's needed to maintain moral orientation. And that gives them existential weight, which keeps building the longer conflicts go unresolved.

If you have difficulty relating to a transgression as massive as the British Post Office scandal, consider instead the moral strain on a devoted single parent who must work two jobs to keep her family afloat, but whose absence at home is contributing to her daughter's depression and failing grades. Or the IT designer whose time-saving AI innovations are costing his closest and most competent friends their jobs. Moral distress often occurs when circumstances make it impossible to live up to our own moral standards, so we feel psychologically trapped and torn. If the overworked parent gives up one of her jobs, she'll be able to tend to her daughter, but the lost wages could leave them both homeless. If the IT designer tries to retract or revise his innovations, management might fire and possibly sue him as well.

In such binds we often make moral concessions: white lies told to give a daughter hope of a weekend together; a Faustian bargain with management to lead a project that could create new jobs for teammates. Or we might rationalize inaction by minimizing the moral cost. A lot of effort can go into making excuses and trying to twist our perceptions of the conflict, all in the hope of shedding moral distress. But despite these efforts, moral residue accrues. The longer the core dilemma persists, the more our thoughts will be clouded by moral indignation and guilt, and the more our bodies will be buffeted by subsequent waves of shame, resentment, and regret.

High-stakes, high-pressure professions like law enforcement or intensive-care and emergency medicine create an especially potent drip of moral distress. The daily choices that these jobs require are rarely simple or morally clear. Is it right to fire on someone who appears to be pointing a gun at you, even if you cannot see whether the weapon is real? Is it right to prescribe or administer a drug that might give an uninsured patient a few more months of life, even if the cost of the drug will bankrupt the patient's family? Was it right during the COVID pandemic, when hospitals were understaffed and undersupplied, to deny treatment to the sickest patients while admitting those most likely to survive?

Each decision that leads to harm or increased suffering leaves a layer of moral residue. And each layer of moral residue serves as a reminder of powerlessness when the next high-stakes case presents itself. The UVA nursing professors Epstein and Hamric point to the dreaded feeling of "here we go again" that surges with each successive moral dilemma. The sheer repetition of moral distress creates a sense of futility that hastens the crescendo effect.

This syndrome of distress in professional settings can lead to several different reactions. Some in medicine and law enforcement become morally numb and emotionally disengaged, perhaps avoiding or handing off situations that require difficult decisions. Others become conscientious objectors, documenting their dissent or reporting ethical conflicts or untenable working conditions. But the most common consequence of repetitive moral distress may be burnout.

We typically use the term "burnout" to describe a state of mental, emotional, and/or physical exhaustion due to prolonged, untenable stress. Caring for a chronically ill family member for months on end without help or relief can cause you to feel burned out. So can a highly demanding academic program that overwhelms you with research requirements and exams that you have difficulty passing. And so can jobs that leave you feeling overworked, impotent, and unappreciated. The moral component of burnout is often overlooked, but in many cases the true cause of burnout is moral injury.

This is especially true for individuals who find themselves caught between the needs of patients or clients, on the one hand, and the fiscal demands of insurers or corporate hierarchies, on the other. The pharmacist who has to deny lifesaving medicine to uninsured customers because they can't afford to pay the full price. The factory foreman who's ordered to cut corners in ways that he knows will result in an unsafe product. The restaurant manager whose boss insists he underpay their immigrant kitchen staff. Trapped in the middle of such conflicts, individuals may find themselves executing direct commands that they believe to be morally wrong. Each time they follow such orders, they'll feel the sting of moral distress.

Every such episode takes a nick out of one's integrity and fills it with moral residue. If the crescendo effect continues unabated, feelings of anger, guilt, shame, and betrayal will mount until the pain becomes pervasive. The resulting tide of moral injury can shatter faith in humanity and throw one's deepest sense of self into doubt.

Moral Trauma and the Smashing of Conscience

Another path to moral injury is acute moral trauma, which can trigger the crescendo effect literally overnight. On January 6, 2021, the whole world witnessed one such cataclysmic event when thousands of American citizens—whose moral outrage was stoked by lies that the 2020 election had been "rigged"—stormed the U.S. Capitol.

For most of the police officers whose job was to protect the Capitol that day, those hours of mortal combat generated profound moral as well as physical anguish. The officers had sworn to serve the very Americans who now inexplicably were turning on them as adversaries. "I sided with the law," Sergeant Aquilino Gonell later reflected. "And I've been a faithful public servant in the Army and as a law enforcement officer for twenty-five years." Yet that day the very people he'd taken an oath to serve descended on him as a mob intent on wrecking and desecrating one of the nation's core symbols of democracy, not to mention physically endangering their own elected leaders and preventing the constitutional transfer of power.

That physical assault and trauma left many officers with serious physical pain and PTSD. Sergeant Gonell's injuries required surgery and forced him to retire from the Capitol Police. But for some, the moral injury was even more debilitating. Four Capitol police officers died by suicide after the January 6 attack. Their families described the officers' sleep deprivation, uncharacteristic anger, and social withdrawal, refusing even the comfort of beloved pets. All these symptoms point to moral injury.

Sergeant Gonell feels most betrayed by the government officials whose lives he and his fellow officers fought to protect. On the fourth anniversary after January 6, he wrote in *The Bulwark*,

> I feel betrayed by the Department of Justice for not moving faster and with more purpose to hold accountable those who inspired the riot that day. I'm sickened that surviving benefits (Public Safety Officers' Benefits) have not been approved for officers who were injured, physically and mentally, in the line of duty.... And I feel let down by the members of Congress who turned their backs

on us even as we saved their lives.... I did my part. They did not do theirs.

Moral trauma occurs when high-stakes events transgress such deeply held beliefs that one's moral compass simply can't withstand the pressure. Unlike lower-key moral distress, which can inundate us with doubt and ambiguity, acute moral trauma often convinces us that we know exactly who's at fault and that the only way to relieve the relentless emotional pain is to do something immediately to atone or to gain retribution.

That *feeling* of moral certainty, though, is not necessarily accurate or stable. The fog of moral trauma, like the fog of war, can distort reality and blind us to facts that might be crystal clear to objective observers. For example, witnesses who experience moral injury as the result of a violent crime might have played only a peripheral role in the actual events or, perhaps like the Capitol police officers who died by suicide, they might have worked heroically to stop the crime, yet they can still feel consumed by guilt.

The Smash and Grab of Distress plus Trauma

The crescendo of moral injury can also be the product of *both* long-term distress and sudden moral trauma. Unfortunately, this dual assault is especially common in marginalized and underprivileged communities.

In the 1990s, the public health researcher Arline Geronimus coined the term "weathering" to describe chronic stress related to social injustice. This stress "literally wears down your heart, your arteries, your neuroendocrine systems, . . . all your body systems so that in effect, you become chronologically old at a young age." Specific causes of weathering include poverty, racial discrimination, and economic and educational injustice, any and all of which make daily life more physically and emotionally draining for marginalized groups than for others. The same principle of weathering can also impact moral well-being, creating its own crescendo effect.

A daily diet of injustice will strain your cognitive and emotional resources, making it more challenging to engage in moral reasoning and to maintain ethical consistency. The underlying social message is this: "You're not worthy enough to belong to the majority, so you don't deserve the privileges others enjoy." On the receiving end, it's like having an internalized report card that's graded continuously and unfairly, marking you as inferior and suspect. As the bad grades add up, you feel more and more like a bad person—and more desperate to escape those bad feelings. When a traumatic event occurs on top of this underlying pressure, the urgent need to relieve stress or simply to survive may overshadow moral considerations. This can lead to decisions that turbocharge the crescendo effect.

What's worse, these conditions often persist across generations, producing a legacy of injustice that can accelerate moral injury even in children.

My dad had stopped whipping me with his belt by the time I reached high school, but the pain of those punishments stayed with me. I carried it when I took off, surfing along the Bodega Coast, when I DJed on weekends, when I studied the music of Prince as if it were my personal lifeline. I never spoke out about the violence I'd suffered. My dad and I both were products of moral trauma passed down over generations, and I didn't think my protests would make any difference. I felt the weight of this isolation, the sense that there was no one to turn to, no safe harbor anywhere. Poverty and racism had stripped away any semblance of security, making it impossible to envision a future where things could be different.

The scarcity of resources magnified my helplessness. There were no counselors, mental health clinics, or even concerned family doctors available to me. Justice and protection, I concluded back then, were luxuries afforded only to white Americans. We Mexicans were supposed to take the abuse, and that was that. We weren't entitled to speak out, request help, or seek change.

All these forces intertwined to create a paralyzing web of moral distress. It wasn't just that I didn't know how to change the system; it was that every element of my existence warned that I had no power to do so. Asking for help, I believed, would only make matters worse.

Today, I know differently. My training has taught me that the crescendo effect *can* be halted. Moral harm can be treated. And we all are entitled to the caring concern, dignity, and help that I once viewed as forbidden luxuries. There are resources available now that I couldn't even imagine when I was young. In fact, the healing prospects for moral injury are more promising by the day.

CHAPTER 6

HEALING

From Moral Distress to Moral Resilience

The soul aids the body, and at certain moments, raises it.

—VICTOR HUGO

Ten years into her teaching career, Lauren Porosoff was familiar with burnout. At three different schools she and her fellow teachers had struggled with classes that were too large, textbooks that were outdated, curricula that prioritized student testing over learning, and shrinking budgets that cut back on the tools and experiences kids most need for a meaningful education. The moral tension between administrative demands and student needs drove many talented teachers into other lines of work, but Lauren concentrated on connecting with her students. She fervently believed in the power of strong learning communities to change lives for the better, and she found joy in the authentic relationships she formed with her students and colleagues.

Lauren's most deeply held moral values directed her to foster harmony through compassion and inclusion. Student success, in her book, wasn't limited to academic excellence or exemplary discipline. One of her favorite middle-schoolers was a boy named Jerome who struggled to read and write, tested poorly, and often got into trouble in her colleagues' classrooms. But Lauren saw a different side of this child in her English class, where he loved to learn and contribute. His insights were genuine and valuable. Even a decade later, when Lauren told me about Jerome, she marveled at the stories he'd written, one in particular about his birth mother in South America and how their mutual love of baseball connected the two of them.

"It was just beautiful and heartbreaking and thoughtful," Lauren told me.

But she and Jerome's Spanish teacher were the only two teachers in the school who recognized this boy's potential. And when he got into serious trouble, they were powerless to help him.

"It was bad," Lauren said. "He had nude photos of a classmate. He showed them to someone else." She made no excuses for his behavior. However, Jerome did not act alone.

"He was not the first or the last who got caught with pictures like this," Lauren recalled, "but only he was expelled."

More to the point, the speed of Jerome's punishment struck her as unjust. Because she considered herself an agent of the school community, Lauren reacted with anger and guilt. "I protested to the principal," she recalled, "but he gave us some, 'Oh, I see things from thirty thousand feet that you don't see on the ground, where you are.'"

What Lauren saw was 360 degrees of moral failure. Even a decade after the fact, her distress was still palpable as we talked. "I remember feeling kind of dead inside. I was disappointed in Jerome, I was angry at him, but how could the school make this decision without even talking to us? They only knew his worst behavior, and people are more than what they do on their worst day."

The betrayal of Jerome, of the girl, and of her own core values as an educator left Lauren feeling gravely disheartened. "What's wrong with me?" she asked her husband. "Why can't I get over this?"

That's when she first learned about moral injury. "My husband's a psychologist, and he works with veterans," Lauren explained.

Soon she was reading Brett Litz's definition of moral injury as "perpetrating, failing to prevent, bearing witness to, or learning about acts that transgress deeply held moral beliefs and expectations." And this rang true to her own experience. "I'm not comparing my job to a soldier's or Jerome's leaving school to an act of war. Yet I do have a deeply held moral belief in helping all students thrive and in cultivating a sense of belonging. Even if Jerome could get a fresh start at a new school, I couldn't escape the feeling that I might have been able to do something that would have led to a better outcome."

Lauren wasn't dealing with the full crescendo effect of moral injury, but she was struggling with very real moral distress. And being able to name this was hugely helpful, she told me, because it made her feel less alone and "weird." If moral distress was common enough to have a name, she reasoned, then "it wasn't my fault that I was so upset about this."

Even better, "because there's literature on it, I could read about it." Reading about moral injury gave Lauren some of the tools she needed to mitigate her distress.

Additional tools emerged from her understanding of contextual psychology, which informed her husband's work. Contextual psychology is transdiagnostic, meaning that solutions aren't specific to one ailment but, instead, tap into our innate ability to heal mental and emotional pain more broadly. Pretty soon, Lauren had compiled several strategies that improved her general well-being *and* helped reduce her moral distress so she could move forward.

The first of these strategies was simply to show herself the same compassion that she was feeling for her students and to acknowledge that she, too, was deeply affected by the transgressions involving Jerome. "When our institutions behave in ways that go against our values," she reflected, "we can give ourselves the support we're so good at giving our students. We can remind ourselves that our hard work was worthwhile and allow ourselves to grieve our losses."

Once Lauren acknowledged her feelings and traced their moral taproots, she experienced a kind of clarity that allowed her to consciously honor her moral orientation as she decided what to do next. One of her first decisions was to try to make amends with Jerome. Not to pretend that he hadn't caused his classmate serious injury, but to remind him that Lauren saw him as more than this mistake, grave as it was, and that she cared about him, as well as the girl, and was there to support them both.

Lauren understood that creativity plays a major role in healing, and she wanted to share this insight with Jerome. She found a cartoon online with the caption "When things get tough . . . make good art." The cartoon pictured absurd examples of things getting "tough," like having your leg eaten by a mutated boa constrictor. Hoping these would give Jerome a laugh as well as encouragement to channel his feelings into art, Lauren ordered a poster of the cartoon and sent it with a personal letter telling him "he was someone who was making good art in my class."

At this point in our conversation, Lauren's voice broke. Her eyes welled up. "I wanted him to see that even though he was leaving our school community, this didn't have to be his ending. It could be a new beginning for him; he could still make good art."

"God," she said when she'd collected herself. "It still hurts."

Lauren's letter couldn't make the transgression not hurt. It didn't change what Jerome had done, nor the way he'd been treated, but he did write back to tell her how much he appreciated what she'd said. And that response fueled another step in her own healing.

"When I wrote my letter," she recalled, "I didn't think I was writing it for myself." But after Jerome wrote back, their exchange became a springboard for her own "good art."

She began by realigning her core values with her teaching practices going forward. This meant making an extra effort to foster authentic connections and a sense of community where everyone belonged, encouraging *all* her students to be creative and take risks. She developed innovative art projects, for example, to help everyone better understand Shakespeare. She showed her respect and concern for each student by giving personal feedback on every assignment. "Even when I feel angry or sad or numb—especially then," she realized, "I can acknowledge those feelings and keep teaching in ways that serve my values."

Lauren's exchange with Jerome also motivated her to honor her values through action for change on a larger scale. She started by writing an article for other educators, titled "Healing from Moral Injury," about her experience with Jerome. That article helped Lauren heal not just because it was cathartic to express what she'd gone through but also because it could change the context for other educators. Going forward, they might be more conscientious in preventing similar transgressions.

Then Lauren began to branch out. She designed values-based workshops to help schools address moral dilemmas and manage conflicts around issues like personal bias. She conducted trainings to foster learning cultures rooted in development rather than punishment. And she created a model for community conflict resolution that she believed could have led to a far better outcome for Jerome.

Lauren's model reflected the three components that had been most instrumental in her own moral healing:

- **Awareness** of how the moral breach impacted each person individually.

- **Care and compassion** for all who were harmed.

- **Accountability** for all involved in the transgression.

It's no accident that these three elements also reflect the principles of restorative justice, which Lauren believes would have led to a better outcome for everyone if they'd been applied in Jerome's case. When I asked her to describe what that might have looked like, she said, "Restorative justice in schools is about acknowledging harm and making repairs. It's informed by the truth and reconciliation idea that often people who harm are themselves harmed, that everyone's voice matters, and ensuring that everyone's getting what they need to heal."

Had Jerome received restorative justice, everyone involved, including the girl he harmed and everyone who knew them both, would have had a chance to speak. Both students' parents, classmates, and teachers would have been able to share the feelings they'd experienced when they learned what had happened. The principal could have presented his perspective. Jerome would have been allowed to describe the peer pressures operating on him at the time and, most important, to express his remorse and make amends to the girl. And the whole community could have worked together, with respect for everyone's moral compass, to restore collective trust and well-being and provide a path back to stability and belonging for both the girl and Jerome.

"Recovery doesn't negate the injury," Lauren emphasized. "But being able to acknowledge the humanity of the person who harmed us, as well as our own humanity, is core to healing for everyone. Even with the injury continuing to exist, we can hold both at once."

"Did you see Jerome again?" I asked as we were wrapping up our conversation.

She sighed. "It was an awful circumstance." Several years after Jerome left the school, the father of a classmate had died by suicide; Lauren saw Jerome at the funeral. "But we were really happy to see each other. I could see that he'd grown and matured. He'd switched schools again and was feeling good about where he was."

She grew thoughtful. "I still tear up thinking about Jerome and making good art. I'm still sad. It's a kind of grief that never really goes away, but it sits alongside a kind of growth."

THE FOUR STAGES OF MORAL HEALING

Lauren's final remark highlighted a crucial point about soul mending: It's not like healing from a cut or recuperating from a cold. The body has a miraculous ability to erase memories of pain that's purely physical, but with moral injury, the injustices that produce distress never completely disappear—and healing doesn't require them to.

As Lauren said, moral health is not a zero-sum game. We humans have the capacity both to hold the history of profound transgression *and* to answer that history by growing in ways that transcend the hurt and move beyond it. This healing process involves reaffirmation of our deepest values, reattachment with others in trusted relationships, recommitment to our true moral orientation, and, through all of this, restoration of our moral balance and integrity. The idea is not to extinguish moral grief and pain but to alchemize it into growth, like green buds sprouting from the charred surface of burnt trees. Psychologists call this post-traumatic growth.

The four basic stages of this process, which we see in Lauren's story, apply to virtually every case of moral healing, including recovery from the full crescendo of moral injury:

Stage 1. Acknowledgment of Transgression

When you're morally injured, you experience a deep internal fracture; your values remain intact, but you feel broken *from* them. Confronting this reality requires more than simply recognizing the experience of harm; it requires active evaluation of both the damage and the need for repair of your moral identity—the violation, the harm done, the victims, and those responsible. Think of this acknowledgment as a quiet pledge to serve as the agent of repair.

You might begin, as Lauren did, by recognizing that you are, in fact, suffering from a form of moral injury. But be honest. It doesn't help to tell yourself that the damage was not "that bad" or that it's not your "fault." When you're in moral distress, the blame and shame and anger you feel are real and must be identified before healing can begin.

It can also help to tell, write, or enact (for instance, through drama or art therapy) the full story of what happened, highlighting the moral values that were violated. This narrative should include cultural context and influences, like the male peer pressure that encouraged Jerome's transgression. Broader perspective and deeper understanding are the goals here.

Stage 2. Relational Repair

Moral transgressions are fundamentally relational in nature; they fracture relationships and threaten the ability of all involved to maintain healthy, trusting human connections. At the same time, safe, sympathetic connections can play a powerful role in calming the fight-or-flight reaction and facilitating healing and resilience. When we have strong social support, the brain takes a little longer to process situations before ringing the amygdala's emotional alarm, and that extra processing often leads to constructive compromises and perspectives, which result in less moral residue. For that reason, relational repair is essential for moral recovery, and this repair begins with your relationship with yourself.

No one is morally perfect or blameless, and few of us would hold others to such standards. Yet we can be merciless in beating ourselves up when *we've* committed an ethical breach. Healing from moral injury, then, requires that we first show ourselves the same compassion that we'd offer a beloved friend or family member. And then we must extend that compassion to others affected by the transgression.

Note that compassion does *not* mean letting anyone "off the hook" or befriending those who've caused you harm. It simply means treating all involved with respect for their human dignity. Why is this necessary? Because moral healing is not a solo process. It requires engagement with those affected, whether directly or symbolically, and engagement is always more productive when everyone involved—from those injured to those culpable—is treated with empathy, grace, and a genuine attempt at understanding. This includes community members, such as family, classmates, staff, or colleagues who might have witnessed or influenced the transgression.

One major obstacle to be aware of here is attribution bias—that tendency to pin moral blame on others without considering the bigger picture of circumstances and unique pressures that might have determined their actions. As we've seen, attribution bias can backfire in two ways: It can lead to harsh, punitive responses (like Jerome's expulsion) that shut down the possibility of reconciliation, or it can so dehumanize the accused that they shed any responsibility and blame their actions entirely on external forces. Effective relational repair requires that we hold individuals to account while also recognizing larger factors, like social injustice or endemic corruption, that might have played a role. Because there's always a larger context. Sometimes it's institutional, like a rigid military or corporate culture. Sometimes it's systemic, involving ingrained practices and attitudes like racism, sexism, or homophobia. Sometimes it's economic, churning resentments and grievances born of income inequality, unfair labor practices, or entrenched poverty.

Sometimes these conditions go back generations. And while we cannot change history, we must actively confront systemic injustices that contribute to today's ethical transgressions. Even if these systems are beyond any individual's control, every one of us can personally commit to becoming an agent for positive change in our shared culture going forward.

Stage 3. Moral Repair

To address the personal crisis of conscience at the heart of moral injury, the third stage of repair focuses on ethical accountability and reconciliation. Many people associate these processes with blame and judgment, but as proactive tools in healing, they instead take on the form of liberation. If moral injury shatters the self, then ethical accountability and reconciliation give us a chance to reassemble the self, not in its past form, but ideally in a stronger, more conscious, and morally robust configuration.

Because moral distress takes root through the internalization of harm—through disturbing memories, thoughts, and emotions—that *internal* weight is the burden that must be released for healing to occur. And that's what ethical accountability makes possible. Instead of remaining fixated on the original violations, this step shifts the focus to moral agency by demanding commitment to a process of renewal: *What are you going to do to give moral meaning to your life* now?

This stage requires a review of the core values that have been compromised and need to be reaffirmed. The simple act of recommitting to a value like compassion, truth, or justice helps repair personal integrity. And that mental process calms the amygdala's stress reactivity, allowing the prefrontal cortex to concentrate on resiliency tasks like learning, emotional regulation, and healing.

Reconciliation is often misunderstood, along with its central component of forgiveness, as a social get-out-of-jail card that excuses wrongdoers. In fact, these steps function morally only when accompanied by honest accounting and genuine acceptance of responsibility.

Forgiveness is not about minimizing or dismissing immoral behavior. Nor does reconciliation erase all memory or record of transgression. The goal here is instead to open a way to moral healing for both the harmed and the wrongdoer, as well as for the broader community or institution involved—to restore integrity where it was lost, create conditions where truth is acknowledged, and make it possible for everyone to push forward with their conscience intact.

Studies in affective neuroscience show that holding on to resentment and anger keeps the amygdala—the brain's threat detection system—highly active, triggering stress responses that can become chronic. This prolonged activation contributes to heightened cortisol levels, anxiety, and even cardiovascular damage. But reconciliation allows for a neurological reset.

Functional MRI research has found that conciliatory actions like asking forgiveness, making amends, and contributing to restitution all activate the brain's precuneus, right inferior parietal regions, and dorsolateral prefrontal cortex in ways that bring emotional relief and balance. Forgiveness is linked to lower blood pressure, reduced cortisol levels, and improved heart health, and it reduces amygdala activation while increasing prefrontal cortex activity. This helps enhance mental flexibility as well as emotional well-being. People who are able to forgive themselves after taking responsibility for their actions also experience lower levels of depression than those who harbor guilt, blame, or shame.

These psychological benefits suggest that moral reckoning is not just a matter of justice but can physiologically break the loop of emotional pain and self-recrimination. In the context of moral injury, forgiveness—whether directed toward oneself or others—can help mend the wounded soul.

For those who've perpetrated harm, reconciliation—whether by service, truth telling, or making amends through reparations—becomes a way to reestablish a sense of self-worth. For people who've been harmed, reconciliation is found by reclaiming agency, setting boundaries, and advocating for justice. Witnesses also have a role; moving from moral paralysis to meaningful action, such as victim advocacy, testimony, or structural ethical reform, prevents complicity from becoming an enduring source of injury. In all cases, reconciliation is not just about processing the injury internally but about taking deliberate, external steps toward broader moral repair. It allows healing to mobilize private remorse into tangible, socially reconstructive action and to shift the morally injured from passive victims of the past to active contributors to a restored future.

In many cases, service becomes a powerful vehicle for reconciliation. Religious traditions have long understood this. Acts of spiritual atonement are rarely solitary. They are enacted through voluntary service to others, to community, and to society. Our psyches know it, too. When we're actively helping others, our brain's stress and threat centers calm down and neural activity related to caregiving and pleasure increases. That's why volunteer work enhances our sense of connection, purpose, and meaning in ways that few other activities do. Neuroscience has now proven that it really is more rewarding to give than to receive.

Accountability, forgiveness, and reconciliation are central to all restorative justice and truth and reconciliation processes because they help reweave the fabric of social trust and mend the collective as well as the individual soul. Extensive studies across psychology, neuroscience, and social science have shown that each of these steps helps to heal the passive suffering that keeps the morally injured stuck in cycles of shame, rumination, and/or alienation. Forgiveness—including self-forgiveness—is also being studied as an evolutionary strategy to resolve the societal stress of interpersonal conflict. The evidence suggests that these processes help mend not only the morally wounded self but also the moral wounds of society. They do this by allowing everyone involved to see each other and themselves, in Lauren Porosoff's words, as "more than what they do on their worst day."

Stage 4. Ethical Realignment

The final stage of moral healing involves long-term change going forward. Not necessarily a change of moral direction, but a conscious adjustment of everyday choices, decisions, and patterns, like Lauren's decision to develop workshops in values-based education to more closely align with her moral orientation.

The goal here is to prevent future moral injury through "corrective experience." Too often, ethical reflection happens only after a crisis, leaving people unprepared to navigate later high-stakes decisions. But when ethical realignment is practiced as a living process, rather than as a onetime reckoning, it strengthens moral resilience and reduces future risk.

This deeper process often brings up existential questions related to one's personal sense of meaning and purpose. For many, this questioning has a spiritual component that dovetails with moral orientation. Those with a caring moral orientation might find purpose by getting involved in local charities or community services. Moral idealists might sign on to work for justice through groups like Human Rights Watch, the American Civil Liberties Union, or others that advance causes they hold dear. Brave risk-takers might channel their pioneering energy into physical or intellectual quests that connect their spiritual values with their need for exploration.

Ethical realignment also means recognizing that moral transgressions tend to occur within unjust structures, like corporate systems or institutions that routinely put people in ethically impossible positions. When there are no mechanisms for organizational or cultural accountability, individuals are left to shoulder the weight of systemic failures alone. True moral healing, then, must extend beyond personal conscience to collective reckoning through personal activism and leadership.

That is the conclusion that's driven the former Capitol police officer Harry Dunn to become an outspoken champion of ethical reform in the aftermath of the moral injury he suffered on January 6, 2021.

"I used to believe in the idea that America was a morally superior country," Harry told me when we spoke early in 2025, "that it would always do the right thing." But after being beaten and vilified by a violent mob of his fellow Americans, Harry began to think his faith in the nation was an illusion.

"I felt like the country had failed me—*me, personally*. The betrayal was deep because it shattered my expectations of people and of the country itself."

Eventually, though, this disillusionment catalyzed Harry's determination to redress his betrayal, not through retaliatory violence, but by helping to repair America's moral fractures. He's written a memoir about his journey as a proud defender of law, order, and the sanctity of the U.S. Constitution. And he regularly speaks out, telling his story on news media, on social media, and through an almost nonstop schedule of live appearances across the country, in small communities and large.

"I've had to adjust my expectations," he told me. "I no longer believe that the U.S. will always choose the morally right path. We've had countless opportunities to do the right thing, and we've failed over and over. That realization caused a lot of my stress, but it also helped me move forward. I don't walk around thinking everyone is a horrible person, but I no longer assume that people will do the right thing. And that shift has helped me emotionally."

"How so?" I asked.

And then Harry said something counterintuitive but profound. "I'm afraid of healing," he said. "That might sound crazy, but my anger and pain are what fuel me. They keep me fighting. If I heal, will I still have that fire? Will I still be driven to fight for what's right? I don't want to ever reach a point where I say, *I'm over January 6*. That scares me."

In fact, Harry's remark told me he'd reached a vital stage in his healing. He was now *using* his moral emotions to help him realign his life choices with his moral compass going forward.

"I'm not stuck in misery every day," he agreed. "But I stay solution oriented. I've shifted my focus to making sure people understand what's at stake. If I can convince even one person to change their view, that's something. The only thing I *can't* do is nothing."

When I asked if he thought the moral injury of January 6—or his recovery—had changed him, Harry again surprised and impressed me.

"No," he said. "It's just made me lean further into who I already was. People who have known me my whole life tell me, *Harry, you've always stood up for what's right*. I've always been someone who fights for the little guy. That part of me hasn't changed; it's just been amplified."

TREATING MORAL INJURY

Questions remain, of course. Lauren and Harry give us a sense of the four stages of healing from moral distress, but what do these stages look like if you're in the midst of advanced, debilitating moral trauma? How long will it take to fully recover? What clinical therapies and practices are most helpful when you're in crisis?

We don't yet have definitive answers to these questions. With triggers that range from catastrophic mass events to hidden, private traumas, every case of moral injury is unique, and few proven treatments have been standardized for this syndrome even today. Outside the military, therapists receive little to no training in this area. Moral trauma still is often confused with PTSD and other psychological conditions, and clinical therapies are only beginning to be designed specifically for moral injury. Studies of long-term outcomes are also in their early phases. But individuals who've survived severe moral injury are plentiful, and their stories offer valuable insights into transdiagnostic strategies that can help.

We know, for starters, that moral injury requires more complex treatment than general counseling. All psychotherapy has a basic goal of relieving personal suffering, but treatment of moral injury must do more. Because moral conflict is woven into the social and spiritual worlds we inhabit, if treatment functions only as an emotional tourniquet, the immediate hemorrhage might be stemmed, but distress will persist, causing moral residue to continue to rise. A clinician might guide a patient to confront their grief over a marital betrayal, for instance, and help them recognize that their guilt is misplaced, teach them how to live with regret without being consumed by it, but none of that will protect the wound from reopening when the next moral betrayal comes along.

Beyond symptom reduction, then, treatment must help the patient restore moral coherence, reclaim moral agency, and challenge the systemic conditions that perpetuate harm. It must cultivate the same skills that helped Lauren Porosoff: *awareness, care and compassion,* and *accountability*. Therapy for moral injury must also serve as a bridge, not just from healing to action, but from personal reckoning to collective repair.

When Wendy first came to me for treatment, we knew we'd find common ground. We both had been Air Force officers in the healing profession and both served on the front lines in Afghanistan at the height of Operation Enduring Freedom. But Wendy was a trauma nurse, which meant that she'd been exposed to the physical savagery of war in ways I could only imagine. Four years after her tour, she was still struggling with a host of symptoms related to moral injury.

Wendy broke down sobbing as she admitted that before her deployment she'd had little sense of the ways that weapons and explosives could torture human beings. In Afghanistan, she'd manage to hold herself together in the bloody and bustling trauma bay at Bagram Air Base as victims of those weapons streamed in, but she'd collapse into a heaving mess in ER staff rooms and back in her quarters when she was off duty. She could not reconcile her deeply caring moral orientation with the daily carnage of war, especially among civilians. And her misgivings were only intensified by the ambiguous nature of our contemporary military engagement, which blurred the lines between combatants and noncombatants. Fighting in crowded cities and densely populated valleys made it nearly impossible to keep the innocent out of harm's way, and the military often minimized civilian lives as collateral damage in the push to achieve military objectives. Wendy could not accept the idea that so much human suffering was warranted.

Although her heart was racked by the sight of wounded and dying coalition forces, the pain inflicted on innocent Afghan children anguished Wendy the most. The memory of one particular Afghan girl haunted her. The child had been about four, her face and body charred nearly beyond recognition.

"I just held her for like an hour. She stared up at me the whole time, at one point barely whimpering." The little girl died in Wendy's arms.

"Oh my gosh, I fucking cried for weeks."

When we met, Wendy was thirty-eight and plagued by guilt and shame. "I did what I was told," she said. "At the time, I thought it was right." But what had the Afghan people done to deserve having their lives shattered? How could she square her patriotism and her pledge to heal people with the human carnage she'd witnessed every day in Afghanistan?

As we talked, it struck me that we shared moral reservations about the war, but Wendy's moral injury had been compounded by her daily exposure to the visceral wounds and suffering of innocent civilians. She could not look away from their agony, and she could not stop remembering the fear in their faces, the ravaged flesh of their bodies, the helpless sounds they made as they lay dying. By comparison, my moral distress in Afghanistan was an ethical abstraction. It came from a broader sense of despair over our nation's policies and moral goals, rather than from personal, immediate trauma. By comparison, I was lucky.

We didn't realize right away that Wendy's core ailment was moral injury. We both assumed she was suffering from PTSD. But unlike many traumatized patients, she wasn't avoidant or hypervigilant. She didn't jump at loud noises, had no memory loss, and expressed none of the distorted beliefs or fears that typically signal PTSD. Instead, she was racked by loss-related stress, anger, remorse, shame, and guilt. Her conscience was under assault from the crescendo effect.

At the time, in 2013, moral injury was still treated as a variation of PTSD. But while I'd found virtual reality assisted exposure therapy helpful for some service members with PTSD, it would have harmed Wendy to virtually reexperience those moments in the field hospital. She carried with her a set of photographs of the mutilations she'd confronted in Afghanistan, and when she shared them with me, even I was deeply disturbed. Reliving those moments, even if we utilized the best available practices for PTSD, was unlikely to ease her grief, her guilt, or her shame. The same was true for cognitive processing therapy, which targets and works to reframe distorted beliefs about the trauma; and for prolonged exposure therapy, which is delivered either traditionally or with virtual reality to reduce the emotional intensity of traumatic memories by gradually confronting avoided experiences. Both these therapies have been shown to help relieve symptoms of PTSD but not moral injury.

Wendy needed therapy that would help her reclaim her sense of meaning through purpose and reconciliation. She needed to rediscover and embrace a reason for living before she could release her emotional pain.

Our first step was to talk through her life story. In this way, I learned that her moral crisis had been preceded by years of moral distress before she even joined the military.

As a civilian intensive care nurse, Wendy had often felt morally conflicted over the treatment she was required to give her patients. She recalled one elderly patient whose family insisted she be given invasive therapies, even though the woman was dying. "You feel like you're hurting your patient and making them suffer even more," Wendy told me. But she had no standing to dispute or disobey her patients' families or doctors' orders; she felt she had to comply. As a result, she'd accumulated a heavy burden of moral residue before she ever set foot in Afghanistan.

Her reason for commissioning into the Air Force had been much the same as mine: She felt drawn to serve her country, to uphold American ideals. So, in our quest to find meaning in her experience, we focused on the true north of her personal mission—to assist in saving lives while treating all patients with compassion. It helped steady her sense of self to recognize that this mission aligned with her caring orientation. She was morally consistent, after all, and her personal cause was just. She had served with honor and distinction.

Seeing the integrity of her personal actions helped assuage Wendy's conscience, even as she continued to grieve the innocent lives lost because of the war. This was an important first step toward recovery.

Over time, she began to see her memories in a new light and to challenge the guilt she carried, though this didn't fully resolve the inner conflict. The part of her moral injury that was unresolved left her questioning her identity and worth, and that required a different therapeutic approach, starting with meditation.

Physiologically, meditation is thought to promote mental well-being by increasing dopamine levels. Its usefulness in moral injury is being studied mostly in the military, where veterans have found that mindfulness meditation helps curb persistent rumination and emotions like guilt, shame, and sorrow, as well as overwhelming distress or feelings of moral failure. Meditation also relieves bodily sensations like chest tightness, stomach discomfort, restlessness, and the heavy, sinking sensation often linked to stress and trauma. In Wendy's case, we gave meditation an assist with VR—virtual reality.

While it hasn't yet been validated as a treatment for moral injury, VR is an excellent tool to help people learn to meditate. The immersive nature of calming VR settings, like serene forests or tranquil beaches, typically makes the practice more vivid, memorable, and effective at reducing anxiety and depression. With Wendy, we used VR meditation to help relieve the self-condemnation that was dominating her perception of herself. She needed to remember that she was more than one set of terrible experiences, that she had access to a much broader range of thoughts, feelings, and possibilities than those memories of Afghanistan. So, in her VR sessions, she was surrounded by soothing, virtual environments designed to facilitate relaxation and mindfulness. Within this immersive atmosphere, she practiced exercises that helped her relax, breathe, and notice her thoughts without judgment. Gradually, the intensity of her ruminative thoughts and emotional distress abated.

Practicing these techniques in the VR setting also helped Wendy learn to meditate on her own, and over time meditation became one of the practices that helped her loosen self-blame and move toward self-compassion. She was better able to manage her emotional responses and build a more balanced sense of self. And she widened her focus to pay attention to the people in her current life, to notice those who needed help, and to imagine ways she might make a positive difference going forward.

Reciprocity in healing and helping is one aspect of moral injury treatment that's distinct from most other mental health therapies. Wendy, like many other moral injury patients, found that helping others was key to her recovery. Years later, when I asked her to reflect on this, she told me, "Early on, I did a lot of volunteering with homeless veterans in the community. I wasn't consciously thinking that I was doing it because of what I'd gone through. I just did it because it felt good to go out and cook for homeless folks, as opposed to feeling bad all the time. I was just looking for things to help me not have to think about what I'd been through. If I wasn't busy, I'd always go back to that."

At the same time, she started going to church with one of the doctors she'd been deployed with, who was grappling with his own moral injury from the war. "Being surrounded by those people at church," she recalled, "picked me up and lifted me out of that place I was in. I also got a dog, and he saved my life."

Wendy's dog is a mutt, part shepherd, part retriever, with thick golden fur that she said always smells like sun-warmed earth after a long walk. "I swear, he knows me better than I know myself. When I start spiraling, he just leans into me, his whole weight pressed up against my side, like he's physically keeping me from slipping too far into my own head. If I'm staring off too long, lost in thought, he nudges my hand, like, 'Hey, come back.' And somehow, I do."

At night, when flashbacks hit, Wendy's dog will curl his body against her, close enough to feel his heartbeat. "It's slow, steady—completely opposite of mine," she explained. "And somehow, without even trying, he slows me down too. I read somewhere that dogs help regulate your nervous system, lower your heart rate, even reduce cortisol or whatever. But I don't need science to tell me what I already know: This dog keeps me tethered to the world."

There's something, too, about this dog's calming effect that has to do with moral acceptance. "It's like he can see straight into me," Wendy told me. "Like he understands everything I don't say out loud. He doesn't try to fix anything. He doesn't need me to explain. He just stays. And some days, that's enough."

All these strands of connection helped Wendy weave the foundation for a new, more resilient civilian life. Unfortunately, healing from moral injury is not "one and done," or even six and done. Looking at her experience differently and re-centering her moral compass helped. So did meditation, volunteering, church, and the deep bond she shared with her dog. But Wendy still could not reconcile her values with her vocation. So she decided to go back to school.

"If you want to continue living a normal life," she explained, "you have to do things that keep you going. For me, that meant getting out of nursing. I had to change course in my life goals."

She became an educator, and one of the first courses she taught was for nurses. Her reasoning mirrored Lauren Porosoff's desire to train other teachers about moral injury. "I wanted nursing students and nurses to be aware of what they were feeling and why. A lot of people leave nursing because they can't figure out what's happening to them. Is it really moral injury they're feeling, or is it PTSD or something else? Even now, a lot of new grads—half of them—leave within the first two years of finishing nursing school. They think every area in nursing is terrible, so they leave without realizing that if they can't be in one area, they can always go to another and still be a nurse."

I wondered if she still struggled with the guilt and shame she'd felt around her deployment, now a dozen years earlier.

"Some things," she said bluntly, "I'm never going to overcome. I'm still on my meds, but some nights I'm still at war in my dreams. But over time, you put it out of your mind because you want to keep going. My focus now is not medicine; it's education."

"You're still orienting your life around helping others," I observed. Like Harry Dunn, she'd changed course but not her core moral orientation. The career change had only reaffirmed and reinforced her core moral values.

"Sometimes that's what you have to do to keep living and keep going."

"Exactly."

Wendy's journey reminded me that moral injury doesn't just go away over time; it remains acute, open-ended, unless confronted with intent. Wendy's healing started not from forgetting the past but from bringing her life back into alignment with her true north.

There is one exciting new tool that I wish had been available when I treated Wendy. It's an innovative form of talk therapy called adaptive disclosure, pioneered by Brett Litz at the Veterans Affairs Boston Healthcare System and now one of the most promising, research-supported approaches to treating moral injury. Rooted in the belief that disclosing and reframing, or "adapting," difficult events can help us move past them to compassion and forgiveness, adaptive disclosure enables patients to tell their story not to force the memories to go away but to recontextualize them within a framework of forgiveness and compassion. This helps break down patients' belief that they'll be shamed and rejected for their role in the violation that caused their pain. It also prompts the nervous system to repair and reintegrate crucial strands of social, emotional, and cognitive functioning that are essential for moral resiliency.

For Andre, a social worker whose morale had shattered under the crushing demands of his job with child protective services, adaptive disclosure therapy proved crucial. The process began with a close examination, guided by his therapist, of the particular moral issues posed by Andre's untenable case load. They pushed past his bitter recollections of taking some kids away from home and leaving others in harm's way, and worked together to uncover the deeper strata of his suffering.

Like most social workers, Andre had gone into this profession with a strong sense of mission. He believed in protecting the weak and giving families the opportunity to mend. While his experiences on the job had often betrayed his caring nature, the therapist reminded him that he still could take pride in his values and in his willingness to accept the responsibility of helping. His pain stemmed not from any flaw in his own moral compass but, rather, from a system so underfunded and understaffed that his every decision involved unbearable trade-offs; for every child he saved, another remained in danger.

The pain was real. Andre still felt each tiny hand in his own, the silence heavy with apprehension, and the question in the child's eyes that he was powerless to answer. But he bore pride, as well as shame, in the same breath. Andre's therapist worked with him to untangle this twist of responsibility, that he might recognize and rekindle his idealism.

Andre was urged to visualize an understanding moral authority—a person who represented compassion and insight. He selected his late aunt, who'd brought him up after the divorce of his parents and who exemplified solidity and compassion for him. By imagining his aunt were present, Andre felt safer confiding his remorse and betrayal. As he spoke, he sensed his aunt's soothing responses and found solace in her understanding.

By emphasizing forgiveness and compassion not solely around

the area of trauma but in all his social interactions, adaptive disclosure helped Andre come to terms with his own experiences *and* fostered healing across his relationships. The therapist explained that human beings are wired to reflect each other, so the more time we spend among people who demonstrate reciprocal respect and concern, the more we tend to care for both our own well-being and others'. This, ideally, is how we develop social trust as children. And even though moral injury can deplete that reservoir, an intentional process of reciprocal connection can help replenish it. For Andre that meant making active social choices that aligned with his true north.

He decided to mentor younger social workers and to volunteer at a neighborhood youth center. These interactions broke down his isolation. And by being surrounded by individuals who made it a point to show each other dignity and respect, he could reclaim these values himself.

Over time, Andre's perspective adjusted. He learned to differentiate his own accountability from the system failures that had overwhelmed him. Where once he'd walked children out of their homes in anguish, he now walked beside younger social workers, steadying them for the burdens he knew too well.

Andre also developed a plan to address the structural causes of his suffering. First, he joined a larger movement of frontline workers. Then, with their support, he lobbied his supervisors at work for reduced caseloads and increased trauma-informed treatment. The group's efforts forced administrators to pay attention to the heavy moral burden carried by child protective services staff, and this advocacy helped Andre transform his suffering into meaning.

In general, when reparative actions lead to change that directly addresses the source of moral injury, such steps can be deeply therapeutic; the channeling of moral distress into meaningful repair restores a sense of agency and coherence. But attempts to change entrenched power structures require careful thought, social support, and logistical planning. Otherwise, they can backfire.

Too often, individuals decide to confront authorities alone, with insufficient reflection or protection. Then, if protests lead to retaliation and loss of professional status, or are simply ignored, a new sense of moral failure can deepen disillusionment. To prevent this, interventions like whistleblowing should always be part of a larger reparatory process combining self-reflection, relational restoration, and a moral community that includes workplace, personal, and neighborhood coalitions.

Adaptive disclosure belongs to a treatment category known as cognitive restructuring, whose goal is to help reduce the burden of guilt and shame that comes with moral injury. Patients learn to untangle the harm that they feel responsible for; to distinguish contributing factors that were beyond their control; and to dismantle the distorted belief that they should have done the impossible. These therapies allow individuals to view themselves with self-compassion rather than condemnation.

But while cognitive restructuring might loosen the grip of self-blame, it does not touch the deeper existential collapse that moral injury often causes. It cannot restore faith in a system that betrayed us, nor can it answer the most profound questions that gnaw at the soul: *If I followed the rules and still caused harm, what does that say about the rules? If I spoke up and was punished for it, is justice even possible?*

A doctor whose best efforts often result in patient deaths can intellectually understand that her decisions are well intentioned, but that knowledge will do nothing to resolve the gut-wrenching feeling that those lives should never have been lost. A journalist who's fired for exposing systemic government corruption can know he did the right thing, but that will do little to soothe the rage and despair of watching the world just roll on, unchanged, after his sacrifice. This is where alternative therapeutic models step in—not to offer solutions, but to help individuals live with the questions that will never have satisfactory answers.

Two alternative therapies often used for moral injury are acceptance and commitment therapy, or ACT, and existential therapy.

Acceptance and commitment therapy does not try to erase pain, nor does it demand resolution. Instead, it asks, *Can you learn to hold your suffering without it becoming the entire weight of your existence?* Where cognitive-based therapies challenge thoughts, ACT teaches individuals how to sit with them without drowning in them. It offers strategies for defusing distressing emotions, for recognizing that moral pain does not have to dictate the course of a life that contains other affirming tributaries.

The doctor haunted by ghosts of the patients she could not save may never be free of those ghosts, but ACT would guide her toward continuing to practice medicine, not because she has forgiven herself, but because her values and the lives she does save demand she continue to try. The journalist may never resolve the contradiction between what his government allows and what is right, but ACT allows him to stay in the fight for his principles without being destroyed by disillusionment.

Existential therapy takes an even more unflinching approach. It does not ask individuals to defuse their suffering, nor does it try to help them reframe it. It meets them where they are and demands engagement with the deepest moral fractures of their soul. It does not offer the comfort of cognitive restructuring or the flexibility of acceptance; it forces a confrontation with meaning itself.

Given the profound sense of betrayal and ethical rupture that defines moral injury, most therapies try to restore a sense of meaning, coherence, and agency in a world that, to the patient, no longer makes sense, but existential therapy aims to make personal sense of the senselessness itself. It is not for those who want to be talked out of their pain, or simply to "cope." Instead, it's for those who need a way to understand why they should continue to exist at all.

What makes this therapy uniquely suited to moral injury is its refusal to soften reality. It asks not, *How can we ease your pain?* but rather, *Now that you've seen what you have seen, what will you do with it?* It acknowledges that some moral wounds cannot be healed, only integrated, and it challenges the patient to shape their life around what remains. Although this approach offers no absolution, no false comfort, for some that's exactly what they need.

For many, moral injury is more than a personal battle. It's often a direct response to external factors like racism, sexism, homophobia, income inequality, and multigenerational domestic abuse. Therapy can help with resilience, emotional regulation, and mental well-being, but some environments cause harm that no amount of internal coping can fix. The Black female manager who's fired without cause can go to therapy, process her pain, learn to carry it more lightly, but if she takes another job with bosses who demean her on account of her race and gender, is she truly healing, or is she merely becoming more efficient at surviving harm?

Abusive households, toxic workplaces, corrupt institutions, and racist and sexist power structures all play outsized roles in moral trauma. They don't just intensify stress; they set up impossible dilemmas that force people to either violate their conscience or suffer for trying to honor their deepest values. Those who crack under such pressure aren't weak, and they don't simply lack the right "coping skills." Their pain comes from being stuck in systems that force them to betray their own sense of right and wrong, over and over again.

As James Baldwin wrote in *Notes of a Native Son*, "The man does not remember the hand that struck him, the darkness that frightened him, as a child; nevertheless, the hand and the darkness remain with him, indivisible from himself forever, part of the passion that drives him wherever he thinks to take flight."

When moral wrongs have been tolerated for generations, even institutionalized by governments and society, the legacy of moral injury cannot be healed through individual treatment alone. Therapy can help process inherited pain, but there's often a fine line between coping and conditioning. If treatment only helps one tolerate moral distress and does nothing to challenge the conditions that create it, then the therapy risks becoming complicit in a cycle that perpetuates harm.

The danger is that we might help individuals become more resilient at surviving morally injurious environments, rather than empowering them to recognize when those environments are fundamentally unjust and need to change. Therapy should not teach people to endure what should never have been asked of them; it should help them reclaim their moral agency, demand better from the institutions that failed them, and ensure that their suffering is not in vain. Real healing means acknowledging the larger forces that shape moral injury and finding constructive ways to push back against them.

This, then, is where treatment must evolve—to empower, equip, and resist, in tandem with healing. The ideal approach integrates personal healing with social awareness, enabling individuals to navigate their pain effectively while also fostering the capacity to engage in systemic reform or to seek more ethical environments, to join with others in challenging the conditions that caused their distress in the first place.

In an era when far too many leaders are motivated by lust for wealth, power, and self-aggrandizement, any real effort to heal our moral epidemic will require a sea change in accountability at the highest levels of government, business, and institutions. This isn't a partisan argument. It's about the fundamental values that shape society, regardless of who's in charge. Moral injury today is a collective crisis that demands collective solutions through renovation of policy, institutional ethics, social norms, and leadership culture. *All of the above.* If we ignore the full scope of this task, we'll just send the traumatized back into the same broken systems that wounded them in the first place. What's needed is a moral reckoning that reaches through every level of society.

CHAPTER 7

RECKONING

The Future of Moral Injury

> When moral deregulation advances because violence and corruption have been institutionalized, including in the behavior of national leaders, then a society can experience *moral collapse.*
>
> —Ruth Ben-Ghiat

The epidemic of moral injury that we face today is spread by institutions that have long prioritized power over ethics, by workplaces that routinely force employees to compromise their values, by communities where racism, sexism, and economic inequality have always been baked into the rules. But the ethical framework that encompasses our daily life has now reached a new breaking point. We can see the casualties in virtually every direction: dedicated civil servants summarily fired without cause; legal residents deported without due process; judges threatened with impeachment for respecting the Constitution; doctors denied the right to provide their patients with the care they need; active service members—military heroes—forced to rely on food stamps; and elected representatives fearing for their lives simply because of their voting record.

Moral assaults like these have become so widespread that it can feel at times as if we were experiencing one *collective* moral injury, with the whole world plunging over an ethical cliff. Somehow, after generations of professed reverence for truth, honor, and civility, we seem to have landed in an era that unabashedly privileges self-interest over the common good, in which systems of commerce, government, even health care and education prohibit ethical compromise, and ordinary citizens around the globe have become resigned to the moral inversion of leaders who equate patriotism with polarization, freedom with censorship, and justice with impunity. Daily headlines trumpet evidence of this inversion in the political celebration of convicted criminals, in CEOs who publicly choose corporate and personal profiteering over the health and safety of their customers, in the punishment of courageous whistleblowers who report corruption, only to be betrayed by the very institutions they're trying to protect.

MORAL FOUNDATIONS UNDER ASSAULT

Remember, back in chapter 2, when I referred to Jonathan Haidt's warning that the human brain requires peer pressure to control our primal inclination toward selfishness? "The most important principle for designing an ethical society," Haidt wrote, "is to *make sure that everyone's reputation is on the line all the time*, so that bad behavior will always bring bad consequences." That's why the leaders of most societies have traditionally modeled—or at least pretended to model—moral virtues like generosity, compassion, respect, and honesty.

But many of today's rulers and influencers have flipped those reputational standards, instead placing so much importance on loyalty and self-aggrandizement that followers are persuaded not just to excuse but to gleefully embrace greed, cruelty, cheating, and deception, so long as they advance their group's agenda. This creates a state that the American historian Ruth Ben-Ghiat calls *"moral deregulation*: a rolling back of civic and ethical norms against defrauding, silencing, bullying, and physically harming others." In this state, everyone's reputation is still on the line, but bad behavior no longer brings bad consequences; instead, it's loudly rewarded. And peer pressure is deployed not to support morality but to divide society for political and economic advantage.

I am not suggesting that polarization is automatically bad for society's moral health. Sometimes it's beneficial, even necessary. According to the political theorist Chantal Mouffe, when divisions are based on healthy disagreement over issues and policies, opponents "will treat each other not as enemies to be destroyed, but as adversaries who will fight for the victory of their position while recognizing the right of their opponents to fight for theirs." This type of issue-based polarization is actually needed in a pluralistic democracy, where diverse groups all have a shared stake in the common good. *E pluribus unum*, the motto on the Great Seal of the United States, means, "Out of many, one." This does *not* suggest that the many should submit to just one race, religion, party, or leader, but that all should collaborate in the struggle to form a more perfect union. That's the spirit of issue-based polarization. But that's not the spirit that dominates the echo chambers of society as I write this chapter in 2025.

Instead, much of our world has split into combative group affinities. As the political scientist Lilliana Mason explains, we are "driven not only by what we think, but also powerfully by who we think we are." And the power of that kind of identification can lure us into groups that demonize each other over perceived differences, which often are not even real.

When ideological conflicts become entwined with social status and belonging, disagreements that begin as civil issue-based negotiations over, say, a local zoning policy or plan to build a neighborhood park can quickly trigger this more divisive group loyalty, pitting factions against one another and devolving into moralized offensives. As one group of researchers explained, such shifts occur "when we can't change what we think or say without losing core relationships or identities." In other words, when we believe the *only* way to get along with our chosen friends is by picking and supporting their "side," as if life were a zero-sum game of winners and losers with no room for ties or compromise. At that point, social affiliation trumps reason, logic, or moral principles.

Once again, group pressure isn't always or necessarily bad for society. The desire to fit in leads to moral regulation that can and often does benefit the common good. The reason most utility bills show homeowners how their electricity usage measures up to their neighbors', for example, is because social comparison nudges big spenders to stop wasting energy. Likewise, if everyone in your congregation gives to charities, you're more likely to donate to the needy, too. These nudges harness peer pressure and the power of reputation to make communities more caring, cohesive, and secure.

But when the price of group identity is lockstep conformity and automatic suspicion of any other party, peer pressure can lead to intolerance and a blinding resistance to innovation and critical thinking, as well as to anyone with different cultural, ideological, or moral views. And conflict theorists who study today's political divisions warn that current demands for group loyalty are also eroding democracy. Why? Because when one rigidly conformist group dominates the contest for influence and power, they do not tend to share power or tolerate dissidence, and that's a recipe for autocracy.

According to Ben-Ghiat, "Authoritarians 'hollow out' institutions by removing anyone not loyal to the leader and the party, but they also hollow out people to the point where they will participate in acts of violence, corruption and sabotage against their compatriots. . . . Moral collapse begins as an individual process and, when the conditions are right, generates new collective norms of behavior that can support large-scale repression."

It's no accident that "divide and conquer" has been a favorite tactic of colonizers and dictators throughout history. But such control rarely comes peacefully. Political polarization based on group identity is often a precursor to armed conflict, as we've seen globally in recent ethnic violence in Rwanda, Kosovo, Sri Lanka, Myanmar, Sudan, and throughout the Middle East, especially in Israel and Gaza.

Moral outrage plays a central role in such group conflicts because it scales up so easily. In 2014 in Myanmar, a young Buddhist cook filed a police report alleging that she'd been raped by two Muslim brothers in the house where she worked. Her claim began to circulate on social media and was picked up by a Buddhist monk famous for his anti-Muslim views. He added the caption "The Mafia is Spreading and Coming to Town." By the next day, armed Buddhist mobs had taken to the streets of the city where the rape had supposedly occurred. Motorcades circled the accused men's address, with drivers spitting on pedestrians and yelling, "Kill the Muslims!" They torched the nearby mosque, looted local businesses, and attacked community residents with swords and spears, killing one Buddhist and one Muslim man. Only after this carnage did the supposed victim tell authorities that she'd been paid to file the claim. She wound up being sentenced to a minimum twenty-one years in prison for "spreading fabricated allegations."

As this story demonstrates, outrage spread by rumor tends to inflame feelings of hostility even in partisans who have no direct connection to the underlying dispute. Through this vicarious process, it can induce a kind of pseudo moral injury that feels both intense and real despite having no basis in lived experience. It's this pseudo moral injury that plays the greatest role in spawning group outrage and polarized violence.

As moral rage spreads socially, it stokes the impression that some other group is the unfair aggressor and one's own group *collectively* is the aggrieved victim. The recent upsurge in hostility toward immigrants in America is an example that particularly disturbs me because of my own immigrant background and work with undocumented workers. The notion that stokes the most outrage against immigrants is the myth that they bring crime to America. In fact, the opposite is true: Crime actually *drops* when immigrant populations rise in U.S. neighborhoods. These workers are not a threat but a vital—and lucrative—feature of the U.S. economy. Apart from the indisputable three-hundred-year-old history of America as a melting pot of immigrants, today's new arrivals perform essential labor that sustains whole industries, including agriculture, construction, food processing, hotels, and restaurants. They also pay into the U.S. government coffers through income and payroll taxes. In 2022 alone, undocumented workers paid nearly $100 billion into federal, state, and local governments. And unlike U.S. citizens, undocumented workers receive few benefits in return for these taxes, since they're not eligible for Social Security or Medicare. These people aren't threatening Americans but *enriching* Americans.

While there's plenty in the immigration system to be outraged about, most of the claims against undocumented workers are flat-out lies. Both sides of the immigration debate know this, but neither will admit it, because to do so would require acknowledging their own complicity in a system built on silent extraction: of labor, of human dignity, and of plausible deniability. The simplest truth of all is that, if politicians truly wanted to end illegal immigration, they'd impose large fines, biometric audits, and corporate accountability on the employers who hire undocumented labor. Then the jobs would dry up, and most undocumented folks would return home. But we don't prosecute the owners. We prosecute the shadows. Because it's easier to exploit shadows not only for power and profit but also for moral outrage.

The grievances that fuel moral outrage are arguably easier to cast with shadows than real people. They are essentially rumors that whip up the fervor of audiences who instantly identify as direct participants—either perpetrating or avenging, even if the inciting event took place thousands of miles away, *even if it never actually happened*. Group outrage and this exploitation of shadow figures thus become key to understanding how bogus accusations and conspiracy theories can go viral and polarize society.

Moral rage is also explosive because it fuels the emotional belief that the only way to reclaim ethical balance is for the victim's group, like the Myanmar mob, to exact revenge not just on the accused individuals but on their whole community. Regardless of the facts, this gladiatorial mindset strips the underlying conflict of human complexity (including personal factors like poverty, bribery, and blackmail between business rivals) and reduces it to a shadow duel between good and evil—that is, between the perception of a moral "us" and the projection of an immoral "them."

Such oversimplification, which can easily hijack both feelings and reason, becomes an especially sinister weapon when spread by anonymous trolls, provocateurs, propagandists, or other conflict entrepreneurs to manipulate mass reactions. That is what happened when a relatively small group of online users in 2020 began spreading lies about rampant election fraud. These lies launched the Stop the Steal movement, which led to the January 6 attack on the U.S. Capitol. Likewise, in Brazil in 2021, "digital militias" of public officials loyal to the incumbent president, Jair Bolsonaro, began concocting outrageous online rumors that ranged from vote rigging and corruption to cannibalism and satanism, all in an attempt to undermine the country's democratic institutions. Even though

Bolsonaro ceded power after losing the 2022 election, thousands of his followers continued to protest for weeks in the mistaken belief that the election had been rigged against their group.

Outrage, unfortunately, is virulently contagious, regardless of whether it's based in truth or in outright lies. Its potency has to do with the illusion of moral righteousness that it confers on those who express and promote their rage. There are now online vigilante groups that operate "in the name of street justice," reporting "bad" behavior ranging from nannies who scroll on their phones while tending children at the playground, to loitering that might indicate the presence of a pedophile. The self-appointed "hunters" in these groups are often hailed reflexively by their followers as heroes and defenders of virtue. That burnishes the accusers' social standing and elevates their moral reputation, which can make outrage addictive.

But this kind of moral grandstanding does not require honesty, proof, or authentic conviction; it's likely to reward accusers even if they have zero evidence to back up their claims or if their outrage is purely performative and fake. That's why lynch mobs can be quick to form around blameless targets, especially in polarized communities where the majority has already demonized a minority. Mob members there gain social standing by fomenting outrage that confirms their group's belief, regardless of the facts. Throughout history, the toxic fusion of mass outrage, moral grandstanding, and moral distortion has led to injustice, violence, and death for countless innocent members of targeted minority groups. This is how Emmett Till, Vincent Chin, Yusef Hawkins, James Byrd Jr., Ahmaud Arbery, and Matthew Shepard all lost their lives.

Yet never before in history has moral outrage found platforms like those that today spread this viral contagion. Between the omnipresence of news and opinion media and the penetration of digital technology, grievance is being pumped through society like emotional gasoline, and the slightest spark ignites wildfire. This is how a lighthearted Twitter thread about a young child learning to use a can opener backlashed into a massive virtual campaign against her father.

"Bean Dad" posted his thread in January 2021 because he thought his daughter's struggle to use a can opener would amuse his followers. But because he'd refused to open the can of beans *for* his daughter, instead giving her this challenge as a "teachable moment," #BeanDad was swarmed online by grandstanding strangers who righteously accused him of child abuse and then dug back through his feed to find a handful of off-color jokes, which they re-tweeted as "proof" that he was also racist, sexist, and homophobic. The viral #BeanDad attack got as many views as news of Donald Trump's phone call pressing Georgia's attorney general "to find 11,780 votes" for him, which occurred around the same time. One might think that more users would feel impacted by Trump's demand to alter the 2020 election results than by Bean Dad's teachable moment, but Twitter amplified the personal outrage against #BeanDad until it had the gravitational social effect of an online lynch mob: His attackers felt that they *belonged* to a morally superior group because they were united in attacking this one total stranger, forcing him to publicly apologize.

Online outrage similarly distorts perceptions of political opponents. Studies have found that Americans who consume divisive content online routinely overestimate the hatred and difference in values that actually exist between Democrats and Republicans. That's because social media tends to highlight extremist caricatures, which drive more online engagement than moderate or conciliatory posts. Also, users who engage the most with online political content are highly partisan, creating the impression that most voters hold extreme views when, in fact, the majority in both parties are more moderate.

The brevity of social media posts, especially on platforms that restrict users to a small number of characters, adds to the distortion of complex moral issues by reducing them to oversimplistic sound bites and memes. Through hyperbolic declarations, doctored imagery, and sensationalist caricatures, many posts make an attention-grabbing impression that accuses a targeted person or group without supplying any actual information or nuance. Then, when these posts go viral, the very act of sharing generates an illusion of involvement, personalizing and amplifying the sharers' moral outrage as if the described offense had directly impacted them. Add the lightning speed and global reach of the internet to this illusion, and a single post can spread the *perception* of grievous moral injury to millions overnight.

As long as society teeters on this ethical precipice, moral injury will continue to metastasize across institutions, families, and communities. Already this epidemic has begun to alter our psychological landscape in ways both subtle and devastating. We see the signs of moral deregulation in increasing normalization of cruelty, in the suspicion that often surrounds expressions of empathy, in the disintegration of community trust and distortions of fairness now routinely used to justify exclusion, and in the outright assault on ethical goals like diversity, equity, and inclusion. When loyalty is twisted into tribalism, cooperation becomes impossible. And when authority is wielded to dominate rather than protect, the very notion of moral accountability erodes until it feels like an outdated relic from a distant era.

The three R's of basic morality—respect, relationship, and reciprocity—are in retreat throughout society today. Communities are fracturing along ideological lines not because of irreconcilable differences but because the moral foundations that make dialogue possible—especially shared assumptions of care and mutual trust—have been systematically undermined. Loneliness and social isolation are at historic highs. Ecoanxiety is spiking, especially among children, as the climate crisis intensifies. And mental health professionals have had to come up with a new term, "political anxiety disorder," for the fear, anger, and helplessness that are stirred by perpetual political outrage and polarization.

These conditions are menacing civic cohesiveness and engagement. Institutions such as universities, libraries, museums, hospitals, humanitarian organizations, and scientific research centers, which have served historically as bulwarks of societal strength and cohesion, are now suddenly under attack. Widespread cynicism has taken root and, with it, a collective moral apathy that whispers, *Why bother?* This apathy is the silent killer of cultural strength. It doesn't arrive with the force of a revolution, but seeps in through layers of unresolved moral residue until we despair—becoming convinced that no amount of soul-searching can help the world recover.

The American promise is that hard work leads to dignity. But when young adults realize they're worse off than their parents, when their ladders to success are blocked by inherited privilege, the result isn't just despair; it's shame. Moral injury here reflects the systemic betrayal of a promise once held to be sacrosanct. Dishonesty in the presence of moral obligation lies at the heart of this injury. And not just for the forsaken, but also for those of us who see the truth and struggle to live beside it. We are all wounded, not just by what's being done, but also by what isn't. By the silence. The pretense. The willful amnesia.

Moral injury is the inevitable consequence in a nation that promises liberty but builds its economy on fear. A state that punishes those it profits from. That predicates one person's success on another's loss. That represents justice not as a human right but as a function of caste. Rights in America now scale with wealth. The poor are bound by the law but not protected by it. The rich are protected by it but no longer bound. This is a moral rupture at the level of the republic: the reinvention of injustice as a national system designed to benefit the ruling class.

If left unchecked, this moral inversion won't just harm the present;

it will destroy our children's future. Anyone raised in a society where cruelty is cheered and honesty jeered and cheating routinely goes unchallenged will almost certainly come to equate moral integrity with weakness. And once the muscle of collective integrity has withered, rugged communities that used to thrive on interdependence will become brittle, incapable of uniting in response to crises, let alone innovating or advancing civilization. History shows us where this road leads. Societies that normalize injustice while silencing moral dissent do not simply stagnate; they collapse from within.

MORAL BRIDGE BUILDING

With so much at stake, another narrative can and must arise—one of human resilience, moral courage, and collective integrity. This narrative is still very much alive in the countless grassroots movements today that defy oppressive regimes, in journalists who leave big news companies rather than betray their ethical commitment to report the truth, in medical professionals who steadfastly uphold their duty of care despite political edicts to withhold or shortchange vital services, and in soldiers, law enforcement officers, and government officials who challenge wrongful orders even at great personal risk. The brave, the just, and the caring models of today are often unsung heroes, but they are all around us, and every one of us possesses the power to join them.

Yes, we are surrounded by complex networks of power that can tempt or compel people to act against their conscience. Yes, many have paid a steep price for attempting to adhere to their highest values, and many more have found themselves injured when those values collided with an indifferent or hostile system. But our human story has always been one of struggling against what is, propelled by a stubborn hope for what could be. Even if we are indeed barreling toward a moment of profound reckoning—one where institutions crumble under the weight of their own contradictions—there is still a chance that this fracture can inspire a renewed sense of shared purpose.

Moral repair cannot occur in isolation. It must grow in relationship, in communities that model moral courage despite disillusionment, with moral bridge building taking place even when society becomes dangerously balkanized. This kind of repair needs educational systems that teach critical moral reasoning alongside historical knowledge so that young people can learn to recognize moral distortion when they see it. It demands that we rethink public discourse, prioritizing platforms and policies that elevate truth and shared understanding over emotional manipulation and ideological pandering. And it insists that we, as individuals, resist the seductive pull of moral passivity—that we recognize the awesome power of conviction to uplift and sway the course of history.

The power of such choices lies not in raw numbers but in the moral solidarity and commitment of the bridge builders. After studying civil rights movements across history, the Harvard political scientist Erica Chenoweth concluded that "most mass nonviolent movements that have succeeded have done so even without achieving 3.5% popular participation." That means that a *tiny* fraction of society, given enough "momentum, organization, strategic leadership, and sustainability," can move the collective conscience of whole nations.

As Ruth Ben-Ghiat explains, "Each time we show solidarity with others, or support those who are protecting the rule of law, helping the targeted, or exposing the lies and the corruption, we are standing up for democratic values of justice, accountability, equality, and more. In doing so, we model the behaviors the authoritarian state wants us to abandon. Joining with others, we transform our individual righteous indignation into a potent moral force for good."

We build bridges not only out of empathy and tolerance but also through disciplined commitment to the practices that make for ethical community in a fractured world. The theologian Parker Palmer co-founded the Center for Courage and Renewal with this collective connection as its mission, and through his work there over three decades he's identified five of these practices. He calls them "Habits of the Heart" and believes they can help us build and strengthen the moral bridges that are so vitally needed today:

- **Remember that we are all in this together.** The first universal step is to dispel the illusion of moral self-containment and engage an ethic of mutual responsibility.

- **Appreciate others.** It is not enough to just celebrate diversity; we need to value otherness to undercut the tribal bias toward conformity and offer a richer engagement, with pluralism seen not as threat but as a moral resource.

- **Hold tension in life-giving ways.** The ability to manage cognitive dissonance is not a soft skill but a civic necessity in a culture that otherwise rewards certainty and punishes complexity.

- **Raise your voice and exercise your personal agency.** In this light, agency is not mere expression but principled action—the refusal to abandon one's moral center under pressure.

- **Create and relate in community.** Real companionship becomes the relational infrastructure through which resilience, dissent, and solidarity are made durable. These are not abstract ideals. They are the social preconditions for resisting moral collapse—and for beginning again, together.

As Palmer explains, "When these five habits become the focus of private conversations and public programs that reach growing numbers of people, they move beyond exhortation and start making a practical contribution to restoring democracy's infrastructure. Change begins when we put time, skill, and energy into the mobilization of the powers of the human heart."

Paradoxically, the pain we experience with moral injury is an exquisite reminder of these powers. If we humans didn't deeply value, need, and care about each other, moral injury wouldn't hurt so much. And perhaps that's the most promising truth of all: Our very anguish validates our desire to connect.

None of this guarantees a happy ending, but it offers an opening for solidarity among those who refuse to accept a world where betrayal and ethical compromise are simply the cost of doing business. When we lead with conscience and community, we are strengthening both each other and ourselves.

CONSTRUCTIVE RESILIENCE

What ultimately stands between us and the moral collapse of society is not ideological purity but a moral stance known as constructive resilience—the conscious decision to act in alignment with our core moral principles even when the social current pulls the other way. The human rights expert Michael L. Penn describes this form of resilience as the ability "to harvest the challenges of life such that they reap benefit, so we don't just suffer for nothing."

The term "constructive resilience" was first used by members of the Baha'i faith, a persecuted religion in Iran, to describe their collective nonviolent response to systemic oppression, but this approach to moral survival is also reflected in the words of the renowned psychologist and World War II concentration camp survivor Viktor Frankl, who coined the term "tragic optimism" for the mindset that accompanies it.

"Everything can be taken from a man but one thing," Frankl wrote in *Man's Search for Meaning*, "the last of the human freedoms—to choose one's attitude in any given set of circumstances, to choose one's own way."

Even during the Holocaust, when millions of people were being ruthlessly incarcerated and tortured, those same people had the power to treat each other with kindness, dignity, and respect. Even when a nation's dictator betrays the constitution of his country, the citizens of that country can still choose to observe and uphold the rule of law. Even when a group is dominated by bullies who humiliate and trample the rights of their opponents, other members of the group can refuse to follow suit. They can come to the aid of the persecuted. They can speak up against injustice. And they can embody kindness, respect, and fairness in the ways they personally *choose* to interact with everyone they encounter in daily life.

Constructive resilience is familiar to former prisoners of war like Vice Admiral James Stockdale, who said that he survived more than seven years in captivity in Vietnam because he'd learned to hold two seemingly contradictory ideas in his mind at the same time. While fully recognizing the brutality of his captors and the bleakness of his prospects, Stockdale nevertheless held on to his moral values along with hope that his situation could improve.

More recently, the journalist Michael Scott Moore relied on the basic principles of constructive resilience to get him through two and a half years in captivity as Somali pirates held him for ransom. Early on, he made a failed attempt to escape. And he seriously considered suicide. But in the end, he said in a 2018 interview, "I made a conscious decision to forgive my guards, to forgive the most immediate people who were causing me pain.... [T]hat was an incredible mental transformation. And once I reordered my brain like that, I no longer had that impulse to kill myself. It was a . . . daily discipline, but it worked.... [T]hat mental orientation was absolutely crucial."

Constructive resilience has been a core practice, too, for countless civil rights activists throughout history. It underlies the very notion of nonviolent protest taught by Mahatma Gandhi and Martin Luther King. As Michael Penn explains, constructive resilience invites us "to reflect upon responses to suffering that is inflicted upon us by others so that our responses would help those who have caused us to suffer and also help ourselves." Such protest is not simply a practice of defiant endurance. Rather, it's an inclusive demonstration of moral conviction and faith whose resonance can transcend ideology, give meaning to suffering, and inspire others, perhaps even moving oppressors to recognize the common ground they share with the oppressed.

The applications of constructive resilience go well beyond political oppression. Sarah Jaquette Ray has been studying this moral stance in the context of climate anxiety. "The reason why we have fear, the reason that motivates us to act like our house is on fire," she explains, "is because there's something that we really love that is under threat." That love, she's found, is a sustaining resource even when the climate crisis seems insurmountable. "It's not that the grief or the despair or the fear go away, but that they can open a door to helping us tap this much more enriching resourcing set of emotions."

The logic behind this approach lies in the mind's neurological biases. "The brain is a pleasure-seeking machine," Ray says. Pleasure is emotionally motivating, rewarding, and soothing. Pleasure helps humans get things done—even difficult things like environmental climate work. The key to remember here—and in all constructive resilience—is that life is not purely black or white, good or bad, frightening or pleasurable. It is *all* of the above, woven into a complex tapestry of emotion and choice. No one of us has the power to fix everything that's wrong with the planet, any more than we have the power to feel good about everything that ever happens to us, but we do have the power to focus our *attention* on the things we can fix and the personal choices and interactions we do feel good about. And we have the necessary power to acknowledge contradictory realities at the same time. As Ray says, "It's true that things are worse. It's true that things are better. It is absolutely both and."

Constructive resilience, then, reframes environmental action to stress the rewards of a healthy planet rather than dwelling solely on the fear of dystopia. In Ray's own life, this shift meant, "I need to make sure I'm feeding the stuff that's in my life that I love, that I'm worried climate change is going to change. So if I make sure that those things are growing, those things are thriving, that is one way to make the problem smaller as well, right? If the things that I love, I'm nurturing and I'm making those things bigger and bigger, like a garden metaphor, right? I'm planting, I'm putting fertilizer, I'm putting the sunlight on the stuff that I love. That is another way to make them resilient to the threats that are going to come around the corner, if not already here."

The same approach led the journalist Ed Yong to take up birdwatching after he burned out covering the coronavirus pandemic for *The Atlantic*. As he explained in 2025, birding became "a salve to all of that moral injury and despair that I was feeling. It doesn't cure it, but it fills my life with wonder and joy, and that acts as a buffer against all the other existential dread and fear that we have to grapple with." This connection with the natural world also replenishes Yong's moral reserves by reminding him what makes life worth living, especially for him as a science reporter facing a climate crisis that current political and corporate policies are escalating. On a daily basis, his communion with birds realigns his life with his moral compass. "It matters, because for those of us who care about biodiversity and diversity and the environment and equality, we need to be connected to the thing that we are fighting for."

Constructive resilience means choosing empathy when dehumanization feels easier. It means advocating for fairness when the system incentivizes bias. It means extending loyalty beyond the narrow confines of ideological tribes and toward the broader, more enduring commitment to a shared humanity and healthy planet. It means holding authority accountable—not with performative outrage, but with an unwavering, principled insistence that leadership serve the collective good and not the consolidation of power.

A NEW ETHOS FOR THE TWENTY-FIRST CENTURY

As I write this, the current status quo is unsustainable. The narratives we live by can either dehumanize and divide or humanize and unify us, and right now the dominant narratives are threatening the moral foundations of our shared future. The antidote to this moral disintegration is not a utopian fantasy of perfect agreement, but the hard, daily work of moral repair. It is the decision, made collectively and repeatedly, to reject the logic of cruelty and reclaim the moral principles that make cooperation, trust, and human flourishing possible.

We need individual healing, but we also need to shape environments where fewer moral injuries occur in the first place. We may never reach a utopia free from ethical dilemmas, but every effort to restore integrity and coherence—whether personal or systemic—is a testament to our ongoing commitment to what is right, rather than what is merely expedient. And in that commitment lies the positive countercurrent to a world that sometimes seems on the brink of abandoning its conscience altogether.

The paradox is that those with the most resources—the billionaires and power brokers who bankroll the autocrats, and the conflict entrepreneurs who drive misinformation, division, and environmental destruction—stand to lose as much in this moral implosion as the average citizen, if not more. Their wealth may insulate them temporarily, but no amount of capital can buy clean air, stable ecosystems, or a society that hasn't corroded itself into dysfunction and violence. No quarterly earnings report matters when supply chains are obliterated by climate catastrophe. No political maneuvering ensures generational dynasties when social trust erodes so completely that civic cooperation becomes impossible. Wealth is powerless in the face of ecological collapse, societal fragmentation, and moral apathy. In that future, the billionaire's heir is no safer than the working-class child.

America has always had a split personality. One version lionizes grit, reinvention, opportunity. The other is a brutal machine of extraction—land, labor, time, even trust. Those who've learned to ride that machine—robber barons a century ago, oligarchs now—lose little sleep over the wreckage, not because they're uniquely monstrous, but because they're insulated. Structurally, socially, and often psychologically, the rich and powerful are protected from the need to reckon with the moral fallout of their privilege. The system doesn't just let them off the hook; it redesigns the hook for their benefit. It turns domination into legacy, philanthropy into sainthood, "wealth creators" into national heroes. This design doesn't encourage reflection, much less remorse.

The people who do suffer—including public defenders, trauma nurses, burned-out social workers, middle managers in corporate settings, idealists in systems designed for denial—are those close enough to feel the moral harm and too far from power to stop it. But stop it we must. For all our sakes.

The path forward demands a new ethos, which I'll call enlightened self-interest at scale. Not in the naive sense of "doing good to feel good," but in the cold, pragmatic realization that collective moral health is the bedrock of any enduring civilization. Remember, moral injury is not confined to veterans, survivors, or marginalized groups. Systemic moral injury, when left untreated, ripples into economic stagnation, public health crises, and intergenerational trauma. It affects everyone.

If the planet's fragile equilibrium continues to unravel—if violence and despair become the default responses to resource scarcity—what will that mean for the billionaires' grandchildren, looking out from their fortified compounds at a world collapsing beyond the gates? This is not a dystopian fiction; it is an impending reality already unfolding in climate migration patterns, geopolitical unrest, and the rise of authoritarianism, which accelerates the breakdown by substituting fear for cooperation. Fear is unsustainable. Cooperation is the only force that, throughout history, has allowed humans to thrive in unpredictable environments.

The call, then, is not to one political party or social class. It is to the human species as a whole. We are stewards of an improbable, breathtakingly rare oasis in the cosmos. To continue treating Earth as an endless resource or a battleground for ideological dominance is to betray not only our moral instincts but our evolutionary inheritance of cooperation and collective problem-solving.

Wealth and power, if wielded responsibly, can become engines of this moral reconstruction. But if they remain tools of short-term gain and *wetiko*, the price will be paid universally. There is no planet rich enough to buy a new atmosphere. No portfolio diversified enough to outrun social collapse. Constructive resilience and moral bridge building are survival strategies that require every stakeholder, from the billionaire to the frontline worker, to recognize that our fates are inextricably interwoven. The planet doesn't negotiate with ideology. But it does respond to every one of our actions.

The choice we face is stark: continue the status quo, with its polarized illusions of separateness, and watch the moral and ecological ground beneath us crumble; or embrace a radical, collective shift toward moral cohesion. The foundations of fairness, compassion, loyalty, and accountable leadership are not quaint ideals. They are the operating principles of a civilization built to last. If we fail to repair and maintain them, it won't just be the vulnerable who suffer. It will, inevitably, be all of us.

This shift requires courage. It requires imagination. But above all, it requires belief that constructive moral resilience is possible, even in the face of profound moral injury. And while the work is hard, there is an often-overlooked silver lining. For even as this work sustains society, its transformative rewards are also deeply personal, because moral bridge-building strengthens our own integrity. Pursuing justice helps us rediscover our shared humanity. And embracing truth and compassion helps us create a future in which everyone, regardless of background or belief, has a shared stake.

This is not work that drains us; it is work that renews us. Because in the end the only way to build this better place we call home is to become better people in the process.

ACKNOWLEDGMENTS

Writing a book can feel and look like a solitary undertaking. That's hardly the case. I started work on this book in 2016 with only my own moral struggles and a sense that this story went beyond my own life and needed to be shared. I am grateful that along the way I met a circle of giants who recognized that this message of moral injury mattered.

Richard Pine, to say that I feel privileged and blessed to have you as my agent, along with the great team at Inkwell, is an understatement. Beyond being peerless, you treated a first-time author as if my words already carried weight. I'm grateful that you felt this book belonged in the world.

Lee Woodruff, you changed the course of my life. You've done this for countless veterans and their families, extending privilege, your voice, courage, and your advocacy for individuals who too often go unseen. I am grateful to count myself among them. I hope that these pages can serve as my repayment.

Carrie Cook, you quickly grasped the significance of this project and set about gathering a dream team to support it. I'm thankful for your steadiness, which guided me through both opportunity and uncertainty. Thank you for your critical insights, feedback, and counsel when the work became most challenging.

ACKNOWLEDGMENTS

Karen Rinaldi, my editor, you brought not just your belief in me and this project but also rigor. You and the HarperCollins team gave this book its runway, demanding the highest standard while offering the kind of on-point feedback and support that makes risk possible.

Aimee Liu, my Robin in this literary caped crusade, you kept time when everything around me threatened to go off-beat. Your confidence, patience, and expertise formed the writing metronome that carried this book through draft after draft. Thank you for lending your incredible skill sets and for being a great human.

Alison, my love, without your unselfishness, your patience, support, encouragement, insightful feedback, and the grace to allow me to retreat into my head whenever this work required my all, this book would not be possible. Day after day, you showed up with your quiet leadership and focus that became the very glue binding our home when it felt like cracks were forming. This book may carry my name, but it carries your efforts, too.

Lauren, I always dreamed of one day being a dad. I never expected to see so much of myself reflected in you. You are a wide-eyed beacon of joy, questions, comedy, and thoughtfulness, yet beneath it all lies a resilience about you that humbles me. Life has asked a lot from you, honey, and you have faced it so far with remarkable grit and grace. What amazes me most is your insight and empathy for others—skill sets that are needed now in the world more than ever. Thank you for being patient with me, kiddo. You are beautiful, sharp, thoughtful, and an extraordinary human. I am truly grateful for you.

Lily, though you may never understand the words printed in these pages, I wanted to document this for the world to see. You make the challenge of being present easy. You brought depth of meaning and purpose to my life that could only have existed with your being. You gave me the option of feeling a kind of pain and strength that came as its own teacher—one that brought new meaning and showed me strength that I never knew I had.

ACKNOWLEDGMENTS

Prince passed a few months after I began writing this book, and though it may sound unusual to place him here, I wouldn't be honest with myself if I didn't. His music was the blueprint of my youth. It was a pulse I returned to when I needed a recalibration, release, or a reminder that being different could be a form of genius. At a time when I was desperate for decompression and intervention, his art gave me both. And it wasn't only Prince—it was the art he built with Wendy, Lisa, Shiela, Susannah, Eric, and all the musicians whose fingerprints shaped his sound all those years. Together they expanded what music could be and gave me emotional medicine when I most needed it. What they created was something more than sound—it was a world. A world that freed me up to reconcile contradictions, to explore vulnerabilities, and to understand that strife could become something beneficial. While plenty of good science can shed light on the relationship between music and wellness, the impact of Prince's music feels beyond research.

I am also forever indebted to the researchers, clinicians, family members, and individuals with lived experience who shared their stories and wisdom with me.

NOTES

Introduction

xi   "Now conscience wakes despair": Milton, *Paradise Lost*, bk. 4.

Chapter 1: Awakening

1   "The real problem of humanity": *Harvard Magazine*, "James Watson and Edward O. Wilson."

5   pandemic death toll: WHO, "COVID-19 Deaths."

5   moral injury was defined broadly: Williamson et al., "Moral Injury."

6   "crimes of obedience": Kelman and Hamilton, *Crimes of Obedience*.

6   "You will discover": Bebinger, "'Moral Injury.'"

7   "tend-and-befriend" response: Taylor, "Tend and Befriend Theory."

7   instead of attempting to fight or flee them: Katz et al., "Beyond Fight, Flight, and Freeze."

7   anterior cingulate cortex: Eisenberger, Lieberman, and Williams, "Does Rejection Hurt?"

8   active in emotional responses: Young and Koenigs, "Investigating Emotion in Moral Cognition."

8   fear and physical trauma: Barnes, Hurley, and Taber, "Moral Injury and PTSD."

10   But fully one-third: Bebinger, "'Moral Injury.'"

NOTES

11 self-harm or suicide: U.S. Department of Veterans Affairs, "VA.Gov | Veterans Affairs."
11 "burden of the lives I took": Copp et al., "Soldier Who Blew Up Tesla."
11 "Self-harm might arise": Bebinger, "'Moral Injury.'"
11 In 2020, about seventeen U.S. veterans: American Addiction Centers, "Suicide Among Veterans."
11 Health-care workers: Awan et al., "Suicide in Healthcare Workers"; Olfson et al., "Suicide Risks of Health Care Workers."
11 So do veterinarians: Chan, "Veterinarians Face Unique Issues."
11 so do first responders: Carson et al., "Analysis of Suicides Among First Responders."
11 predators and victims alike: Fani et al., "Moral Injury in Civilians"; Pritchard and King, "Comparison of Child-Sex-Abuse-Related."
12 plane accidents happen: Durgut, "Code of Conduct and Air Traffic Control."
12 children in their charge: Svoboda, "Moral Injury Is an Invisible Epidemic."
12 journalists and photographers: Reuters Institute for the Study of Journalism, "Emotional Toll on Journalists."
12 border patrol agents: Brooks and Greenberg, "Mental Health and Wellbeing"; DeMarco, "Growing At-Risk Group for Moral Injury."
12 Legal defenders: Svoboda, "Moral Injury Is an Invisible Epidemic."
12 high burnout rate: Svoboda, "Moral Injury Is an Invisible Epidemic."
12 epidemic of moral distress: Svoboda, "Moral Injury Is an Invisible Epidemic."
13 half the nation's wealth: O'Donnell, "Are We Living in the Gilded Age 2.0?"
14 help each other survive: Putnam, *Bowling Alone*, 19.
16 "Understanding the simple fact": Haidt, *Righteous Mind*, 4.
17 "heck of a toll on me": Rose, "Another Boeing Whistleblower."
17 "I can't do this any longer": Smoak, "Another Tragic Whistleblower Death."
18 whistleblower Philip Haney: Smoak, "Another Tragic Whistleblower Death."
20 you didn't resist: Leonhardt, "Morning: 'I Froze.'"
21 "bystander effect": Jacobs, "Would You Jump In to Stop an Assault?"
21 crescendo effect: Epstein and Hamric, "Moral Distress, Moral Residue."
24 "that misfit it": Sophocles, line 230.
24 "mark of Cain": *The New Oxford Annotated Bible*, Genesis 4:11–15.
25 More than five billion people: Van Bavel et al., "Social Media and Morality."
25 half our waking hours online: Statista, "Time Spent Online Worldwide 2023."

25 kill themselves on camera: Young, "How a Teenager Pushed a Vulnerable Man."
25 commit terrorist acts: *FRONTLINE*, "Rise and Fall of Terrorgram."
26 outweigh the positives: Van Bavel et al., "Social Media and Morality."
26 online stalking: Lever, "What Is Doxxing?"
27 Around the world: Bengali, "Muslims Faced Hatred and Violence in Sri Lanka."
28 law has few remedies: American Bar Association, "Doxing and Online Harassment."
28 "ecoanxiety": American Psychological Association, "Mental Health and Our Changing Climate."
28 75 percent said they were frightened: Hickman et al., "Young People's Voices on Climate Anxiety."
29 "go into pretty severe depression": Hidden Brain Media, "Wellness 2.0."
29 "There's that complicity factor": Hidden Brain Media, "Wellness 2.0."
29 "I don't want to die": Hickman et al., "Young People's Voices on Climate Anxiety."
30 numbers worsen every year: UN News, "Climate and Weather Related Disasters Surge."
30 expected to top one billion: World Economic Forum, "Climate Refugees."
30 supply chain worldwide: World Economic Forum, "How Climate Change Is Accelerating."
30 trend toward political polarization: Putnam, *Bowling Alone*, 428.

Chapter 2: Evolving

35 "It can hardly be disputed": Darwin, *Descent of Man*, chap. 4.
36 "would be so incorruptible": Plato, *Republic*, 2.360c.
36 "to *make sure that everyone's reputation*": Haidt, *Righteous Mind*, 86.
36 "What is moral is everything": Émile Durkheim, The Division of Labor in Society, 331.
37 stress and anxiety: Pohling and Diessner, "Moral Elevation and Moral Beauty."
37 healthier aging: Pohling and Diessner, "Moral Elevation and Moral Beauty."
37 "proper behavior of a person": Online Etymology Dictionary, "Moral."
39 *groups* need for survival: University of Texas at Austin, "Morals."

39	inherently "prosocial":	Litz, "Moral Injury."
41	whether it feels right or wrong:	Haidt, *Righteous Mind*, 53.
41	"*feelings* that urge us":	Churchland, *Conscience*, 5.
42	"That voice of conscience":	Churchland, *Conscience*, 177.
43	"All animals must have the basic circuitry":	Churchland, *Conscience*, 22.
44	"to yield something rather new":	Churchland, *Conscience*, 21.
44	"In the evolution of the mammalian brain":	Churchland, *Conscience*, 21.
44	to the candy:	Suttie, "Finding Morality in Animals."
44	sometimes for hours:	Schultz, "Leave No Dolphin Behind."
44	grieve for their dead:	Wrage et al., "Ubuntu in Elephant Communities."
45	hurt another monkey:	Wade, "Scientist Finds the Beginnings of Morality."
45	"Attachment begets caring":	Churchland, *Conscience*, 49.
45	"they had to start really punishing":	Gambino, "How Humans Became Moral Beings."
45	"second-person morality":	Tomasello, "Origins of Human Morality."
46	"When everyone in a group":	Haidt, *Righteous Mind*, 239.
46	"A 'we is greater than me' morality":	Tomasello, "Origins of Human Morality."
47	bullying is discouraged:	Hamlin, "Moral Judgment and Action"; Bloom, "Moral Life of Babies."
48	its own infancy:	May et al., "Neuroscience of Moral Judgment."
48	unique to mammals:	Churchland, *Conscience*, 30.
48	won the lottery:	Harbaugh, Mayr, and Burghart, "Neural Responses to Taxation."
49	moral foundations theory:	Haidt, *Righteous Mind*, 146.
49	six moral foundations:	Haidt, *Righteous Mind*, 179.
51	"One of the greatest truths":	Haidt, *Righteous Mind*, 32.
52	Paleolithic foes:	Otterbein, "Earliest Evidence for Warfare?"
52	"Love for one's family members":	Christakis, "Neurobiology of Conscience."
53	"If our sociality motivates caring":	Churchland, *Conscience*, 21.
53	"I really believed":	Schroeder and Herr, "Interview with Michael Herr."
54	"Our collective unconscious":	YouTube, "Vietnam War Documentary—First Kill."
54	"They never explored":	Schroeder and Herr, "Interview with Michael Herr."

55 They account for more than one-fifth: Burton and Saleh, "Antisocial Behavior and Mental Health." Also Kiehl and Hoffman, "The Criminal Psychopath: History, Neuroscience, Treatment, and Economics."
55 antisocial activity online: Moor and Anderson, "Systematic Literature Review."
55 "a lack of feelings of guilt": Churchland, *Conscience*, 129.
56 their own amoral impulses: May et al., "Neuroscience of Moral Judgment."
56 executives had psychopathic traits: Babiak, Neumann, and Hare, "Corporate Psychopathy."
56 "so reveled in firing people": Mukunda, "Psychopaths Who Lead Us."
57 died by suicide: Bilton, "How Elizabeth Holmes's House of Cards Came Tumbling Down."

Chapter 3: Civilizing

59 "If civilization is to survive": King, "Civilization's Great Need."
60 a kind of coevolution: Shweder, "Cultural Psychology."
62 disinterested in human interactions: Norenzayan, "Does Religion Make People Moral?"
62 supernatural authority: Norenzayan, "Does Religion Make People Moral?"
63 "to bring about the rule": Yale Law School, "Code of Hammurabi."
64 "sacredness [as well as morality generally]": Haidt, *Righteous Mind*, 299.
65 weight of transgression: Shay, *Odysseus in America*, 152–53.
66 run into the millions: N4CM, "Horrors of the Church."
67 sacred "tradition": Fox-Genovese and Genovese, "Divine Sanction of Social Order."
68 institution of slavery: Swarns, "Catholic Order Pledges $100 Million."
69 separating church and state: Norenzayan, "Does Religion Make People Moral?"
70 just society *prevents* moral harm: Rawls, *Theory of Justice*.
71 "the least representative populations": Henrich et al., "Weirdest People in the World?," 61–83.
72 detached from the big picture: Henrich et al., "Weirdest People in the World?," 72.
72 Henrich's research team tested: Henrich et al., "Weirdest People in the World?," 72.

73 99 percent of human history: Narvaez, "Having, Doing, and Being of Moral Personality."
73 "disposes each citizen to isolate himself": Putnam, *Bowling Alone*, 24.
73 "the cult of the individual": Marske, "Durkheim's 'Cult of the Individual.'"
74 "a spontaneous weakening": Marske, "Durkheim's 'Cult of the Individual.'"
74 "The story of social capital": Putnam, *Bowling Alone*, 5.
75 student debt at their age: Minkin et al., "Key Milestones for Young Adults."
75 80 percent lower than for white families: Kochhar and Moslimani, "Wealth Gaps Across Racial and Ethnic Groups."
75 political conspiracies, and hate groups: Jetten et al., "Consequences of Economic Inequality."
76 social behavior for millennia: Van Bavel et al., "Social Media and Morality."
77 digital "connection": Van Bavel et al., "Social Media and Morality."
77 TV, and radio combined: Van Bavel et al., "Social Media and Morality."
77 inclusivity and acceptance: Van Bavel et al., "Social Media and Morality."
77 online hatred they consume: Bilewicz and Soral, "Hate Speech Epidemic."
77 "Pizzagate": Hsu, "Comet Pizza Gunman Pleads Guilty."
78 real-world social interaction: Phang et al., "Investigating Affective Use."
79 hate speech often breeds: Karim et al., "Social Media Use and Its Connection."
79 yet to return to pre-pandemic levels: Roth, "Social Isolation in America?"; Gallup, "Loneliness in U.S. Subsides."
79 70 percent since 2003: U.S. Department of Health and Human Services, "Our Epidemic of Loneliness and Isolation."
79 morally sustainable standards: U.S. Department of Health and Human Services, "U.S. Surgeon General Releases New Framework."

Chapter 4: Socializing

81 "About morals, I know only": Hemingway, *Death in the Afternoon*, chap. 1.
87 "Between them, the circuitry": Churchland, *Conscience*, 68.
88 acts of generosity: Harbaugh et al., "Neural Responses to Taxation."
88 viewed as more trustworthy: ScienceDaily, "Behaviors and Traits That Influence Social Status."
89 vital to our physical and mental health: ScienceDaily, "Behaviors and Traits That Influence Social Status."

89 Studies have found that people: Haidt, *Righteous Mind*, 71.
90 bear to contemplate it: Haidt, *Righteous Mind*, 40.
90 Empathy is the secret agent: Schalkwijk, "New Conceptualization of the Conscience"; Solms, "Hard Problem of Consciousness."
93 "Morality and dignity go": Sacks, *Morality*, 232.
93 "not the same": Azarian, "Morals, Not Memories, Define Who We Are."
93 who we are to each other: Schalkwijk, "New Conceptualization of the Conscience"; Solms, "Hard Problem of Consciousness."
97 "I know it when I see it": Lattman, "Origins of Justice Stewart's 'I Know It.'"
98 courage, leadership, and personal honor: Command and Leadership Resource Network, "What Were Some of the Leadership Characteristics."
99 core traits of temperament: Exploring Your Mind, "Cloninger's Theory of Personality."
101 collective impact on our core personality: Schalkwijk, "New Conceptualization of the Conscience"; Solms, "Hard Problem of Consciousness."
101 These *character* traits: Exploring Your Mind, "Cloninger's Theory of Personality."
103 "That boy who shot me": Peralta, "Malala Yousafzai."
103 "One child, one teacher": Husain, "Malala."
104 three-quarters of its adult volume: Narvaez, "Having, Doing, and Being of Moral Personality"; Panda and Mahapatro, "Brain Growth in the First Year."
104 selfish desires and frustrations: Narvaez, "Having, Doing, and Being of Moral Personality."
104 more anxious, insecure, and distrustful: Narvaez, "Having, Doing, and Being of Moral Personality."
105 suspicious of outsiders: May et al., "Neuroscience of Moral Judgment."
105 long-term moral injury: Litz, "Moral Injury."
106 students from diverse backgrounds: May et al., "Neuroscience of Moral Judgment."
109 9 percent of U.S. adults: National Institute of Mental Health, "Personality Disorders."
109 4 percent of the general population: Werner et al., "Epidemiology, Comorbidity, and Behavioral Genetics of Antisocial Personality Disorder and Psychopathy."
109 psychopathy has stronger genetic roots: Blackburn, "Personality Disorder and Psychopathy."

110 consider themselves unimpeachable: ScienceDaily, "Extreme Antisocial Personality Predicts Gang Membership."

111 They dubbed these moral models: Walker and Hennig, "Differing Conceptions of Moral Exemplarity."

112 deception or manipulation: Walker and Hennig, "Differing Conceptions of Moral Exemplarity."

116 "Once any person, book": Haidt, *Righteous Mind*, 317.

116 Reena Virk: Dickson and Burgmann, "After Almost 19 Years, Kelly Ellard Admits Role."

116 John Chau: Sohn, "Inside the Story of John Allen Chau's Ill-Fated Trip."

116 Lance Armstrong: Bike Tips, "Cycling's Darkest Hour."

118 "with regard to their own social status": Caspers et al., "Moral Concepts Set Decision Strategies."

Chapter 5: Hurting

121 "We are spinning our own fates": James, *Principles of Psychology*, chap. 4.

121 State corrections director: Pilkington, "Prison Officers Traumatized."

122 British Post Office: ITV News, "Post Office Victims on Reality of Scandal."

122 "the crescendo effect": Epstein and Hamric, "Moral Distress, Moral Residue."

123 for causing harm to others: Basile et al., "Deontological and Altruistic Guilt."

130 "Moral challenges": Litz, "Moral Injury," 187–99.

130 "either incredulity about the state": Litz, "Moral Injury," 187–99.

131 "Environmental problems are often": Hidden Brain Media, "Wellness 2.0."

132 taxing us mentally and emotionally: Caspers et al., "Moral Concepts Set Decision Strategies."

132 "transaction costs": Putnam, *Bowling Alone*, 135.

132 "A well-connected individual": Putnam, *Bowling Alone*, 20.

133 "society was focused more": Putnam, *Bowling Alone*, 25.

133 78 percent of those polled: Gallup, "Views of State of Moral Values."

133 racism as a moral problem: Gallup, "Record-High 50% of Americans Rate U.S. Moral Values."

133 traditional-individualistic moral biases: Kivikangas et al., "Moral Foundations and Political Orientation."

NOTES | 213

134 "Honesty, civic engagement, and social trust": Putnam, *Bowling Alone*, 137.

136 "I hope someone slits your throat": Andrews, *I Know Who You Are*, 102.

137 lynching of more than sixty-five hundred: Fox, "Nearly 2,000 Black Americans Were Lynched During Reconstruction."

137 militias that support white supremacy: Southern Poverty Law Center, "White Nationalist."

137 Palestinians in Gaza: "Over 60,000 Palestinians Have Died in the Israel-Hamas War, Gaza's Health Ministry Says," Associated Press.

138 "told too late": Diaz, "Alice Munro's Daughter Says Her Mother."

138 "We don't always love": Dederer, *Monsters*, 8–9.

140 moral *distress*: Epstein and Delgado, "Understanding and Addressing Moral Distress."

140 victims broke down and attempted suicide: Kavi, "UK Post Office Scandal Report."

140 banding together to sue the Post Office: *Financial Times*, "Post Office Campaigner Alan Bates Threatens Further Legal Action."

141 claims still remained unpaid: BBC News, "Post Office Horizon IT Scandal Compensation."

142 "here we go again": Epstein and Hamric, "Moral Distress, Moral Residue."

143 they'll feel the sting of moral distress: Epstein and Hamric, "Moral Distress, Moral Residue."

144 "I sided with the law": Gonell, "I Was Nearly Killed on Jan. 6th."

144 suicide after the January 6 attack: Jackson, "4 Capitol Police Officers Have Died."

144 even the comfort of beloved dogs: Dewan, "He Killed Himself After the Jan. 6 Riot."

145 "I feel betrayed": Gonell, "I Was Nearly Killed on Jan. 6th."

145 "literally wears down your heart": Davies, "How Poverty and Racism 'Weather' the Body."

Chapter 6: Healing

149 "The soul aids the body": Hugo, *Les Misérables*, pt. 3, bk. 5, chap. 2.

153 "Healing from Moral Injury": Porosoff, "Healing from Moral Injury."

159 responses that can become chronic: Blair, "Considering Anger from a Cognitive Neuroscience Perspective."

159 emotional relief and balance: Ricciardi et al., "How the Brain Heals Emotional Wounds."

159 cortisol levels, and improved heart health: Toussaint et al., "Forgiveness, Stress, and Health."

159 increasing prefrontal cortex activity: Witvliet et al., "Compassion-Focused Reappraisal."

159 harbor guilt, blame, or shame: Hall and Fincham, "Self-Forgiveness."

160 neural activity related to caregiving and pleasure increases: Inagaki et al., "Neurobiology of Giving Versus Receiving Support."

161 societal stress of interpersonal conflict: Ricciardi et al., "How the Brain Heals Emotional Wounds."

168 reducing anxiety and depression: Ma et al., "Effectiveness of Immersive Virtual Reality."

177 "The man does not remember": Baldwin, "Many Thousands Gone."

Chapter 7: Reckoning

179 "When moral deregulation advances": Ben-Ghiat, "We Are Living Through Moral Collapse."

180 "The most important principle": Haidt, *Righteous Mind*, 86.

181 "*moral deregulation*: a rolling back": Ben-Ghiat, "We Are Living Through Moral Collapse."

181 "will treat each other": Mouffe, "Books Interview: Chantal Mouffe."

181 "driven not only by what we think": Mason, "Ideologues Without Issues."

182 "when we can't change": Stray, et al., "The Algorithmic Management of Polarization and Violence on Social Media."

183 "Authoritarians 'hollow out' institutions": Ben-Ghiat, "We Are Living Through Moral Collapse."

183 precursor to armed conflict: Van Bavel et al., "Social Media and Morality."

183 In 2014 in Myanmar: Waheed, "Rape Used as a Weapon in Myanmar."

183 "spreading fabricated allegations": *Straits Times*, "Myanmar Convicts Five over Fake Rape Claim That Sparked Riots."

184 Crime actually *drops*: Brennan Center for Justice, "Debunking the Myth of the 'Migrant Crime Wave.'"

184 undocumented workers paid nearly $100 billion: Institute on Taxation and Economic Policy, "Tax Payments by Undocumented Immigrants."

185 shadow duel between good and evil: Knight First Amendment Institute, "Algorithmic Management of Polarization."

185 manipulate mass reactions: Knight First Amendment Institute, "Algorithmic Management of Polarization."

185 the Stop the Steal movement: Decker and Cohen, "U.S. 'Stop the Steal' Messages."

185 undermine the country's democratic institutions: Global Voices, "Undertones."

186 protest for weeks in the mistaken belief: Nicas, "Brazil Counted All Its Votes."

186 tending children at the playground: Ensor, "New York City's Nannies Aren't Alright."

186 outrage is purely performative and fake: Van Bavel et al., "Social Media and Morality."

187 grievance is being pumped through society: MacGillis, "How Social Media Apps Could Be Fueling Homicides."

187 "Bean Dad": Di Placido, "Ballad of 'Bean Dad.'"

187 "to find 11,780 votes": CNN Politics, "Read the Full Transcript."

187 majority in both parties are more moderate: Van Bavel et al., "Social Media and Morality."

188 Loneliness and social isolation: U.S. Department of Health and Human Services, "Our Epidemic of Loneliness and Isolation."

188 Ecoanxiety is spiking: Speare-Cole, "Eco-Anxiety Rife Among Children."

189 "political anxiety disorder": Bronfman and Sagarin, "Should Political Anxiety Disorder Be a Diagnosis?"

191 "most mass nonviolent movements": Chenoweth, "Questions, Answers, and Some Cautionary Updates."

191 "Each time we show solidarity": Ben-Ghiat, "We Are Living Through Moral Collapse."

193 "When these five habits": Palmer, *Healing the Heart of Democracy*, xxiv.

193 "to harvest the challenges of life": Egli, "Interview with Dr. Michael Penn."

194 "Everything can be taken from a man": Frankl, *Man's Search for Meaning*, 86.

194 "I made a conscious decision": Davies, "Journalist Held Captive by Pirates."

195 "to reflect upon responses": Egli, "Interview with Dr. Michael Penn."

195 "The reason why we have fear": Hidden Brain Media, "Wellness 2.0."

196 "a salve to all of that moral injury": Marchese, "Ed Yong Wants to Show You."

REFERENCES

American Addiction Centers. "Suicide Among Veterans—Why Are Veterans at a Higher Risk of Suicide?" americanaddictioncenters.org/veterans/suicide-among-veterans.

American Bar Association. "Doxing and Online Harassment: Considerations, Precautions, and Mitigation." www.americanbar.org/groups/litigation/committees/business-torts-unfair-competition/articles/2021/doxing-online-harassment-precautions-mitigation/.

American Psychiatric Association. "Updates to DSM-5-TR Criteria and Text." www.psychiatry.org/psychiatrists/practice/dsm/updates-to-dsm/updates-to-dsm-5-tr-criteria-text.

American Psychological Association and ecoAmerica. "Mental Health and Our Changing Climate: Impacts, Implications, and Guidance." March 2017. doi.org/10.1037/e503122017-001.

Andrews, Lori. *I Know Who You Are and I Saw What You Did: Social Networks and the Death of Privacy*. Simon & Schuster, 2012.

Associated Press. "Over 60,000 Palestinians Have Died in the Israel-Hamas War, Gaza's Health Ministry Says." *PBS NewsHour*, July 30, 2025. https://www.pbs.org/newshour/world/over-60000-palestinians-have-died-in-the-israel-hamas-war-gazas-health-ministry-says.

Aviation File. "Code of Conduct and Air Traffic Control." www.aviationfile.com/code-of-conduct-and-air-traffic-control-an-ethical-perspective/.

Awan, Sana, Mufaddal Najmuddin Diwan, Alifiya Aamir, et al. "Suicide in Healthcare Workers: Determinants, Challenges, and the Impact of COVID-19." *Frontiers in Psychiatry* 12 (Feb. 2022): 792925. doi.org/10.3389/fpsyt.2021.792925.

REFERENCES

Azarian, Bobby. "Morals, Not Memories, Define Who We Are." *Scientific American*, Sept. 29, 2015. www.scientificamerican.com/article/morals-not-memories-define-who-we-are/.

Babiak, Paul, Craig S. Neumann, and Robert D. Hare. "Corporate Psychopathy: Talking the Walk." *Behavioral Sciences & the Law* 28, no. 2 (2010): 174–93. doi.org/10.1002/bsl.925.

Baldwin, James. "Many Thousands Gone." In *Notes of a Native Son*. Beacon Press, 1955.

Barnes, Haleigh A., Robin A. Hurley, and Katherine H. Taber. "Moral Injury and PTSD: Often Co-Occurring yet Mechanistically Different." *Journal of Neuropsychiatry and Clinical Neurosciences* 31, no. 2 (2019): A4–103. doi.org/10.1176/appi.neuropsych.19020036.

Basile, Barbara, Francesco Mancini, Emiliano Macaluso, Carlo Caltagirone, Richard S. J. Frackowiak, and Marco Bozzali. "Deontological and Altruistic Guilt: Evidence for Distinct Neurobiological Substrates." *Human Brain Mapping* 32, no. 2 (2011): 229–39. doi.org/10.1002/hbm.21009.

BBC News. "Post Office Horizon IT Scandal Compensation Hits £1Bn." June 9, 2025. www.bbc.com/news/articles/cev4mw43w13o.

Bebinger, Martha. "'Moral Injury': Gaining Traction, but Still Controversial." WBUR, June 25, 2013. www.wbur.org/news/2013/06/25/moral-injury-research.

Ben-Ghiat, Ruth. "We Are Living Through Moral Collapse. How Democrats Can Strike Back." *Lucid*, Substack, March 16, 2025. lucid.substack.com/p/we-are-living-through-moral-collapse.

Bike Tips. "Cycling's Darkest Hour: The Lance Armstrong Doping Scandal Explained." March 28, 2023. biketips.com/lance-armstrong-doping-scandal/.

Bilewicz, Michał, and Wiktor Soral. "Hate Speech Epidemic: The Dynamic Effects of Derogatory Language on Intergroup Relations and Political Radicalization." *Political Psychology* 41, no. S1 (2020): 3–33. doi.org/10.1111/pops.12670.

Bilton, Nick. "Exclusive: How Elizabeth Holmes's House of Cards Came Tumbling Down." *Vanity Fair*, Sept. 6, 2016. www.vanityfair.com/news/2016/09/elizabeth-holmes-theranos-exclusive.

Blackburn, Ronald. "Personality Disorder and Psychopathy: Conceptual and Empirical Integration." *Psychology, Crime & Law* 13, no. 1 (2007): 7–18. doi.org/10.1080/10683160600869585.

Blair, R. J. R. "Considering Anger from a Cognitive Neuroscience Perspective." *Cognitive Science* 3, no. 1 (2012): 65–74. doi.org/10.1002/wcs.154.

Bloom, Paul. "The Moral Life of Babies." *New York Times*, May 5, 2010. www.nytimes.com/2010/05/09/magazine/09babies-t.html.

Bobrov, Liron Hakim. "Content Moderators: The Cost of Burnout." *ActiveFence*, Jan. 19, 2023. www.activefence.com/blog/content-moderators-cost-of-burnout/.

Brennan Center for Justice. "Debunking the Myth of the 'Migrant Crime Wave.'" Sept. 26, 2024. www.brennancenter.org/our-work/analysis-opinion/debunking-myth-migrant-crime-wave.

Bronfman, Elisa T., and Johanna D. Sagarin. "Should Political Anxiety Disorder Be a Diagnosis?" *Psychology Today*, Feb. 2025. www.psychologytoday.com/us/blog/aligning-for-growth/202502/should-political-anxiety-disorder-be-a-diagnosis.

Brooks, S. K., and N. Greenberg. "Mental Health and Wellbeing of Border Security Personnel: Scoping Review." *Occupational Medicine* 72, no. 9 (2022): 636–40. doi.org/10.1093/occmed/kqac108.

Burton, B., and F. M. Saleh. "Antisocial Behavior and Mental Health." *Psychiatric Times* 37, no. 10 (2020).

Carson, Leslie M., Suzanne M. Marsh, Margaret M. Brown, Katherine L. Elkins, and Hope M. Tiesman. "An Analysis of Suicides Among First Responders—Findings from the National Violent Death Reporting System, 2015–2017." *Journal of Safety Research* 85 (June 2023): 361–70. doi.org/10.1016/j.jsr.2023.04.003.

Caspers, Svenja, Stefan Heim, Marc G. Lucas, et al. "Moral Concepts Set Decision Strategies to Abstract Values." *PLOS ONE* 6, no. 4 (2011): e18451. doi.org/10.1371/journal.pone.0018451.

Chan, Melissa. "Veterinarians Face Unique Issues That Make Suicide One of the Profession's Big Worries." *Time*, Sept. 12, 2019. time.com/5670965/veterinarian-suicide-help/.

Chenoweth, Erica. "Questions, Answers, and Some Cautionary Updates Regarding the 3.5% Rule." Harvard Carr Center for Human Rights Policy, April 2020.

Christakis, Nicholas A. "The Neurobiology of Conscience." *Nature* 569, no. 7758 (2019): 627–28. doi.org/10.1038/d41586-019-01658-w.

Churchland, Patricia S. *Conscience: The Origins of Moral Intuition*. W. W. Norton, 2019.

CNN Politics. "Read the Full Transcript and Listen to Trump's Audio Call with Georgia Secretary of State." Jan. 3, 2021. www.cnn.com/2021/01/03/politics/trump-brad-raffensperger-phone-call-transcript/index.html.

REFERENCES

Command and Leadership Resource Network. "What Were Some of the Leadership Characteristics of George Patton?" www.clrn.org/what-were-some-of-the-leadership-characteristics-of-george-patton/.

Copp, Tara, Rio Yamat, Alanna Durkin Richer, and Colleen Long. "Soldier Who Blew Up Tesla at Trump Hotel Left Note Saying Blast Was to Be a 'Wake Up Call' for US." *AP News*, Jan. 3, 2025. apnews.com/article/cybertruck-explosion-trump-hotel-las-vegas-6c85af85255753db497f2cd344fb2ace.

Darwin, Charles. *The Descent of Man, and Selection in Relation to Sex*. John Murray, 1871.

Davies, Dave. "How Poverty and Racism 'Weather' the Body, Accelerating Aging and Disease." NPR, March 28, 2023. www.npr.org/sections/health-shots/2023/03/28/1166404485/weathering-arline-geronimus-poverty-racism-stress-health.

Davies, Dave. "Journalist Held Captive by Pirates Says Focus and Forgiveness Were Crucial." NPR, July 30, 2018. www.npr.org/2018/07/30/633965533/journalist-held-captive-by-pirates-says-focus-and-forgiveness-were-crucial.

Decker, Benjamin T., and Adi Cohen. "U.S. 'Stop the Steal' Messages Reverberate to Brazil, and Back." *Tech Policy Press*, Oct. 27, 2022. techpolicy.press/u-s-stop-the-steal-messages-reverberate-to-brazil-and-back.

Dederer, Claire. *Monsters: A Fan's Dilemma*. Knopf, 2023.

DeMarco, Michele. "A Growing At-Risk Group for Moral Injury and Moral Distress." *Psychology Today*, April 8, 2024. www.psychologytoday.com/intl/blog/soul-console/202306/a-growing-at-risk-group-for-moral-injury-and-moral-distress.

Dewan, Shaila. "He Killed Himself After the Jan. 6 Riot. Did He Die in the Line of Duty?" *New York Times*, July 29, 2021. www.nytimes.com/2021/07/29/us/police-suicides-capitol-riot.html.

Diaz, Jaclyn. "Alice Munro's Daughter Says Her Mother Did Nothing to Stop Abusive Stepfather." NPR, July 8, 2024. www.npr.org/2024/07/08/nx-s1-5032827/alice-munro-daughter-abuse-stepfather.

Dickson, Louise, and Tamsyn Burgmann. "After Almost 19 Years, Kelly Ellard Admits Role in Killing Reena Virk." *Times Colonist*, May 4, 2016. www.timescolonist.com/local-news/after-almost-19-years-kelly-ellard-admits-role-in-killing-reena-virk-4636017.

Di Placido, Dani. "The Ballad of 'Bean Dad' Shows the Cruel, Petty Side of Twitter." *Forbes*, Jan. 5, 2021. www.forbes.com/sites/danidiplacido/2021/01/05/the-ballad-of-bean-dad-shows-the-cruel-petty-side-of-twitter/.

Durgut, M. "Code of Conduct and Air Traffic Control." *Aviation File*. www.aviationfile.com/code-of-conduct-and-air-traffic-control-an-ethical-perspective/.

Durkheim, Émile. *The Division of Labor in Society*. 1893. Reprint, translated by W. D. Halls. Free Press, 1984.

Egli, Glenn. *CO·HERE*, podcast, episode 4, "Interview with Dr. Michael Penn." Green Acre, May 13, 2020. www.greenacre.org/co-here-episode-4-constructive-resilience-part-2/.

Eisenberger, Naomi I., Matthew D. Lieberman, and Kipling D. Williams. "Does Rejection Hurt? An fMRI Study of Social Exclusion." *Science* 302, no. 5643 (2003): 290–92. doi.org/10.1126/science.1089134.

Ensor, Josie. "New York City's Nannies Aren't Alright." *Airmail*, May 24, 2025. airmail.news/issues/2025-5-24/the-nannies-arent-alright.

Epstein, Elizabeth G., and Sarah Delgado. "Understanding and Addressing Moral Distress." *OJIN: The Online Journal of Issues in Nursing* 15, no. 3 (2010). doi.org/10.3912/OJIN.Vol15No03Man01.

Epstein, Elizabeth G., and Ann Baile Hamric. "Moral Distress, Moral Residue, and the Crescendo Effect." *Journal of Clinical Ethics* 20, no. 4 (2009): 330–42. www.semanticscholar.org/paper/Moral-Distress%2C-Moral-Residue%2C-and-the-Crescendo-Epstein-Hamric/423995950913b97e83554efd6533dfb88ff95694.

Exploring Your Mind. "Cloninger's Theory of Personality." exploringyourmind.com/cloningers-theory-of-personality/.

Fani, Negar, Joseph M. Currier, Matthew D. Turner, et al. "Moral Injury in Civilians: Associations with Trauma Exposure, PTSD, and Suicide Behavior." *European Journal of Psychotraumatology* 12, no. 1 (2021): 1965464. doi.org/10.1080/20008198.2021.1965464.

Financial Times. "Post Office Campaigner Alan Bates Threatens Further Legal Action." Nov. 5, 2024. www.ft.com/content/ddof41d4-26a3-4280-b923-07af8681a98e.

Fox, Alex. "Nearly 2,000 Black Americans Were Lynched During Reconstruction." *Smithsonian Magazine*, June 18, 2020. www.smithsonianmag.com/smart-news/nearly-2000-black-americans-were-lynched-during-reconstruction-180975120/.

Fox-Genovese, Elizabeth, and Eugene D. Genovese. "The Divine Sanction of Social Order." *Journal of the American Academy of Religion* 55, no. 2 (1987): 211–34. doi.org/10.1093/JAAREL/LV.2.211.

Frankl, Viktor. *Man's Search for Meaning*. Washington Square Press, 1984.

FRONTLINE. "The Rise and Fall of Terrorgram." www.pbs.org/wgbh/frontline/documentary/the-rise-and-fall-of-terrorgram/.

Gallup. "Loneliness in U.S. Subsides from Pandemic High." April 4, 2023. news.gallup.com/poll/473057/loneliness-subsides-pandemic-high.aspx.

Gallup. "Record-High 50% of Americans Rate U.S. Moral Values as 'Poor.'" June 15, 2022. news.gallup.com/poll/393659/record-high-americans-rate-moral-values-poor.aspx.

Gallup. "Views of State of Moral Values in U.S. at New Low." June 9, 2023. news.gallup.com/poll/506960/views-state-moral-values-new-low.aspx.

Gambino, Megan. "How Humans Became Moral Beings." *Smithsonian Magazine*, March 3, 2012. www.smithsonianmag.com/science-nature/how-humans-became-moral-beings-80976434/.

Global Voices. "Undertones: Brazil Copes with 'Digital Militias' Ahead of Tense Elections." Oct. 27, 2022. globalvoices.org/2022/10/27/undertones-brazil-copes-with-digital-militias-ahead-of-tense-elections/.

Gonell, Aquilino. "I Was Nearly Killed on Jan. 6th. Four Years Later, I Feel Betrayed All Over Again." *Bulwark*, Jan. 6, 2025. www.thebulwark.com/p/january-6th-four-years-later-aquilino-gonell-feel-betrayed.

Haidt, Jonathan. *The Righteous Mind*. Penguin Books, 2013.

Hall, Julie H., and Frank D. Fincham. "Self-Forgiveness: The Stepchild of Forgiveness Research." *Journal of Social and Clinical Psychology* 24, no. 5 (2005): 621–37. doi.org/10.1521/jscp.2005.24.5.621.

Hamlin, J. Kiley. "Moral Judgment and Action in Preverbal Infants and Toddlers: Evidence for an Innate Moral Core." *Current Directions in Psychological Science* 22, no. 3 (2013): 186–93.

Harbaugh, William T., Ulrich Mayr, and Daniel R. Burghart. "Neural Responses to Taxation and Voluntary Giving Reveal Motives for Charitable Donations." *Science* 316, no. 5831 (2007): 1622–25. doi.org/10.1126/science.1140738.

Harvard Magazine. "James Watson and Edward O. Wilson: An Intellectual Entente." Sept. 10, 2009. www.harvardmagazine.com/2009/09/james-watson-edward-o-wilson-intellectual-entente.

Hemingway, Ernest. *Death in the Afternoon*. Scribner's, 1932.

Henrich, Joseph, Steven J. Heine, and Ara Norenzayan. "The Weirdest People in the World?" *Behavioral and Brain Sciences* 33, no. 2–3 (2010): 61–135.

Hickman, Caroline, Elizabeth Marks, Panu Pihkala, et al. "Young People's Voices on Climate Anxiety, Government Betrayal, and Moral Injury: A

Global Phenomenon." *SSRN Electronic Journal*, Sept. 7, 2021. doi.org/10.2139/ssrn.3918955.

Hidden Brain Media. "Wellness 2.0: When It's All Too Much." Jan. 20, 2025. hiddenbrain.org/podcast/wellness-2-0-when-its-all-too-much/.

Hsu, Tina. "Comet Pizza Gunman Pleads Guilty to Federal and Local Charges." *Washington Post*, March 24, 2017. www.washingtonpost.com/local/public-safety/comet-pizza-gunman-to-appear-at-plea-deal-hearing-friday-morning/2017/03/23/e12c91ba-0986-11e7-b77c-0047d15a24e0_story.html.

Hugo, Victor. *Les Misérables*. Translated by Isabel F. Hapgood. 2nd ed. Canterbury Classics, 2025.

Husain, Mishal. "Malala: The Girl Who Was Shot for Going to School." *BBC News*, Oct. 6, 2013. www.bbc.com/news/magazine-24379018.

Inagaki, Tristen K., Kate E. Byrne Haltom, Shosuke Suzuki, et al. "The Neurobiology of Giving Versus Receiving Support: The Role of Stress-Related and Social Reward–Related Neural Activity." *Psychosomatic Medicine* 78, no. 4 (2016): 443–53. doi.org/10.1097/PSY.0000000000000302.

Institute on Taxation and Economic Policy. "Tax Payments by Undocumented Immigrants." itep.org/undocumented-immigrants-taxes-2024/.

ITV News. "Post Office Victims on Reality of Scandal: Suicide Attempts and Bankruptcy." Jan. 4, 2024. www.itv.com/news/2024-01-04/post-office-victims-on-reality-of-scandal-suicide-attempts-and-bankruptcy.

Jackson, Jon. "4 Capitol Police Officers Have Died by Suicide Since the Insurrection." *Newsweek*, Aug. 2, 2021. www.newsweek.com/3-capitol-police-officers-have-died-suicide-since-january-6-insurrection-1615452.

Jacobs, Andrew. "Would You Jump In to Stop an Assault?" *New York Times*, April 3, 2021. www.nytimes.com/2021/04/03/science/bystander-effect.html.

James, William. *The Principles of Psychology*. Vol. 1. Henry Holt, 1890.

Jetten, Jolanda, Kim Peters, Belén Álvarez, et al. "Consequences of Economic Inequality for the Social and Political Vitality of Society: A Social Identity Analysis." *Political Psychology* 42, no. S1 (2021): 241–66. doi.org/10.1111/pops.12800.

Karim, Fazida, Azeezat A. Oyewande, Lamis F. Abdalla, Reem Chaudhry Ehsanullah, and Safeera Khan. "Social Media Use and Its Connection to Mental Health: A Systematic Review." *Cureus* 12, no. 6 (2020): e8627. doi.org/10.7759/cureus.8627.

REFERENCES

Katz, Carmit, Noga Tsur, Anat Talmon, and Racheli Nicolet. "Beyond Fight, Flight, and Freeze: Towards a New Conceptualization of Peritraumatic Responses to Child Sexual Abuse Based on Retrospective Accounts of Adult Survivors." *Child Abuse & Neglect* 112 (Feb. 2021): 104905. doi.org/10.1016/j.chiabu.2020.104905.

Kavi, Aishvarya. "UK Post Office Scandal Report." *New York Times*, July 10, 2025. https://www.nytimes.com/2025/07/10/world/europe/uk-post-office-scandal-report.html.

Kelman, Herbert C., and V. Lee Hamilton. *Crimes of Obedience: Toward a Social Psychology of Authority and Responsibility*. Yale University Press, 1990.

Kiehl, K. A., and M. B. Hoffman. "The Criminal Psychopath: History, Neuroscience, Treatment, and Economics." *Jurimetrics* 51, no. 4 (2011): 355–97.

King, Martin Luther, Jr. "Civilization's Great Need." 1949. Martin Luther King Jr. Research and Education Institute, Stanford University. kinginstitute.stanford.edu/king-papers/documents/civilizations-great-need.

Kivikangas, J. Matias, Belén Fernández-Castilla, Simo Järvelä, Niklas Ravaja, and Jan-Erik Lönnqvist. "Moral Foundations and Political Orientation: Systematic Review and Meta-Analysis." *Psychological Bulletin* 147, no. 1 (2021): 55–94. doi.org/10.1037/bul0000308.

Knight First Amendment Institute. "The Algorithmic Management of Polarization and Violence on Social Media." knightcolumbia.org/content/the-algorithmic-management-of-polarization-and-violence-on-social-media.

Kochhar, Rakesh, and Mohamad Moslimani. "Wealth Gaps Across Racial and Ethnic Groups." Pew Research Center, Dec. 4, 2023. www.pewresearch.org/2023/12/04/wealth-gaps-across-racial-and-ethnic-groups/.

Lattman, Peter. "The Origins of Justice Stewart's 'I Know It When I See It.'" *Wall Street Journal*, Sept. 27, 2007. www.wsj.com/articles/BL-LB-4558.

Leonhardt, David. "The Morning: 'I Froze.'" *New York Times*, Aug. 22, 2023. www.nytimes.com/2023/08/22/briefing/rape-victims-trauma-response-biden-hawaii.html.

Lever, Rob. "What Is Doxxing?" *U.S. News & World Report*, Dec. 16, 2021. www.usnews.com/360-reviews/privacy/what-is-doxxing.

Litz, Brett T. "Moral Injury: State of the Science." *Journal of Traumatic Stress* 38, no. 2 (2025): 187–99. doi.org/10.1002/jts.23125.

Litz, Brett T., and Hannah E. Walker. "Moral Injury: An Overview of Conceptual, Definitional, Assessment, and Treatment Issues." *Annual Review of Clinical Psychology* 21 (May 2025): 251–77. doi.org/10.1146/annurev-clinpsy-081423-022604.

Ma, Jingni, Dongrong Zhao, Naihong Xu, and Jinmei Yang. "The Effectiveness of Immersive Virtual Reality (VR) Based Mindfulness Training on Improvement Mental-Health in Adults: A Narrative Systematic Review." *Explore* 19, no. 3 (2023): 310–18. doi.org/10.1016/j.explore.2022.08.001.

MacGillis, Alec. "How Social Media Apps Could Be Fueling Homicides Among Young Americans." ProPublica, Aug. 8, 2023. www.propublica.org/article/social-media-violence-young-americans.

Marchese, Jess. "Ed Yong Wants to Show You the Hidden Reality of the World." *New York Times*, Feb. 22, 2025. www.nytimes.com/2025/02/22/magazine/ed-yong-interview.html?smid=em-share.

Marske, Charles E. "Durkheim's 'Cult of the Individual' and the Moral Reconstitution of Society." *Sociological Theory* 5, no. 1 (1987): 1–14. doi.org/10.2307/201987.

Mason, Lilliana. "Ideologues Without Issues: The Polarizing Consequences of Ideological Identities." *Public Opinion Quarterly* 82, no. S1 (2018): 866–87. doi.org/10.1093/poq/nfy005.

May, Joshua, Clifford I. Workman, Julia Haas, and Hyemin Han. "The Neuroscience of Moral Judgment: Empirical and Philosophical Developments." In *Neuroscience and Philosophy*, edited by Felipe De Brigard and Walter Sinnott-Armstrong, 17–47. MIT Press, 2022. www.ncbi.nlm.nih.gov/books/NBK583720/.

Milton, John. *Paradise Lost*. Edited by Gordon Teskey. Norton, 2020.

Minkin, Rachel, Kim Parker, Juliana Menasce Horowitz, and Carolina Aragão. "Key Milestones for Young Adults Today Versus 30 Years Ago." Pew Research Center, Jan. 25, 2024. www.pewresearch.org/social-trends/2024/01/25/key-milestones-for-young-adults-today-versus-30-years-ago/.

Moor, Lily, and Joel R. Anderson. "A Systematic Literature Review of the Relationship Between Dark Personality Traits and Antisocial Online Behaviours." *Personality and Individual Differences* 144 (July 2019): 40–55. doi.org/10.1016/j.paid.2019.02.027.

Mouffe, Chantal. "The Books Interview: Chantal Mouffe." *New Statesman*, Nov. 2009. Archived at web.archive.org/web/20091123033245/http://www.newstatesman.com/books/2009/11/agonistic-democracy-bnp-post.

Mukunda, Gautam. "The Psychopaths Who Lead Us." *Forbes*, Sept. 26, 2024. www.forbes.com/sites/gautammukunda/2024/09/26/the-psychopaths-who-lead-us/.

Narvaez, Darcia. "The Having, Doing, and Being of Moral Personality." *The Philosophy and Psychology of Character and Happiness*, Jan. 1, 2014. www.academia.edu/46844111/The_Having_Doing_and_Being_of_Moral_Personality.

REFERENCES

National Institute of Mental Health. "Personality Disorders." www.nimh.nih.gov/health/statistics/personality-disorders.

New Oxford Annotated Bible: New Revised Standard Version with Apocrypha. 5th ed. Edited by Michael D. Coogan. Oxford University Press, 2018.

N4CM. "The Horrors of the Church and Its Holy Inquisition." April 7, 2016. churchandstate.org.uk/2016/04/the-horrors-of-the-church-and-its-holy-inquisition/.

Nicas, Jack. "Brazil Counted All Its Votes in Hours. It Still Faces Fraud Claims." *New York Times*, Nov. 10, 2022. www.nytimes.com/2022/11/10/world/americas/brazil-election-fraud.html.

Norenzayan, Ara. "Does Religion Make People Moral?" *Behaviour* 151, no. 2–3 (2014): 365–84. doi.org/10.1163/1568539X-00003139.

O'Donnell, Edward T. "Are We Living in the Gilded Age 2.0?" *History*, June 15, 2018. www.history.com/articles/second-gilded-age-income-inequality.

Olfson, Mark, Candace M. Cosgrove, Melanie M. Wall, and Carlos Blanco. "Suicide Risks of Health Care Workers in the US." *JAMA* 330, no. 12 (2023): 1161–66. doi.org/10.1001/jama.2023.15787.

Online Etymology Dictionary. "Moral—Etymology, Origin & Meaning." www.etymonline.com/word/moral.

OpenAI. "Investigating Affective Use and Emotional Well-Being on ChatGPT." cdn.openai.com/papers/15987609-5f71-433c-9972-e91131f399a1/openai-affective-use-study.pdf.

Otterbein, Keith F. "The Earliest Evidence for Warfare?" *Current Anthropology* 52, no. 3 (2011): 439. doi.org/10.1086/659742.

Palmer, Parker. *Healing the Heart of Democracy*. John Wiley & Sons, 2024.

Panda, S., and S. Mahapatro. "Brain Growth in the First Year." In *Encyclopedia of Evolutionary Psychological Science*, edited by T. K. Shackelford and V. A. Weekes-Shackelford. Springer, 2021. doi.org/10.1007/978-3-319-19650-3_805.

Peralta, Eyder. "Malala Yousafzai: 'I Believe in Peace; I Believe in Mercy.'" NPR, Oct. 7, 2013. www.npr.org/sections/thetwo-way/2013/10/07/230196881/malala-yousafzai-i-believe-in-peace-i-believe-in-mercy.

Phang, Jason, Michael Lampe, Lama Ahmad, et al. "Investigating Affective Use and Emotional Well-Being on ChatGPT." OpenAI. cdn.openai.com/papers/15987609-5f71-433c-9972-e91131f399a1/openai-affective-use-study.pdf.

Pilkington, Ed. "Prison Officers Traumatized by Rate of Executions in US Death Penalty States." *Guardian*, April 28, 2024. www.theguardian.com/world/2024/apr/28/prison-guard-trauma-execution-death-penalty.

Plato. *Republic*. Translated by Benjamin Jowett. Internet Classics Archive. www.classics.mit.edu/Plato/republic.html.

Pohling, Rico, and Rhett Diessner. "Moral Elevation and Moral Beauty: A Review of the Empirical Literature." *Review of General Psychology* 20, no. 4 (2016): 412–25. doi.org/10.1037/gpr0000089.

Porosoff, Lauren. "Healing from Moral Injury." *Learning for Justice*, no. 51 (Fall 2015). www.learningforjustice.org/magazine/fall-2015/healing-from-moral-injury.

Pritchard, Colin, and Edward King. "A Comparison of Child-Sex-Abuse-Related and Mental-Disorder-Related Suicide in a Six-Year Cohort of Regional Suicides." *British Journal of Social Work* 34, no. 1 (2004): 99–113. doi.org/10.1093/BJSW/BCH021.

Putnam, Robert D. *Bowling Alone*. Simon & Schuster, 2020.

Rawls, John. *A Theory of Justice*. Rev. ed. Harvard University Press, 1999.

Reuters Institute for the Study of Journalism. "The Emotional Toll on Journalists Covering the Refugee Crisis." reutersinstitute.politics.ox.ac.uk/our-research/emotional-toll-journalists-covering-refugee-crisis.

Ricciardi, Emiliano, Giuseppina Rota, Lorenzo Sani, et al. "How the Brain Heals Emotional Wounds: The Functional Neuroanatomy of Forgiveness." *Frontiers in Human Neuroscience* 7 (Dec. 2013): 839. doi.org/10.3389/fnhum.2013.00839.

Rose, Joel. "Another Boeing Whistleblower Says He Faced Retaliation for Reporting 'Shortcuts.'" NPR, April 12, 2024. www.npr.org/2024/04/12/1244147895/boeing-whistleblower-retaliation-shortcuts-787-dreamliner.

Roth, Adam R. "Social Isolation in America? A 20-Year Snapshot." *Socius* 10 (Jan. 2024): 23780231241228445. doi.org/10.1177/23780231241228445.

Sacks, Jonathan. *Morality*. Basic Books, 2020.

Schalkwijk, Floris. "A New Conceptualization of the Conscience." *Frontiers in Psychology* 9 (Sept. 2018): 1863. www.frontiersin.org/articles/10.3389/fpsyg.2018.01863/full#B52.

Schroeder, Eric James, and Michael Herr. "Interview with Michael Herr: 'We've All Been There.'" *Writing on the Edge* 1, no. 1 (1989): 39–54. www.jstor.org/stable/43158633.

Schultz, Colin. "Leave No Dolphin Behind: Dolphin Pod Carries Injured Member Until She Stops Breathing." *Smithsonian Magazine*, Jan. 25, 2013. www.smithsonianmag.com/smart-news/leave-no-dolphin-behind-dolphin-pod-carries-injured-member-until-she-stops-breathing-6342625/.

ScienceDaily. "Behaviors and Traits That Influence Social Status, According to Evolutionary Psychologists." June 3, 2020. www.sciencedaily.com/releases/2020/06/200602183412.htm.

ScienceDaily. "Extreme Antisocial Personality Predicts Gang Membership, Finds Study Based on Survey of Male Prisoners." Nov. 9, 2011. www.sciencedaily.com/releases/2011/11/111109104206.htm.

Shay, Jonathan. *Odysseus in America*. Scribner, 2002.

Shweder, Richard A. "Cultural Psychology: What Is It?" In *Cultural Psychology: Essays on Comparative Human Development*, edited by J. W. Stigler, R. A. Shweder, and G. Herdt, 1–43. Cambridge University Press, 1990.

Smoak, Breezy. "Another Tragic Whistleblower Death—OpenAI Whistleblower Suchir Balaji." Constantine Cannon, Dec. 20, 2024. constantinecannon.com/whistleblower/whistleblower-insider-blog/another-tragic-whistleblower-death-openai-whistleblower-suchir-balaji/.

Sohn, Tim. "Inside the Story of John Allen Chau's Ill-Fated Trip to a Remote Island." *Smithsonian Magazine*, Oct. 21, 2018. www.smithsonianmag.com/history/inside-story-john-allen-chaus-ill-fated-trip-remote-island-180970971/.

Solms, Mark. "The Hard Problem of Consciousness and the Free Energy Principle." *Frontiers in Psychology* 9 (Jan. 2018): 2714. doi.org/10.3389/fpsyg.2017.02714.

Sophocles. *Sophocles II: Ajax, The Women of Trachis, Electra, Philoctetes, The Trackers*. Edited and translated by Mark Griffith, Glenn W. Most, David Grene, and Richmond Lattimore. University of Chicago Press, 2013.

Southern Poverty Law Center. "White Nationalist." www.splcenter.org/fighting-hate/extremist-files/ideology/white-nationalist.

Speare-Cole, Rebecca. "Eco-Anxiety Rife Among Children as 78% Found to Be Worried About Climate Change." *Independent*, Feb. 3, 2025. www.independent.co.uk/climate-change/news/greenpeace-children-homes-b2690913.html.

Statista. "Time Spent Online Worldwide 2023." www.statista.com/statistics/1380282/daily-time-spent-online-global/.

Stavrou, Athena. "Suicide, Exile Abroad, and Prison: The Stories Behind the Post Office Scandal." *Independent*, Jan. 9, 2024. www.independent.co.uk/news/uk/home-news/post-office-scandal-mr-bates-b2475510.html.

Straits Times. "Myanmar Convicts Five over Fake Rape Claim That Sparked Riots." March 20, 2015. www.straitstimes.com/asia/se-asia/myanmar-convicts-five-over-fake-rape-claim-that-sparked-riots.

Stray, Jonathan, Ravi Iyer, and Helena Puig Larrauri. "The Algorithmic Management of Polarization and Violence on Social Media." Knight First Amendment

Institute at Columbia University, August 22, 2023. www.knightcolumbia.org/content/the-algorithmic-management-of-polarization-and-violence-on-social-media.

Stroud, Court. "Sgt. Aquilino Gonell: The Immigrant Who Defended Democracy on Jan. 6." *Forbes*, Oct. 30, 2024. www.forbes.com/sites/courtstroud/2024/10/30/sgt-aquilino-gonell-the-immigrant-who-defended-democracy-on-jan-6/.

Suttie, Jill. "Finding Morality in Animals." *Greater Good*, July 9, 2013. greatergood.berkeley.edu/article/item/morality_animals.

Svoboda, Elizabeth. "Moral Injury Is an Invisible Epidemic That Affects Millions." *Scientific American*, Sept. 19, 2022. www.scientificamerican.com/article/moral-injury-is-an-invisible-epidemic-that-affects-millions/.

Swarns, Rachel L. "Catholic Order Pledges $100 Million to Atone for Slave Labor and Sales." *New York Times*, March 15, 2021. www.nytimes.com/2021/03/15/us/jesuits-georgetown-reparations-slavery.html.

Taylor, Shelley E. "Tend and Befriend Theory." In *Handbook of Theories of Social Psychology*. Vol. 1, edited by Paul A. M. Van Lange, Arie W. Kruglanski, and E. Tory Higgins, 32–49. SAGE Publications, 2012.

Tomasello, Michael. "The Origins of Human Morality." *Scientific American*, Sept. 1, 2018. doi.org/10.1038/scientificamerican0918-70.

Toussaint, Loren L., Grant S. Shields, and George M. Slavich. "Forgiveness, Stress, and Health: A 5-Week Dynamic Parallel Process Study." *Annals of Behavioral Medicine* 50, no. 5 (2016): 727–35. doi.org/10.1007/s12160-016-9796-6.

United Nations Office for the Coordination of Humanitarian Affairs—Occupied Palestinian Territory. "Humanitarian Situation Update #296 | Gaza Strip." June 11, 2025. www.ochaopt.org/content/humanitarian-situation-update-296-gaza-strip.

University of Texas at Austin. "Morals." *Ethics Unwrapped*. ethicsunwrapped.utexas.edu/glossary/morals.

UN News. "Climate and Weather Related Disasters Surge Five-Fold over 50 Years, but Early Warnings Save Lives—WMO Report." Sept. 1, 2021. news.un.org/en/story/2021/09/1098662.

U.S. Department of Health and Human Services. "Our Epidemic of Loneliness and Isolation." www.hhs.gov/sites/default/files/surgeon-general-social-connection-advisory.pdf.

U.S. Department of Health and Human Services. "U.S. Surgeon General Releases New Framework for Mental Health & Well-Being in the Workplace." Oct. 20, 2022. doi.org/10/20/us-surgeon-general-releases-new-framework-mental-health-well-being-workplace.html.

U.S. Department of Veterans Affairs. "VA.Gov | Veterans Affairs." General Information. www.ptsd.va.gov/professional/treat/cooccurring/moral_injury.asp.

Van Bavel, Jay J., Claire E. Robertson, Kareena del Rosario, Jesper Rasmussen, and Steve Rathje. "Social Media and Morality." *Annual Review of Psychology* 75 (Jan. 2024): 311–40. doi.org/10.1146/annurev-psych-022123-110258.

Wade, Nicholas. "Scientist Finds the Beginnings of Morality in Primate Behavior." *New York Times*, March 20, 2007. www.nytimes.com/2007/03/20/science/20moral.html.

Waheed, Anealla. "Rape Used as a Weapon in Myanmar to Ignite Fear." Al Jazeera, Oct. 28, 2015. www.aljazeera.com/features/2015/10/28/rape-used-as-a-weapon-in-myanmar-to-ignite-fear.

Walker, Lawrence J., and Karl H. Hennig. "Differing Conceptions of Moral Exemplarity: Just, Brave, and Caring." *Journal of Personality and Social Psychology* 86, no. 4 (2004): 629–47. doi.org/10.1037/0022-3514.86.4.629.

Wellable. "2024 Employee Wellness Industry Trends Report." www.wellable.co/resources/employee-wellness-industry-trends-reports/2024/.

Werner, Kimberly B., Ian W. Few, and Kathleen K. Bucholz. "Epidemiology, Comorbidity, and Behavioral Genetics of Antisocial Personality Disorder and Psychopathy." *Psychiatric Clinics of North America* 38, no. 4 (2015): 727–40. https://www.ncbi.nlm.nih.gov/pmc/articles/PMC4649950/.

WHO. "COVID-19 Deaths." COVID-19 Dashboard. data.who.int/dashboards/covid19/deaths.

Williamson, Victoria, Dominic Murphy, Andrea Phelps, David Forbes, and Neil Greenberg. "Moral Injury: The Effect on Mental Health and Implications for Treatment." *Lancet Psychiatry* 8, no. 6 (2021): 453–55. doi.org/10.1016/S2215-0366(21)00113-9.

Winsper, Catherine, Nisha Bilgin, Sarah Thompson, et al. "The Prevalence of Personality Disorders in the Community: A Global Systematic Review and Meta-Analysis." *British Journal of Psychiatry* 216, no. 2 (2020): 69–78. doi.org/10.1192/bjp.2019.166.

Witvliet, Charlotte Van Oyen, Ross W. Knoll, Nova G. Hinman, and P. A. DeYoung. "Compassion-Focused Reappraisal, Benefit-Focused Reappraisal, and Rumination After an Interpersonal Offense: Emotion-Regulation Implications for Subjective Emotion, Linguistic Responses, and Physiology." *Journal of Positive Psychology* 5, no. 3 (2010): 226–42. doi.org/10.1080/17439761003790997.

World Economic Forum. "Climate Refugees—the World's Forgotten Victims." June 18, 2021. www.weforum.org/agenda/2021/06/climate-refugees-the-world-s-forgotten-victims/.

World Economic Forum. "How Climate Change Is Accelerating the Global Food Crisis." July 11, 2023. www.weforum.org/agenda/2023/07/climate-change-is-accelerating-the-global-food-crisis-we-must-act-now-to-protect-the-most-vulnerable/.

Wrage, Birte, Dennis Papadopoulos, and Judith Benz-Schwarzburg. "Ubuntu in Elephant Communities." *Journal of the American Philosophical Association*, Dec. 12, 2023, 1–22. doi.org/10.1017/apa.2023.24.

Yale Law School. "The Code of Hammurabi." Avalon Project. avalon.law.yale.edu/ancient/hamcode.asp.

Young, Liane, and Michael Koenigs. "Investigating Emotion in Moral Cognition: A Review of Evidence from Functional Neuroimaging and Neuropsychology." *British Medical Bulletin* 84 (2007): 69–79. doi.org/10.1093/bmb/ldm031.

Young, Robin. "How a Teenager Pushed a Vulnerable Man into Livestreaming His Suicide." WBUR, Dec. 19, 2024. www.wbur.org/hereandnow/2024/12/19/discord-suicide.

YouTube. "Vietnam War Documentary—First Kill." youtu.be/mom573MxXXw?si=1GXINTomzloeBqeI.

INDEX

acceptance and commitment therapy (ACT), 175
acute moral trauma, 143–145. *See also* post-traumatic stress disorder (PTSD)
adaptive disclosure, 171–174. *See also* cognitive restructuring
adventurousness, 100
Afghanistan, author's deployment in, xi–xvi
agency, xix, 129, 173–174, 193
aggression, 51–54
agreeableness, 100
Ali, Muhammad, 112
Alison (author's wife), 107
altruism, reciprocal, 46
American Psychiatric Association, 13
American society
    distrust and despair in, 31–32
    fractures in, xx
    political anxiety disorder, 188–189, 194–195
    political partisanship, 133–134
    political polarization, 30–33, 182–183
    political polarization in, 30–33
Amun (Big God), 64

amygdala, 48–49, 52–53, 85, 125
analytic thought, 72
Andre (case story), 171–173
anger, 123
anterior cingulate cortex, 7–8
antisocial personality disorder (ASPD), 109–110
Armstrong, Lance, 116
artificial intelligence (AI), 78
assisted exposure virtual reality therapy, 166–169
atonement, xv, 65–66, 160
attachment, 45
attribution bias, 106–107, 135–137, 157
authoritarians, 182–183

Baha'i faith, 193
Balaji, Suchir, 18
benevolence (*ren*), 69
Ben-Ghiat, Ruth, 181, 182–183, 191
betrayal, as hallmark of moral violation, 12–13
bias, 131. *See also* attribution bias
Big Gods. *See also* religion/spirituality
    as all knowing, 62–63
    civil order maintained through, 64

Big Gods (*continued*)
   of Egypt, 64
   purging troubled souls, 65
   of Western world, 64
Boehm, Christopher, 45
Bowling Alone (Putnam), 74–75, 132
brain. *See* human brain
brave, the, 111–112
British Post Office scandal, 140–141
burnout, 142–143, 149
bystander effect, 21

caring, the, 112
Center for Courage and Renewal, 193
character, 101–104, 107–108
Chau, John, 116
Chenoweth, Erica, 191
Cher eezi (shamanic deity), 62
chronic stress, 145–146
Churchland, Patricia, 41, 52–53, 55, 87
Cicero, 37
civil order, 64
civil rights activists, 194
civil society, 69–71
climate anxiety, 28–30, 195–196
Code of Hammurabi, 63
cognitive behavior therapy, xvi
cognitive dissonance, 130–132, 193
cognitive restructuring, 174–175. *See also* adaptive disclosure
collective conscience. *See* conscience
collective identities, 50, 52. *See also* group identity
collective social instincts, 61
community, creating, 193
compassion, 172–173
conflict entrepreneurs, online, 26–28
Confucius, 69

congruence, 88
conscience
   addressing personal crisis of, 158
   attention to, 33
   coevolution of personal and collective, 67
   congruence, 88
   defined, 36–37
   empathy, 90–92
   gravitational pull of, 97–98
   as identity's compass, 85–92
   intuition and, 40–41
   as mind's referee, 86–87
   moral identity and, 87
   personal, xviii, 86
   prioritizing concern for others, 88–89
   protecting one's, 88
   reason and, 41
   self-control and, 45
   tests of, 20–21
Conscience (Churchland), 41
constructive resilience
   applications of, 194–195
   civil rights activists and, 194
   climate anxiety and, 195–196
   empathy and, 196–197
   examples of, 193–194
   as survival strategy, 199–200
contextual psychology, as transdiagnostic, 151–152
cooperative harmonists, 112
cooperativeness, 47–49, 50, 103
courage, 113
COVID-19
   family medicine residents during, 1–2
   moral assault of, 3–5
crescendo effect, 21–22, 121–122
cultures, approach to morality, 59–60

Damasio, Antonio, 89–90
Dederer, Claire, 138
Dee (case story), 93–97, 110
defense coalitions, 50
deontology, 15–16
despair. *See* helplessness and despair
Diagnostic and Statistical Manual of Mental Disorders (DSM), 13–14
digital shielding, 76–77
digital technology
   artificial intelligence (AI) and, 78
   attribution bias, 136
   empathy and, 78
   human interaction and, 78–79
   individualism and, 75
   mental lynch mob effect, 77
   moral effects of, 26–27
   moral outrage accelerated with, 77–78
   pervasiveness of, 24
   reptilian instincts and, 78–79
   safety and, 79–80
   social media, 24, 26–27, 77–78, 136
   social safeguards, 76
dignity, 50
disease prevention, 50
dishonesty, 189
dissonance, sense of, xiii
distress. *See* moral distress
divine will, 67–68
dopamine, 100
Dunlap, Al, 56
Dunn, Harry, 162–163
Durkheim, Émile, 36, 73

ecoanxiety, 28–30, 188–189
Educated (Westover), 119
emotional overload, 85
emotional pain, managing, xvi
emotions, disturbing moods, 23
empathy, 78, 90–92, 104–107, 124, 196–197
enlightened self-interest, 198–200
Enlightenment, The, 69–70
Epstein, Elizabeth, 122, 142
ethical dilemmas, 57–58
ethical reflection, 161
ethics
   about: overview, 60–61
   Big Gods and, 62–64
   challenges to, 131
   of children, 97
   described, 38
   encompassing our daily life, 179
   formalizing rules of social conduct, 61
   governing society, 69–71
   religion's stranglehold on, 69–70
eudaimonia (flourishing/happiness), 69
excommunication, 105–106
existential therapy, 175–176

faith, loss of, 24
familismo, 59
family nurturing, 49–50
father-son relationships, 83–84, 113–115, 146–147
fight-flight-freeze response, 6–8, 90, 156
First Babylonian Dynasty, 63
forgiveness, 37, 159–161, 172–173, 194
Framework for Workplace Mental Health and Well-Being, 79
Frankl, Viktor, 193–194
Fugitive Slave Act of 1793, 68

Geronimus, Arline, 145–146
Gibbons, Ian, 56–57

global warming, anxiety over, 28–30
Gonell, Aquilino, 144–145
goodness, xviii, 36–37, 71, 86, 91, 103
Graham, Jesse, 49
group aggression, 53
group identity, 61, 67. *See also* collective identities
group loyalty, 36, 40, 52–53, 133, 182–183
group pressure. *See* peer pressure
group strength, 50
guilt, 123

"Habits of the Heart," 193
Haidt, Jonathan, 16, 36, 49, 51, 116, 180
Hamric, Ann, 122, 142
Haney, Philip, 18
Hare, Robert D., 56–57
harmonists, 50, 112, 119–120
Heine, Steve, 71
helplessness and despair, xiv, 28, 126, 147, 188–189
Hennig, Karl, 111
Henrich, Joe, 71
Herminia (author's mother), 82–83
Herr, Michael, 53–54
Himmler, Heinrich, 57
holistic thought, 72
Holmes, Elizabeth, 56–57
Homer, 65
hopelessness, 122
hostility highs, 53, 54
human brain
    amygdala, 48–49, 52–53, 85, 125
    anterior cingulate cortex, 7–8
    dopamine levels, 100
    evolution of, 43–45
    growth of, 104
    information processing of, 72
    mammalian, evolution of, 44–45
    serotonin levels, 100
human evolution
    ethical dilemmas and, 57–58
    us-versus-them division, 52
    violence and, 51–52
human impulses, contest between, 35–36

idealists, self-directed, 111
identity
    centrality of, 129
    collective, 50, 52
    conscience and, 87
    crisis of, 24
    group, 61, 67
    as hyperconnected, 117
    moral. *See* moral identity
    morals as pillars of, 3
    social, 97
    tribal, 61
immoral commands, victim of, 19–20
Indian Removal Act of 1830, 68
indignant anger, 123
individualism, 131–133
    digital technology and, 75
    effects of, 74–75
    holistic vs analytic thought, 72
    individual rights and, 71–72
    Industrial Revolution and, 73–74
    rise of, 71–74
individualistic bias, 131
individualists-collectivists study, 117–118
individuality, cult of, 73
Industrial Revolution, 73–74
insula, 89

interpersonal conflict, 160–161
intuition, 40–41

January 6 insurrection, 143–145, 162–163
Jim Crow, 137
Joseph, Craig, 49
just, the, 111

Kant, Immanuel, 69
Kirkpatrick, Christopher, 18

Lauren (author's daughter), 107
li (proper conduct), 69
Liliana (author's daughter), 126–129
Litz, Brett, 10, 11, 130–131, 171
Livelsberger, Matthew, 11
Locke, John, 69
loneliness, 23, 78–79, 188
love hormone, 7
lynch mob effect, 77

Macbeth effect, 89
MacLean, Paul, 43
mammalian brain. *See* human brain
Marks, Elizabeth, 28
Mason, Lilliana, 181
Meacham, Jon, 68
meditation, 168
mental lynch mob effect, 77
mirror neurons, 90–91
Monsters (Dederer), 138
Moore, Michael Scott, 194
moral absolutism, 15–16
moral acceptance, 170
moral agency, 92
moral apathy, 189
moral assaults, examples of, 179–180
moral betrayal, xvi, 6, 28–29, 71, 92
moral breakdown, 4

moral bridge building, 190–193, 199–200
moral certainty, 117, 145
moral challenges
  cognitive dissonance and, 130–132
  moral decoupling, 137–139
  as part of human condition, 130
  political partisanship and, 133–134
moral choices, xvii, 10, 17, 36, 57, 87
moral codes, wide variance in, 3
moral compass, 116–117
moral compromises, 135–137
moral conflict, xx
  antisocial personality disorder and, 109–110
  children in, 119
  countries with sustained, 33
  emotional turmoil of, 41
  psychological effects of, 53
  resolution of, 9
  as self-perpetuating, 137
  social strain of, 10
  unresolved, 124–126
moral decoupling, 137–139
moral deregulation, 180–181, 188
moral development of children, 96, 119
moral disorientation, 22–23
moral distress
  British Post Office scandal, 140–141
  burnout and, 142–143
  channeling into meaningful repair, 173–174
  example of. *See* Porosoff, Lauren
  invisible epidemic of, 12
  as natural response, 18
  in professional settings, 142

moral distress (*continued*)
    as second stage of moral pain, 18–19
    Sophie's choice moment in, 19–20
moral diversity, 15, 16
moral elevation, 37
moral emotions, 122–126
moral evolution, 42
moral foundations, 49–51, 86
moral frustration, 130–131
moral grandstanding, 186
moral healing
    acknowledging moral transgressions, 155–156
    engagement with those affected, 157
    ethical realignment, 161–163
    path forward, 197
    proactive tools for, 158–161
    relational repair, 156–158
    soul mending and, 155
moral identity
    author's experience with, 95–97
    in balance, 93
    conscience and, 87
    example of, 93–97
    internal conflict, 8
    social identity and, 93
moral injury
    about: overview, xvi–xix
    acute moral trauma and, 143–145
    author's experience with, xi–xvi
    burnout and, 142–143
    causes of, xviii
    as collective crisis, 177–178
    defined, 5, 151
    distress in professional settings, 140–142
    institutionalized, 66–67
    intergenerational fallout, 67
    long-term distress, 145–146
    mechanics of, 4
    as occupational hazard, 11–12
    occurrences of, xvii
    personal conscience, xviii
    post-traumatic stress disorder and, 5–6, 9
    psychological damage of, 17
    psychological hallmarks of, 22–24
    religion/spirituality and, 17
    as response to external factors, 176–177
    responses from, xviii
    symptoms, 6
    treatment of. *See* treatment for moral injury
moral integrity, 88–89, 93
moral intuitions, rooted in instincts, 42
moral judgment, 23
moral licensing, 115–117
moral masquerading, 119–120
moral narcissism, 116–117
moral neuroscience, scientific study of, 47–49
moral obligation, 73, 189
moral orientation
    as adaptive, 112
    controlling thoughts and decisions, 117
    defined, 98
    determining how we think, 118–119
    ethical realignment, 161
    temperament and, 99–101
moral outrage
    as contagious, 186–187
    grievances that fuel, 185
    immigration debate and, 184
    reclaiming ethical balance, 185–186
    role in group conflicts, 183

social media and, 187–188
spread by rumor, 183–184
moral pain, 18–19, 98
moral problems, defined, 13–14
moral reconstruction, 199
moral repair, 158–161, 191
moral residue, 124–126, 130, 140–141
moral righteousness. *See* righteousness
moral stress, 14, 18, 130
moral transgressions, 155–156
moral trauma
    acute, 143–145
    chronic stress and, 145–146
    collective, 14–15
moral values, 39
moral wellness, 37
moralis, 37–38
morality. *See also* ethics
    cultural approaches to, 59–60
    divine will and, 67–68
    genetic evolution of, 85–86
    moving away from spirituality, 70
    as pillars of our identity, 3–5
    primal sense of, 45
    as prosocial, 39–40
    second-personal, 45–46
    spiritualization of, 62–64, 67–68
    three R's of, 38, 104, 188
    universal elements of, 35–36
    universal purpose of, 39
    weaponizing, 31
Mouffe, Chantal, 181
Mukunda, Gautam, 56
Munro, Alice, 137–138
Murthy, Vivek, 79
mutual responsibility, 193

Nacho (author's father), 83–84, 112–115, 146–147
National Institute of Mental Health, 109
natural selection, 42, 85–86
neighbor, defined, 35
neurotransmitter norepinephrine, 100
Norenzayan, Ara, 62, 71

Odyssey, The (Homer), 65
online communications, 24
online conflict entrepreneurs, 26–28
othering, 137
otherness, 193
oxytocin, 7

Pakistan, 101–102
Palmer, Parker, 192–193
Palo Alto Veterans Affairs Medical Center, xix–xx
parental anguish, 127
patriotism, 31
peer pressure, 154, 156, 180–182
Penn, Michael L., 193, 194, 195
perseverance, 100
personal conscience. *See* conscience
personal violations, 14–15
personality disorders, 109–110
Plato, 36
pleasure, 195
polarization
    as beneficial, 181
    issue-based, 181–182
    political, 30–33, 182–183
political anxiety disorder, 188–189, 194–195
political partisanship, 133–134
political polarization, 30–33, 182–183
Porosoff, Lauren
    burnout and, 149
    designing values-based workshop, 153–154
    disheartened feelings, 150–151
    exchange with Jerome, 152–153

Porosoff, Lauren (*continued*)
  fostering harmony, 149–150
  honoring her moral orientation, 152
  mitigation tools, 151–152
  reacting to Jerome's punishment, 150
  realigning core values, 152–153
  struggling with moral distress, 149–151
post-traumatic stress disorder (PTSD), 5–9, 166–167
prefrontal cortex, 125
prosocial instincts, 47–49
psychopathy, 55–57, 109
purification, 65–66
Putnam, Robert, 74–75, 132, 134

Ramses II, 64
Ray, Sarah Jaquette, 29, 131–132, 195–196
reason, 41
reciprocal altruism, 46
reciprocity, 104
reconciliation, 158–160
Reconstruction, 137
relate, 104
relational repair, 156–158
religion/spirituality. *See also* Big Gods
  atonement, xv, 65–66, 160
  Christian claims of divine will, 67–68
  influence on slavery, 67–68
  moral injury and, 17
  morality and, 62–64, 67–68
  purification and, 65–66
ren (benevolence), 69
reptilian brain, 43, 78–79
respect, 104
restorative justice, in schools, 154
righteousness, 16, 22, 63, 66, 111, 115–117, 186
risk-takers, 111–112, 119–120

Sacks, Jonathan, 93
Samaritan, story of, 35–36
second-personal morality, 45–46
self-blame, 126, 127, 169, 174
self-control
  conscience and, 45
  early development of, 45–46
self-directed idealists, 111
self-directedness, 102
self-forgiveness, 160–161
self-harm/suicide
  described, 23–24
  post-traumatic stress disorder and, 11–12
  whistleblowers and, 17–18
self-importance, 125
self-interest
  common good vs, 179–180
  enlightened, 198–200
self-knowledge, as protective buffer, 98
self-preservation, 95–96
self-protectiveness, 100
self-punishment, 11
self-transcendence, 103
self-transcendent risk-takers, 111–112
serotonin levels, 100
service, as ritual of belonging and gratitude, xiv–xv
shared virtue, 69, 89
Shay, Jonathan, xvi, 6
shell shock. *See* post-traumatic stress disorder (PTSD)
slavery, institution of, 67–68
social capital, 14, 88–89
social disconnection, 23
social identity, 93

social isolation, 79, 188
social media. *See* digital technology
social order, 50
social rejection, 105
social reputation, power of, 61
social trust, 173
society. *See* American society
sociopathy, 109
Socrates, 69
Sonoma County Regional Hospital, 1
Sophie's Choice (film), 19
soul mending, 155
Southern Poverty Law Center, 137
spirituality. *See* religion/spirituality
Stewart, Potter, 97
Stockdale, James, 194
stress responses, for physical survival, 6–8. *See also* moral stress
suicide. *See* self-harm/suicide
survival strategies
    constructive resilience as, 199–200
    fight-flight-freeze response, 6–8, 90, 156
survivor's exultation, 54

talk therapy. *See* adaptive disclosure
Taylor, Shelley, 7
team bonding, 50
technology. *See* digital technology
temperament, 99–101, 111–112. *See also* character
tend-and-befriend response, 7
Theranos, 56–57
Tocqueville, Alexis de, 73
Tomasello, Michael, 45–46
tragic optimism, 193–194
trauma, 143–145. *See also* moral trauma; post-traumatic stress disorder (PTSD)
treatment for moral injury
    about: overview, 163–164
    acceptance and commitment therapy (ACT), 175
    adaptive disclosure, 171–174
    Andre's journey, 171–173
    assisted exposure virtual reality therapy, 166–169
    career change, 170–171
    cognitive restructuring, 174–175
    dog/pet support, 169–170
    existential therapy, 175–176
    of inherited pain, 177
    long-term outcomes, 164
    meditation, 168
    reciprocity in healing and helping, 169
    as variation of PTSD, 166–167
    Wendy's journey, 164–171
trust, as form of social capital, 88–89
Tuva group, 62

UCSF Sutter Health Family Medicine Residency, xx
undocumented migrants, systemic wrongs against, xiv

Valdovinos, Michael (author)
    Afghanistan deployment, xi–xvi
    Alison (wife) and, 107
    on family and community ties, 59–60
    father. *See* Nacho (author's father)
    Lauren (daughter) and, 107
    Liliana (daughter) and, 126–129

Valdovinos, Michael (*continued*)
   losing connection with himself, 84–85
   moral distress of, 146–147
   moral identity of, 95–97
   mother. *See* Herminia (author's mother)
   panic attacks, 81–82, 84–85
   return to civilian life, xix–xx
values-based workshops, 153–154
ventromedial prefrontal cortex, 7–8, 89–90, 93
Veterans Affairs Boston Healthcare System, 10
violence, human evolution and, 51–52
Virk, Reena, 116
virtual reality therapy, 166–169
virtues, 86

Waal, Frans de, 51
Walker, Lawrence, 111
warfare, xvii, 64–65
weathering, 145–146
Weill Cornell Medical College, xix–xx
WEIRD (Western, Educated, Industrialized, Rich, and Democratic) societies, 71–73
Wendy (case story), 164–171
Westover, Tara, 119
whistleblowers, moral injury of, 17–18
Wynn, Karen, 47

Yong, Ed, 196
Yousafzai, Malala, 101–102

ABOUT THE AUTHOR

MICHAEL VALDOVINOS is a licensed psychologist, board-certified in behavioral and cognitive psychology by the American Board of Professional Psychology. A former U.S. Air Force psychologist, he has spent more than two decades building national mental health programs for veterans, directing clinical systems at leading medical institutions and pioneering the use of immersive technologies in trauma treatment. His expertise extends to shaping digital safety and mental health policy on a global scale. He has advised governments, NGOs, and technology leaders. His work bridges psychology, innovation, and social impact, bringing human insight to some of today's most urgent challenges.

See more at www.michaelvaldovinos.com.